YAMAHA
STREET BIKES 1955–2009

Other Titles in the Crowood MotoClassic Series

YAMAHA

STREET BIKES 1955–2009

COLIN MACKELLAR

THE CROWOOD PRESS

First published in 2010 by
The Crowood Press Ltd
Ramsbury, Marlborough
Wiltshire SN8 2HR

www.crowood.com

British Library Cataloguing-in-Publication Data
A catalogue record for this book is available from the British Library.

ISBN 978 1 84797 163 0

Designed, typeset and edited by Focus Publishing,
Sevenoaks, Kent

Printed and bound in Singapore by Craft Print International Ltd

Contents

Introduction

I approached this book with some trepidation. Despite having written several Yamaha books before, this one would have to be different in nature. This would be tricky. It was clear to me that writing the exhaustive, definitive history of Yamaha streetbikes would be impossible without reaching Encyclopedia Britannica-like proportions when doing full justice to the hundreds of different models Yamaha has produced since the first YA1 left the assembly line in February 1955. Consequently, I have focused on the mainstream motorcycle product lines that formed the heart of Yamaha's export drive over the last five decades. As a result, the company's large number of scooters and lightweight small capacity motorcycles are scarcely mentioned in this book.

Rather than detailed technical analyses of each bike, I have described the evolution of the mainstream motorcycle ranges in the context of the competitive, commercial, political and legislative forces at work, influencing the decision Yamaha took as a company. Formed as the post-war Japanese economic boom gained momentum, Yamaha experienced the highs and lows of the shifting consumer fortunes of the 1960s and 1970s, struggled to remain profitable as the yen soared in value in the 1980s, and wrestled with the long Japanese recession of the 1990s. Their weapon in this battle for commercial success was a continuously evolving portfolio of motorcycles, several of which could rightly be claimed to have changed the direction of motorcycle development over the years. It is this saga I have tried to capture.

Colin MacKellar, 2010

Acknowledgements

I was very fortunate to have obtained the assistance of Onabe san and Miyaji san of the Yamaha public relations office. Miyaji san was able to provide me with reference material from the early days of Yamaha history as well as some of the rare photographs from this time. His willingness to try to help with any of the detailed questions that I had, despite a heavy workload and many competing priorities, was a source of great encouragement.

Karlheinz Vetter of Yamaha Germany allowed me to rummage through their press archive in search of photographs and illustrations for the book, once again at the expense of his own valuable time. Sjaak Lucassen, intrepid explorer, provided me with three of my favourite photographs in the book, taking his R1 where none have dared before.

I was guided throughout the recreation of the Yamaha roadbike story by the collective works of the motorcycling press of the last sixty years. The arrival of Joe Parkhurst's *Cycle World* in February 1962 marked the start of a new generation of motorcycle journalism, characterized by objective criticism, genuine enthusiasm and vivid articulation. The Palace Coup at *Cycle* in 1966 saw the CW genes take the place of owner Floyd Clymer's tips on how to ride a motorcycle facing backwards. The scene was set for *Cycle*, under Phil Schilling and Cook Neilson, to become the most authoritative and instructive English language motorcycle publication of the 1970s and 1980s. The grimy fingernails of *Motorcycle Mechanics* in the UK gave way to *Bike* as the leading British motorcycle magazine, later spawning focused, irreverent, entertaining yet totally honest periodicals such as *Performance Bikes*. Complementing the glossies there has always been the perennial *Motorcycle News*, scooping the world as a weekly newspaper. Without the history of motorcycling captured in the pages of these excellent publications, Yamaha Streetbikes would have been a very hard story to tell.

No book on Yamaha can fail to mention Ludy Beumer and his excellent classicyams website. Ludy's own personal involvement with Yamaha Europe from its earliest days, as well as his vast network of contacts throughout the world, make him the Oracle of all things Yamaha. I am again indebted to him for his assistance and willingness to allow me access to his vast collection of memories and material.

Friends and family were no less important to getting this done. Cyber-support was forthcoming from Christine and Shanny; their injections of advice and encouragement were welcome fuel as inspiration occasionally waned. Sometimes it's not just what is said, but also what is not said that counts. The lack of complaint about a house littered with boxes of research material, and life with a partner who only appears at meal times is a true sign of forbearance and support. Marian, bedankt!

1 Birth of the Yamaha Motorcycle Company

The Yamaha Motorcycle Company was born in deed, if not in name, at around 11am on Monday 26 April 1954. It was the regular monthly meeting to review the business operations of Nippon Gakki Co. (Japan Musical Instrument Manufacturing Co.), with senior management coming together in the Tokyo head office in the Ginza district.

There was a feeling of subdued excitement in the room, as it was rumoured that the company president, Genichi Kawakami, was to make a pronouncement on a subject that had been dominating management meetings for the last few months. In November 1953, Kawakami had

Torakusu Yamaha, organ builder, Nippon Gakki's first president, father of Yamaha.

issued a highly confidential internal memo, outlining his intentions to consider diversification of the current product portfolio to add motorcycle manufacture to the musical instruments' business that had been the core of the company since it was formed in 1897. A feasibility study had been initiated at Nippon Gakki to consider the alternative engine designs that could be adopted, and two engineers were dispatched to Europe to visit and report on the motorcycle industry there, and how it might be applied to the Japanese market. They spent most of their time in Germany and France; at the French Motobecane plant they were welcomed and treated with interest and respect, while at the DKW plant they met some ridicule for countenancing motorcycle manufacture when their skills and experience lay in piano construction.

By March 1954 the engineers were back in Japan and reporting on their observations of assembly lines and mass production. Despite the scepticism they had met, Kawakami was convinced that Nippon Gakki's future lay with motorcycles. His conviction was enough; it would be so.

Kawakami was a very focused individual, self-confident and decisive, cast in the mould of his father Kaichi Kawakami, the third president of Nippon Gakki. Kaichi Kawakami had rescued the company from the destructive natural disasters of earthquakes and fires in the early 1920s, and coped with the ensuing bitter industrial disputes that had paralysed the company for months at a time. Kawakami had been asked to take over the company in 1927, just after the start of the modern Showa era in Japan; this period was to see the country fall under the yoke of militarism in

Kaichi Kawakami could not prevent pre-war Nippon Gakki from being coerced into becoming an industrial military supplier of propellors.

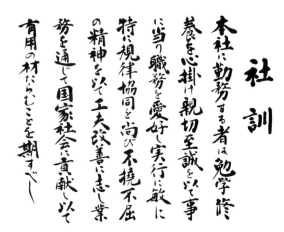

Kawakami's company pledge: 'Strive to bring a relentless spirit of innovation.'

the 1930s, leading to the devastation of World War II and the resulting loss of everything on capitulation in August 1945. He was also to oversee the initial steps towards recovery before illness and death brought his son, Genichi, into the position of president in September 1950.

Post-war Depression

Post-war Japan was a desperate place. The massive air raids that had been unleashed on Japan during the last year of the war had resulted in almost total destruction of the major cities, and massive loss of life. In a few hours on the night of 10 March 1945, firebombs killed about 100,000 people and destroyed a million homes in Tokyo. Many Japanese cities were categorized as suffering from greater than 50 per cent devastation. As the war ended, the surviving population did not escape the horrors inflicted on all of the defeated nations, exposed to unimaginable suffering caused by acute housing and food shortages, with food from neighbouring countries no longer available and harvests failing.

The country sank into the deep mood of desperation they called *kyodatsu*. The first winter after defeat was a tough one, with families crammed into the few remaining brick buildings, living in the catacombs of railway stations and subject to the daily fight for survival, dominated by a continuous search for fuel and food. Fish and rice, which had comprised the pre-war staple diet, were very scarce, as the fishing fleet had been largely destroyed and the USSR had grabbed large swathes of the fishing grounds as the war ended. Almost no food was imported to help during the first six months of occupation, despite an estimated 870,000 tonnes needed to feed the population. General MacArthur, the Supreme Commander Asia Pacific, effectively Japan's ruler and President during the Occupation, sent his famous telegram to Washington: 'Send me food or send me bullets!' Melodramatic as it sounded, it was extremely close to reality.

Nippon Gakki survived the war, but it was a close-run thing. The company had been placed under army management in August 1938, and most of the production facilities in Hamamatsu were converted, to support the munitions industry through the fabrication of wooden and metal propellers. This had been part of the business line since 1921, but with the aggressive plans of the military government, the production of pianos

Genichi Kawakami, who turned Nippon Gakki into Yamaha, announcing his fact-finding global tour.

became increasingly marginalized. By 1944 it was producing 1,300 propellers per month, using machine tools imported from the USA before the start of the war. In total the factory produced 28 per cent of all the propellers delivered to the Japanese air force during the war.

Hamamatsu was targeted for bombing, and on 19 May 1945 a heavy raid seriously damaged the plant; after this, a start was made to disperse the surviving company assets. The factory was evacuated to Komyo in Iwata county, the move taking place on 31 July 1945, and as a result the precision tools of the propeller trade survived the war intact. At the start of occupation they were immediately impounded by the Allied powers, but they were to remain unused, locked in the factory now known as the Sakura factory in Iwata. Soichiro Honda was born on 17 November 1906 in Komyo, and destiny was to keep Honda and Yamaha close.

Under the Occupation, Nippon Gakki, like many Japanese companies, struggled to re-establish pre-war business, though they were hampered by the lack of raw materials, lack of invest-

ment capital, and a society that had more important things on its mind than musical instruments. To make matters worse, in 1949 the US introduced tight monetary policies in order to curb inflation and build a stable base for reconstruction. Known as the Dodge line, it also had the effect of throwing the country into a recession, as money once again became scarce. As the company fought for survival it was dealt another blow when Kaichi Kawakami, its president, but also its spiritual figurehead after the trials and tribulations of two decades of leadership, became ill in September 1950. The task of saving the company fell to his son Genichi, who had supervised the Tenryu and Iwata plant during the war.

Bust Turns to Boom

The company's future hung in the balance, but world events were to be the saviour of Nippon Gakki and many other Japanese companies. As the Korean war took hold in 1950, the USA needed a strong base to launch their defence of the Western world against the perceived menace of Red China.

A proud moment. The design team reveals their prototype for Yamaha's first motorcycle.

A rapid improvement in the economy developed, resulting in greater employment and an improved standard of living, stimulating a consumer spending spree. Bust had turned to boom, and by 1953 industrial production had returned to pre-war levels and the scene was set for the astonishing Japanese economic growth that was to last into the 1970s.

Business started to pick up at Nippon Gakki, but the issue occupying the management was how best to capitalize on the booming economy that was developing. They received some good news at the end of 1952, when the order impounding the machinery that had been used to produce the variable pitch metal propellers during the war was rescinded, and the company was free to use the machinery as they saw fit, provided it was for non-military purposes. Some of the ideas considered were sewing machines, ships' propellers and scooters, but all were rejected. In the meantime an idea had taken root in the mind of Genichi Kawakami, and was beginning to dominate the direction in which he felt the company should move. He was convinced the future lay in two-wheeled motorized transport: Nippon Gakki would become a motorcycle manufacturer.

There was little empirical evidence to support such a move. Japan was flooded with motorcycle manufacturers, most of whom had been established during the early 1950s boom. It was a bold move to enter a market with 200 competitors, starting from scratch and with no experience of the associated engineering or technology. But Kawakami was a quick learner and he expected the same from his staff, so ignorance was considered the least of his concerns. Knowledge and expertise were a natural process, and the drive was there to obtain both. The company would learn from the acknowledged masters of the industry, located in Europe, so the two senior engineers were sent to Europe at the start of 1954 to observe and learn. In the boardroom of the Ginza office, in April 1954, with Sakura trees in full bloom in the streets outside – powerful symbol of new life in Japanese culture – Kawakami set out his plans to enter the motorcycle manufacturing business, backed by new management appointments and capital investment in new equipment. The die had been cast.

Kawakami's instructions were unequivocal. The engineering team were to find the right motorcycle and copy it exactly. Only in this way did he feel they would be able to match the quality of the motorcycles in the European marketplace, for this was to be the way the company would distinguish itself from the dozens of competitors already in the Japanese market. Having decided to build a motorcycle with a two-stroke engine due to its mechanical simplicity, several alternatives were considered – although in reality there was only one choice that made sense. The DKW RT125 had been cloned by many other manufacturers, the most famous being the BSA Bantam. Copyright was not a problem, as all licence rights had been forfeited by the German motorcycle industry as part of the war reparations. The DKW could be, and was, freely copied by others.

The First Nippon Gakki 125cc Motorcycle

Showing commendable maturity as leader, despite the enormous commercial risks at stake, Kawakami's Zen-like words 'to work carefully is to work quickly' guided the team working from a secure room within the Nippon Gakki engineering department. The RT125 was chosen in late June 1954, and by September a pre-production unit was built and sent on a 10,000km (6,200 miles) shakedown ride. Kawakami joined the riders to get a feeling for the motorcycle on which the future of his company rested. A factory assembly line was built in what was to be known as the Hanama Factory in Shizuoka Prefecture, and on 11 February 1955 the first Nippon Gakki 125cc motorcycle left the assembly line, ready for delivery. The whole company turned out to witness the first commercial motorcycle leaving the company on the back of the delivery lorry.

The Yamaha Motor Co. Ltd

On 1 July 1955, a new company was established to handle the motorcycle division. It was called the Yamaha Motor Co. Ltd in honour of the founding father of Nippon Gakki, Torakusu Yamaha, whose organ-building business had been the seed that had grown into Nippon Gakki.

The new single-cylinder 125 machine was identified as the Yamaha YA1, but soon earned the name *Akatombo*, or Red Dragonfly, due to its distinctive brown-red paintwork. The colour was

Shake-down tests and a little sightseeing. Pre-production YA1s at the Kaikoen gate in Komorro.

The finished product: the Yamaha YA1.

one of the legacies of the GK design team that had been approached to produce distinctive cosmetics for the bike, building on their background in industrial design. Despite the instructions to provide an exact copy of the RT125, the engineering team had persuaded Kawakami to sanction a little free thought and they had been allowed to develop a four-speed gearbox with a slicker gear-change, allowing neutral to be selected directly from any gear. It was a small enhancement, but psychologically important, strengthening the self-confidence of the design team for models to come.

The problem facing the new company was getting their product to market in the swarm of competing products in the marketplace. Initial sales were sluggish, given the lack of sales outlets as well as a price level that was up to 15 per cent higher than the competition. What was needed was publicity that would raise the profile of company and motorcycle, and this was found in the annual Mount Fuji races due to be held on 10 July 1955. Won by Honda in 1953 and 1954, Yamaha entered eleven machines in the 125 class, and won the race out of a field of forty-nine

machines from sixteen manufacturers, with seven YA1s in the first ten finishers. The performance was repeated four months later at the first Asama Highlands race.

Such complete domination resulted in a surge of interest from the market, and established both the strong link with racing in the company ethos and the bitter rivalry with Honda that has continued to this day. By the end of 1955, with the new 175cc YC1 on the way, it looked as if Kawakami's gamble had paid off and Yamaha Motor Co. had established itself as a leading player in the Japanese market.

By February 1956, the YC1 was also ready for production. This was a clone of the DKW RT175, with no attempt made to improve the technical aspects of the bike. There were two rival design teams that looked at different cosmetic options for the motorcycle, but the final production design was close to an exact copy of the DKW. With the race successes of 1955 fresh in the public's mind, the YC1 immediately started to sell well and the factory was soon struggling to meet demand for the three machines, a bored-out 127cc machine called the YB1 also having been

ABOVE: The first YA1 commercial delivery; the factory closed for all employees to savour this historic moment.

BELOW: The spoils of racing. The team proudly displays their trophies after the first Asama race.

Yamaha's second motorcycle the 175cc YC1.

introduced from July 1955. They enlisted the help of some of their more successful dealers, who supplied extra hands to keep the assembly lines running flat out.

The New Street 250cc Twin

Meanwhile Kawakami's drive for progress was undiminished by the success of the YA1 and YC1. He had his eyes firmly set on the next step to market domination, a 250cc twin. In January 1956 he had authorized the establishment of the Nippon Gakki Research Centre, located in an old silk cocoon warehouse in Hamamatsu. Its initial goal had been to develop the YA1 engine for competition, as Kawakami was certain there would be a strong challenge to the company in the 1956 races on Mount Fuji and Asama Plains.

By painstaking trial and error, but also applying the knowledge gained by the company in the tuned lengths of trombones, new exhausts and cylinders were developed that boosted power output to 10bhp, double that of the standard engine. The new YA1s were unbeatable, taking the first eight places at the Fuji 125 race, and first two places at Asama. They even dominated the 250 class at both races.

With the competition side secured, the small research team was strengthened to work on the new street 250 machine. An Adler MB250 was acquired to be used as the model to be cloned, but the design team, brimming with confidence from their success so far, made a strong pitch to be freed to make their own design decisions. A GK designer and a chassis engineer were ushered into Kawakami's office to make their case, reappearing shortly afterwards with Kawakami's blessing. 'If you want to do it that much, go ahead' were his words of encouragement.

It is debatable if this was the right decision, because the YD1, as it was to be known, was a remarkably unattractive machine, following the direction taken with the YC1, in the production of a utilitarian motorcycle. It was a trend that was adopted by many of the contemporary Japanese manufacturers. Rather than a cradle frame, a pressed-steel chassis was used with integrated rear mudguard. A rather flimsy swing-arm and twin shock rear suspension marked the move away from the plunger-type suspension of the YA/YC chassis. All the mounting points for the engine were integrated into the frame. The bulk of the frame coupled to the enclosed chain-case for the final drive chain gave the impression of bulk and weight. A twin-cylinder engine was developed, sharing the 54 × 54mm bore and stroke of the Adler, in contrast to the unorthodox 52 × 58mm of the YA series. The engine design was complex, with a vertically split crankcase, requiring the crankshaft halves to be built up in each crankcase half, before being splined together at assembly. The 14bhp that the engine provided at 6,000rpm

was passed to the rear wheel via a four-speed gearbox. Weighing in at 140kg (308lb), it was in fact quite a light machine for the 250cc capacity, but its appearance belied this. Even the Japanese struggled a little with its unusual appearance, providing it with the nickname of *Bunbuka Chagama*, or 'tea kettle'.

The extra complexity of the twin pushed the design team just a little too far, given their only nascent understanding of two-stroke engineering. Despite being subjected to the traditional shakedown tests, as well as a two-day journey by Kawakami san from Hamamatsu to Tokyo to announce the launch of the bike, reports soon started to arrive of serious problems with the crankshaft assembly. The spline coupling of the two crankshafts was inadequate, and ultimately 3,000 machines had to be recalled to be updated; inevitably this tarnished the image of the company, although it minimized the fallout by way of its quick, no-nonsense response to the problem. Despite the quality issues, the YD1 was heralded as a success both by the public and the press – helped no doubt by the open courting of the press by the company, which included making available test machines for journalists.

The start of a famous legacy: the YD1 was Yamaha's first two-stroke twin.

Model	YA1	YA2	YA3
Year	1955	1957	1960
Capacity (cc)	123	123	123
Configuration	2-s 1 cyl	2-s 1 cyl	2-s 1 cyl
Induction	piston port	piston port	piston port
Bore × stroke (mm × mm)	52 × 58	52 × 58	52 × 58
Gearbox	4-speed	4-speed	4-speed
Final drive	chain	chain	chain
Frame	plunger	pressed steel	pressed steel
Wheelbase (mm, in)	1,290 (50.8)	1,245 (49)	1,245 (49)
Dry weight (kg, lb)	95 (209)	108 (238)	104 (229)
Power (bhp)	5.6 @ 5,000rpm	6.5 @ 6,000rpm	6.8 @ 6,000rpm
Torque (kgm)	0.96 @ 4,000rpm	0.96 @ 4,900rpm	0.98 @ 4,900rpm
Top speed (km/h, mph)	85 (53)	85 (53)	85 (53)

Model	YC1	YD1	YD2
Year	1956	1957	1959
Capacity (cc)	175	247	247
Configuration	2-s 1 cyl	2-s 2 cyl	2s 2 cyl
Induction	piston port	piston port	piston port
Bore × stroke (mm × mm)	62 × 58	54 × 54	54 × 54
Gearbox	4-speed	4-speed	4-speed
Final drive	chain	chain	chain
Frame	pressed steel	pressed steel	pressed steel
Wheelbase (mm, in)	1,285 (50.6)	1,270 (50)	1,270 (50)
Dry weight (kg, lb)	118 (260)	140 (309)	140 (309)
Power (bhp)	10.3 @ 5,500rpm	14.5 @ 6,000rpm	14.5 @ 6,000rpm
Torque (kgm)	1.6 @ 3,400rpm	1.9 @ 4,000rpm	1.9 @ 4,000rpm
Top speed (km/h, mph)	110 (68)	115 (71)	115 (71)

Model	YDS1
Year	1959
Capacity (cc)	246
Configuration	2-s 2 cyl
Induction	piston port
Bore × stroke (mm × mm)	56 × 50
Gearbox	5-speed
Final drive	chain
Frame	cradle frame
Wheelbase (mm, in)	1,285 (50.6)
Dry weight (kg, lb)	120 (265)
Power (bhp)	18 @ 7,500rpm
Torque (kgm)	1.9 @ 6,000rpm
Top speed (km/h, mph)	140 (87)

ABOVE: The engine assembly line in 1957.

BELOW: President Kawakami(right) doing his own quality control on the first YD1.

Open day for the press.
YD1 test day organized
by Yamaha.

Consolidating the Line-up

With three basic designs launched in the 125, 175 and 250 class, it was time to consolidate the line-up and this resulted in the production of the YA2 in November 1957. It bore a strong resemblance to the YD1, also using a pressed-steel frame and rear swing arm, with a leading link front fork that was also becoming fashionable in Europe at the time. Most novel feature was the presence of an electric start motor, not often fitted to contemporary motorcycles, and certainly not on a bike of such small capacity.

Completing the line-up was a larger-bore 260cc version of the YD1 called the YE1, which arrived in July 1958. Yamaha had by now become a major force in the marketplace, ranking in sixth place in the table of manufacturers, with a total of 15.811 units produced in 1957; however, this was still a long way behind market leader Honda, who were building over 70,000 motorcycles per year. Nevertheless Kawakami, ever keen to push forwards, was looking at expanding his operations beyond the shores of

Japan, with the USA a clear target for the future. Given the success of the strategy of linking racing success to a model launch, Kawakami arranged for Yamaha to enter the 1958 race on Catalina Island just off the California coast, a track similar to the Fuji and Asama events, with a mix of dirt and paved surfaces. This legendary race, the first for Yamaha outside Japan, saw Fumio Ito take the YD 250, which had won the 1957 Asama race, to sixth place, despite falls and pit stops for oiled plugs.

Shortly after the race, Frank Cooper was appointed as the Yamaha distributor for the US, based in Los Angeles, and early in 1959 was provided with the new YD2 and YA3 machines for sale in the US. While the YA3 differed only in detail from the YA2, the YD2 featured a totally redesigned engine to facilitate high-volume assembly that was envisioned when the US market was entered. In addition to a new crank and crankcase assembly, the clutch was moved to the end of the crankshaft, where it was to remain on Yamaha twins for the next ten years, much to the

Moving on. The YA2 successor to the Red Dragonfly.

First sketch for the new export twin in the making, the YD2.

frustration of the owners of TD production racers that were to be produced during the 1960s. The clutch span at engine speed, and fluffed gear changes, could result in major damage to the crankshaft. Another ingenious item was the combined dynamo and electric starter specially developed by Hitachi.

The 250 Sports Model

Although the YD2 was a good representative of the design style employed by the majority of Japanese manufacturers at the end of the 1950s, it was not suitable for extending the link with racing that Yamaha had adopted from its inception. Indeed the 250 racers that had been so successful at the 1957 Asama had borne little resemblance to the street bike. Most visible was the use of a cradle frame, rather than the pressed steel component on the street bikes. With such an obvious difference between the models, successes in racing would be difficult to link to the street machines. So it was decided that a 250 Sports model would be built, with such a strong link to racing that there would be kits offered for sale to convert the street bike to racing on dirt-track or tarmac.

This was a truly momentous decision, as it was to form the basis for Yamaha's marketing philosophy for the next fifteen years, and would lead to their support for racing that was to see the race world flooded with Yamaha race bikes with a street-based heritage. It was the essence of Kando, later to be adopted by Yamaha as their corporate mission.

The frame was a duplex design with twin tubes running under and behind the engine and a single backbone tube running over the engine from the top of headstock to the rails for the rear sub-frame. An extra 'tension pipe' was bolted between the bottom of the headstock and the sub-frame/backbone joint. The front forks from the YD2 were adopted, with hydraulic twin rear shock absorbers. At the 1957 Asama race there had been Yamaha 250cc machines running with both 54 × 54mm dimensions as well as 56 × 50mm, with the race being won by the 54mm model, but with two of the machines with the short-stroke engine behind it. It was decided to adopt the short-stroke engine for the production machine, distinguishing it from the YD2 and offering the possibility to increase the engine power output through the increase of engine speed.

The engine layout was similar to the YD2, with vertical crankcases and the clutch mounted on the left-hand end of the crankshaft. Cylinder design was standard contemporary two-stroke, with inlet and outlet port and two transfer ports on opposite sides of the cast-iron cylinder. Quite revolutionary, however, was the use of two separate 22mm Mikuni carburettors, rather than the single twin-barrelled design that had been used on previous 250 twins. Another unusual feature was the five-speed gearbox, with most contemporary motorcycles of this capacity equipped with just four gears. Certainly, with the view to tuning the bike through the kits that would be available, the extra gear would be very welcome, as extra power was usually obtained at the expense of a narrower power-band, with extra gears needed to keep the engine on the boil.

The resulting bike was unquestionably a milestone in Japanese motorcycle design. The 20bhp performance of the engine matched the clean lines of the chassis, with the stunning cream and gold colour scheme being the icing on the cake. For the first production runs of the bike it was known as the 250S, but after 3,000 units had been produced it was christened the YDS1, and under this identity was exported to the US and Australian markets. The appearance of the bike was to set the standard for the other Japanese manufacturers as they consolidated their domestic market position and explored new markets abroad.

For Yamaha, it was a machine that could justifiably lead the drive into new export markets, headed by Australia and the USA. Already in Sep-

The pride of the Yamaha factory, lined up to take on the world outside of Japan: from the top, the 250, model YD2, the 250S that was to become the YDS1 and the 125cc YA3.

Manufacturer : YAMAHA MOTOR CO., LTD.
Hamamatsu, Japan
Exporter : NIPPON GAKKI CO., LTD.
Hamamatsu, Japan

ABOVE: Not an enormously imposing HQ, but this was Yamaha International Corporation in June 1960.

BELOW: All smiles as the tape is cut and Yamaha officially arrives in the USA.

Pre-YIC advert from Yamaha distributor Frank Cooper.

tember 1958, the first steps had been taken with the creation of a full Yamaha de Mexico subsidiary in Mexico City. Just a month previously Nippon Gakki had opened a representative's office in Los Angles, but Frank Cooper was heading the exclusive distributorship deal that he had been awarded earlier in the year. This was not to be a happy relationship, with Kawakami feeling that Yamaha needed to control the complete approach to the US market, rather than relying on 'agents', as the distributors were called. In June 1960, Yamaha International Corporation was launched, as a full subsidiary of Yamaha Japan, and exports to the US could be ramped up accordingly. A bitter legal wrangle developed between Cooper and Yamaha, ultimately being resolved in 1961, with Yamaha claiming breach of contract when Cooper also started to sell Bultacos in the US.

With the YDS1 as their flagship motorcycle, Yamaha were set to expand their business dramatically. By 1960, Japan had become the largest motorcycle producing nation of the world, with annual production of almost 1.5 million machines. Yamaha had established themselves as one of the top five companies, helped by the acquisition of Showa and Kitagawa, the latter having fallen on hard times after holding second place in the market during the mid-1950s. Yamaha was poised to move into the 1960s with a strong domestic market position, firm manufacturing base and a focused and determined management team, intent on continuing the rapid growth of the company. It had been an incredible six years of expansion; the challenge was to replicate this in the unknown world outside Japan.

2 The Early Years

Yamaha's spectacular growth in the years leading up to 1960 was to be mirrored by spectacular business failures at the start of the decade, which by 1962 brought the company to the brink of bankruptcy. Perhaps the culprit was over-confidence garnered from the success of the first years of their existence – though in truth the danger signs could have been spotted if there had been the inclination within the company to analyse its design and manufacturing performance. As it was, the drive was to the future, with little interest in the past.

It is clear that by 1960, the company was stretched very thin in the drive ahead. Whilst the Japanese motorcycle industry was the largest in the world, it was still divided between more than twenty manufacturers. The inevitable shake-out had started at the close of the 1950s, with Yamaha snapping up Kitagawa Sangyo, manufacturers of a 250cc clone of the Sunbeam S8 500cc twin.

Shortly after this, Showa, a venerable name in the Japanese industry, ran into financial difficulties and became part of the Yamaha operation in April 1960. A year earlier Showa themselves had taken over Hosk, manufacturers of a strong-selling 500cc ohc vertical twin. Wisely, Yamaha left the Hosk manufacturing plant intact and continued to market the bike under its original name until 1963. All the same, Yamaha needed to integrate and consolidate the Showa and Kitagawa acquisitions, without compromising their own organic growth.

Despite these takeovers, Yamaha's ambitions in the domestic market were still not fulfilled, and they felt they needed to be a player in the booming scooter and moped market. The scooter market was dominated by two companies, Shin Mitsubishi with their Silver Pigeon, and Fuji Sangyo with the Rabbit. The scooter market had flared strongly in the 1950s, but was over its peak by the time Yamaha launched their attempt to carve

So innocent in the studio, but the SC1 almost destroyed Yamaha.

The threat of bankruptcy, started by the SC1 problems, was almost sealed by the MF1 in 1961.

themselves a share. The Yamaha SC1 arrived in March 1960, with some quite radical ideas packaged around the 175cc engine from the YC1. Equipped with a semi-automatic transmission and forced engine cooling in the scooter packaging around a monococque chassis, Yamaha played up the innovative nature of the design.

The market was convinced and the SC1 sold well, until numerous problems were reported with the transmission, and inadequate engine cooling. Demand slumped, many compensation claims were submitted and honoured, and the SC1 was dropped from the line-up by the end of the year. To make matters worse, Yamaha had also built a 50cc moped, the MF1, spurred on, no doubt, by Honda's creation of what was to become the most popular motorcycle in history, the 50cc Cub. Once again, Yamaha decided that innovation was the key to success, and in the eight-month design, development and production period, produced a monococque design

with a single shock rear suspension. It caught the market by storm, with production of 300 units per month from the simultaneous launch with the SC1.

Dealers were desperate for the new bike; one report of the time states: 'There were many dealers who put cash in their money belts, drove a truck to the factory to buy the mopeds, and waited in a hotel until they were ready.' But the MF1 also turned out to have serious design problems, including a tendency for the monococque beam to fracture and break at the headstock. Again a massive number of claims for replacement of broken parts and compensation flooded in, which, together with the on-going troubles with the SC1, swamped the factory and dramatically hit production levels.

Finally, in July 1960, Yamaha launched their first outboard engines for motorboats, with all the focus and attention that is needed for a new product in an untried market.

Printed in Japan

Yamaha Scooter 175

Model SC-1	Fuel Tank Capacity .... 8ℓ (2.08 gallon)
Overall Length .... 1770 mm (69.7″)	Starting System .... Starter Dynamo
Overall Height .... 660 mm (26.0″)	Engine .... C2 2 Stroke Engine
Overall Width .... 980 mm (38.6″)	Cylinder .... Single Cylinder System
Wheel Base .... 1260 mm (49.6″)	Ignition System .... Battery Ignition
Net Weight .... 133 kg (293 lbs)	Clutch .... Torque Converter
Maximum Speed .... 90 km/h (56 m.p.h.)	Fuel Consumption .... 40 km/ℓ (94 mile/gallon)
Brake Efficiency ...... 14 m/50 km/h (26.2/22 m.p.h.)	Motor Oil Mixing Ratio .... 20 : 1

Yamaha moped MF-1

Model MF-1	Fuel Tank Capacity .... 4ℓ (1.04 gallon)
Overall Length .... 1685 mm (66.05″)	Starting System .... Starter Dynamo
Overall Height .... 885 mm (34.09″)	Engine .... F1 2 Stroke Engine
Overall Width .... 660 mm (26.0″)	Cylinder .... Single Cylinder System
Wheel Base .... 1130 mm (44.5″)	Ignition System .... Battery Ignition
Net Weight .... 65 kg (143 lbs)	Clutch .... Multi-plate Clutch
Maximum Speed .... 70 km/h (45 m.p.h.)	Fuel Consumption ...... 75 km/ℓ (184.6 mile/gallon)
Brake Efficiency .... 7 m/35 km/h (23′/22 m.p.h.)	Motor Oil Mixing Ratio .... 20 : 1

Partners in crime, the SC1 and MF1 together in a 1961 Yamaha sales brochure.

Flat out MF1 production in 1960.

The company was in desperate shape, as costs from the guarantee claims and replacements from the scooter and moped adventure rose dramatically and revenue dropped from falling production output. Year-on-year, output and revenue dropped 10 per cent, with share prices tumbling and no dividend payments for shareholders. By the summer of 1961, the Yamaha domestic sales network was close to collapse, caused by dealer bankruptcies and desertions as the demand for Yamaha motorcycles plummeted. Similar conditions had, in the past, resulted in other manufacturers failing completely or being acquired. Kawakami's response was to appoint a new sales director to rebuild the sales network and establish the trust of the dealers, who were critical to Yamaha's road to market. Hisao Koike was plucked from the Nippon Gakki division and placed in charge of this critical recovery plan.

The plan to re-establish an effective sales organization was based on the establishment of Yamaha-backed wholesale dealerships throughout Japan, responsible for supplying the retail dealerships in their region. This worked well, although there were some enterprising wholesale dealers who also offered retail sales, compromising the trust of the retail outlets they were intended to support. Dealers were also poached by other manufacturers offering better terms. It was a volatile time in the Japanese market, but the sales structure that had been put in place by Koike was able to save the domestic sales network from total meltdown.

The YA5

As the reorganization started to take effect in Japan, export market growth took off. The dispute in the USA with the first US distributor was resolved, and Yamaha International took full responsibility for developing their network of dealers. The model range consisted of the YDS1 and YD2, with a few MF1s also being delivered in the USA and sold as 'Lightning 50s'. While the failures had been mounting up with the scooter and moped models, thankfully there had been a small success with the introduction of the YA5 that had arrived in April 1961. This was the fourth of the YA series, although the use of the number four as a model number was avoided by Yamaha, because the Japanese word for 'death' sounds very similar to *shi* , the Japanese for 'four'. Given the financial troubles of the company at the time, they couldn't risk anything deterring potential customers.

The first overt link between Yamaha race bikes, the TD1 at Suzuka and their street twins, the YDS2.

The YA5 heritage was to be found in the acquisition of Showa in 1960. Showa's trademark was the use of the two-stroke engine with rotary valve induction, considered at the time to be the most effective way to extract higher power levels from a given engine capacity. Showa had produced good power levels with their racing machines, although they lacked the reliability needed to be a race winner. Yamaha had immediately adopted the rotary valve for the GP racers they had in preparation for a visit to Europe in 1961, to compete in the 125 and 250 classes. These machines were to form the basis for the Yamaha GP challenge that resulted in world championships with the RD56 and later the V4 125 and 250cc machines, all fitted with rotary valve induction.

Yamaha decided to bring this same technology to the street with the YA5, adopting the short stroke 56 × 50mm cylinder dimensions of the racers. In general, the chassis was quite similar to its predecessor, although the leading link front forks were replaced by heavier oil-damped telescopic units. The rotary valve and carburettor were fitted to the right-hand end of the crankshaft, behind the conventional engine covers, resulting in a slightly wider engine. Extra support came in the form of a tube extending from an engine mounting point just under the cylinder, up to lugs on the frame under the headstock, as used on the YD2. Power output had jumped by a massive 50 per cent, resulting in almost 10bhp at 6,000rpm in contrast to the 6.8bhp produced by the YA3, but a four-speed transmission was still used, with revised gear ratios. Unfortunately, somewhere along the line the YA5 had also gained 13kg (28.6lb), taking the edge off the extra performance.

The YD3

Fortunately for Yamaha the bike was a success, with no major design flaws, and it helped save the company from going under. After a year of sales in Japan it was felt safe to introduce it to the US market, and from 1962 it joined its big brothers, the 250s, sporting the crossed tuning forks instead of company name in support of Yamaha's drive to build a corporate identity and instantaneously recognizable logo in the USA. The 250s themselves had also undergone a facelift, which included the adoption of the Yamaha tuning fork logo on the fuel tank. The YD3 hit the market in November 1961, with the YDS2 following just four months later.

Apart from the new logo on the fuel tank and the startling white-wall tires on the YD3, it appeared to be very similar to its predecessor. In fact there were numerous changes to the engine, intended primarily to simplify the manufacturing process and improve the reliability of the engine. The use of a different crankshaft design, with a labyrinth seal at the connection of the two crankshaft halves, as well as 'parkerized' piston rings and conrods with extra oil slots in the big-end and little-end eyes, illustrates the amount of effort the company put into the new engine. A complete new transmission was designed and a Mikuni

Not sure these rockers will be too interested in the YD3 in the foreground.

carburettor with integrated choke was introduced for the first time. Subtle improvements to the chassis included new brake linings as well as a larger diameter drum, front and back, resulting in special praise from contemporary road testers.

In fact the YD3 was seen as an excellent bike by the press once they realized it was intended to be a tourer rather than a sports bike. Both the brakes and also the suspension and engine performance came in for praise, although there was some mild criticism of the bike's weight. Not only was it the actual weight, but its bulk, too, gave the impression of its being a staid, slow and unexciting ride. Sharing the limelight with its brother the YDS2, it came up looking distinctly dated. It was the best of the look that had originated in the 1950s, with styling heavily influenced by car design, resulting in press steel frames, chain cases, flared mudguards and enclosed engines.

But with the arrival of the YDS1, motorcycles were to forge their own style, especially the sports models, emphasizing the lean and mean associated with performance. With the arrival of the YDS2, the sports 250 hit its stride.

The YDS2

Feeling that they had the basics covered with the YDS1, Yamaha made an evolutionary step when building its successor. Despite having one of the best power-to-weight ratios in the 250cc street bike market, it was felt that a few more bhp would put the gloss on the 'sports' epithet. The new cylinders and heads, with modified porting, increased power output by 20 per cent, with the engine delivering a claimed 22bhp at 7,500rpm. Throughout the model range, Yamaha were fitting conrods with oil slots cut in the big- and little-end eyes, and the YDS2 had the same modification. Initially the same carburettors were used to feed the engine, but before the bike was released for export, the Mikuni VM20SH – as had been used on the YD3 – was fitted, complete with choke system for cold starts. The distinctive air-filter shrouds were modified a little to provide greater protection from dirt and dust without compromising air flow into the engine.

The transmission design was unaltered, but underwent a few detail changes as some owners of the YDS1 had experienced problems with the

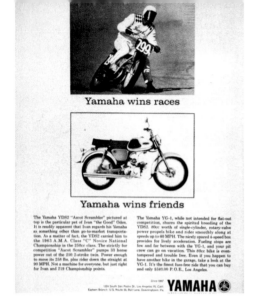

Yamaha adverts were starting to link unlikely bedfellows such as the Ascot Scrambler and the YG1.

Everyone's happy. Floyd Clymer has a glossy cover and Yamaha have the YDS2 on countless US newsstands.

transmission jumping out of gear. There was also a slightly higher primary gear reduction ratio, slowing the gears on the primary shaft, resulting in slicker gear changes. Initially, no further changes were made to the five-speed in the gearbox, but after a year of production new ratios were introduced, more compatible with the changed primary gearing.

On the chassis, the greatest attention was paid to the brakes, with a twin leading drum brake fitted to the front wheel. This provided far better stopping power than the simple brakes fitted to the European competition. Already the sophistication of the Yamaha and Honda street machines was casting a shadow over the traditional motorcycle manufacturers.

Despite gaining 5kg (11lb) over the YDS1 due to the new brakes and stronger wheel spokes, the straight-line performance of the YDS2 was significantly better. Quarter-mile elapsed time, the standard yardstick for performance, showed it flashing through the lights in under 17sec. Such a time was only matched within the 250 class by the Ducati Diana, with most 350 machines struggling to come even close.

Top speed and acceleration were good, but the handling was less assured. The suspension was too soft and under-damped, and this, more than anything else, limited the performance of the YDS2. This didn't concern the motorcycle press, who were very enthusiastic in both the USA as well as Europe, where the YDS2 was leading the push into the homeland of the non-Japanese competition.

The YDT1

Despite having two models already available for the 250 class, Yamaha felt there might be room for a third, combining the best of both worlds. There had been some comments about the lack of an electric start on the YDS2, despite the YD3 and the YA5 having this feature. Predictably, the YD3 had also been criticized for its dated appearance, so the obvious solution was to put a YD3 engine in a YDS frame: the end result was the YDT1.

It was offered for sale in the USA and the emerging markets in Europe throughout 1963 and 1964, but was dropped from the line going into 1965. This left just the YDS series, with its close links to racing success, to represent Yamaha in the 250 class. A 260cc version of the bike was also built and sold in the Japanese market, but the YET1 was even less successful and was withdrawn along with the YDT1. A similar approach had been adopted for the 125 class, with a YAT1 being produced with a newly designed tubular frame. The intention was that the bike would be a full sports model along the lines of the YDS series. The YA5 engine was tweaked to deliver 11bhp, but the performance was inadequate as the new chassis had increased the weight of the bike, and 125 sports bikes from Tohatsu and Bridgestone were faster. By increasing the bore by 1mm a 127cc version was also produced called the YBT1, but this, along with the YAT1, only lasted a single year of production.

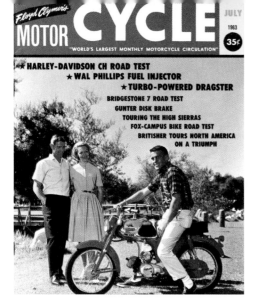

The drive to capture the hearts of young America was in full swing by July 1963.

Future president Hisao Koike leads a 1964 fact-finding mission to evaluate the US market.

While Yamaha were making inroads into their target export markets, they were still a long way behind market leaders Honda in terms of production figures. In the six-month period between April and September 1962, Honda had produced 564,109 motorcycles, compared to just 69,797 rolling out of Yamaha factories. Indeed Yamaha was in third place, trailing behind Suzuki, although well ahead of fourth-placed Tohatsu. Analysis of the breakdown of the Honda numbers revealed the massive 40 per cent share of the Honda 50cc step-through Cub, which had been introduced in 1958 and been a stunning success. In 1960, Honda had built a factory in Suzuka solely for this model, with a capacity of 50,000 units per month!

The MF2, MJ2

The failure of the MF1 meant that Yamaha were an outside player in this booming sector of the market, but the company was determined to redress this. The MF2 was announced in April 1962, essentially adopting the standard set by Honda with the pressed steel step-through frame, leading link front fork and swing-arm rear suspension. The air-cooled, single-cylinder 49cc engine with rotary valve induction had a three-speed gearbox and produced just 4.5bhp. A 55cc variation, the MJ2, appeared a couple of months later. Many manufacturers produced slightly larger versions of 50cc machines to overcome a Japanese law forbidding 50cc machines from carrying passengers.

Given the success of Honda in this market, almost all of the remaining manufacturers produced clones of the Cub, and the domestic market became very crowded. Yamaha was one of the more successful companies in opening up an export market, so they were keen to stimulate as great a demand in the US and Europe as that which Honda had achieved, leading to the Cub's success. From the middle of 1962, the MJ2 went on sale at just $285, marketed in the USA as the 'Riverside 55', together with an 'off the road' variant called the 'Omaha Trail'.

The MJ2 was a competent but undistinguished runaround, suitable for anyone looking for small, easy-to-use, unintimidating three-speed transport for zipping around the neighbourhood. The Omaha turned out to be a rather good equivalent for off-road use on forest trails and tracks, with sufficient power and torque to get the rider through the rough stuff. The engine had been tuned to run smoothly at slow speeds, with a massive rear sprocket to make the most of the modest power output. In fact there were twin rear sprockets mounted on the rear wheel, making it possible to shorten the chain, move to the other sprocket and use the bike around town when not out in the wilds of the US. The concept worked in the USA and the bike sold well.

Model	SC1	MF1	MF2
Year	1960	1960	1962
Capacity (cc)	175	50	50
Configuration	2-s 1 cyl	2-s 1 cyl	2-s 1 cyl
Induction	piston port	piston port	piston port
Bore × stroke (mm × mm)	62 × 58	40 × 40	40 × 40
Gearbox	torque converter	3-speed	3-speed
Final drive	shaft	chain	chain
Frame	monocoque	pressed steel	pressed steel
Wheelbase (mm, in)	1,260 (49.6)	1,130 (44.5)	1,140 (44.9)
Dry weight (kg, lb)	133 (293)	70 (154)	75 (165)
Power (bhp)	10.3 @ 5,500rpm	3 @ 8,000rpm	4.6 @ 7,500rpm
Torque (kgm)	1.45 @ 4,000rpm	0.3 @ 4,500rpm	0.47 @ 6,000rpm
Top speed (km/h, mph)	90 (56)	67 (42)	70 (44)

Model	MJ2	YF1	YJ1
Year	1962	1964	1964
Capacity (cc)	55	50	60
Configuration	2-s 1 cyl	2-s 1 cyl	2-s 1 cyl
Induction	piston port	rotary valve	rotary valve
Bore × stroke (mm × mm)	42 × 40	40 × 40	42 × 42
Gearbox	3-speed	4-speed	4-speed
Final drive	chain	chain	chain
Frame	pressed steel	pressed steel	pressed steel
Wheelbase (mm, in)	1,140 (44.9)	1,140 (44.9)	1,145 (45)
Dry weight (kg, lb)	72 (159)	75 (165)	79 (174)
Power (bhp)	5 @ 7,500rpm	4 @ 8,000rpm	4.9 @ 7,000rpm
Torque (kgm)	0.5 @ 6,000rpm	0.4 @ 6,000 rpm	0.5 @ 6,000rpm
Top speed (km/h, mph)	72 (45)	75 (47)	80 (50)

Model	YG1	H1	YA5
Year	1963	1965	1961
Capacity (cc)	73	86	123
Configuration	2-s 1 cyl	2-s 1 cyl	2-s 1 cyl
Induction	rotary valve	rotary valve	rotary valve
Bore × stroke (mm × mm)	47 × 42	50 × 44	56 × 50
Gearbox	4-speed	4-speed	4-speed
Final drive	chain	chain	chain
Frame	pressed steel	pressed steel	pressed steel
Wheelbase (mm, in)	1,145 (45)	1,145 (45)	1,250 (49.2)
Dry weight (kg, lb)	82 (181)	92 (203)	119 (262)
Power (bhp)	6 @ 7,000rpm	8 @ 7,000rpm	9.3 @ 6,000rpm
Torque (kgm)	0.65 @ 5,000rpm	0.85 @ 5,000rpm	1.22 @ 4,500rpm
Top speed (km/h, mph)	83 (52)	93 (58)	95 (59)

(continued…)

Model	YAT1	YDS2	YDS3
Year	1963	1962	1964
Capacity (cc)	123	246	246
Configuration	2-s 1 cyl	2-s 2 cyl	2-s 2 cyl
Induction	rotary valve	piston port	piston port
Bore × stroke (mm × mm)	56 × 50	56 × 50	56 × 50
Gearbox	4-speed	5-speed	5-speed
Final drive	chain	chain	chain
Frame	pressed steel	duplex cradle	duplex cradle
Wheelbase (mm, in)	1,265 (49.8)	1,290 (50.8)	1,295 (60)
Dry weight (kg, lb)	123 (271)	125 (276)	128 (282)
Power (bhp)	11 @ 7,000rpm	22 @ 7,500rpm	23 @ 7,500rpm
Torque (kgm)	1.22 @ 5,500rpm	2.14 @ 6,000rpm	2.3 @ 6,000rpm
Top speed (km/h, mph)	105 (65)	145 (90)	140 (87)

Model	YD3	YDT1	YM1
Year	1961	1963	1965
Capacity (cc)	247	247	305
Configuration	2-s 2 cyl	2-s 2 cyl	2-s 2 cyl
Induction	piston port	piston port	piston port
Bore × stroke (mm × mm)	54 × 54	54 × 54	60 × 54
Gearbox	4-speed	4-speed	5-speed
Final drive	chain	chain	chain
Frame	duplex cradle	duplex cradle	duplex cradle
Wheelbase (mm, in)	1,255 (49.4)	1,290 (50.8)	1,295 (60)
Dry weight (kg, lb)	142 (313)	140 (309)	151 (333)
Power (bhp)	17.2 @ 6,000rpm	18 @ 6,000rpm	25.5 @ 7,000rpm
Torque (kgm)	2.4 @ 4,500rpm	2.4 @ 4,500rpm	2.7 @ 6,000rpm
Top speed (km/h, mph)	120 (75)	130 (81)	145 (90)

The YG1

With the YD3, YDS2 and YDT1 in the 250 class, the YA5 in the 125, and MJ2 and MJ2T tiddlers, Yamaha seemed to be well represented in the small bike classes. However, there was in fact one more capacity class they wanted to enter: the 90cc. Japanese manufacturers had started producing motorcycles for this class in 1960, when licensing regulations in Japan were changed. Until that time, no license was needed for machines up to 50cc, but this was changed, making it mandatory for all riders to undergo a test to obtain a license. But many who went through the effort of passing their test in Japan wanted a 'real' motorcycle rather than the utilitarian step-throughs. Since sales tax was exempted in Japan on bikes with a capacity under 90cc, manufacturers started to produce sporty sub-90cc bikes to cater for this small but growing segment of the market.

Late in 1961, Yamaha had started work on the YG1, a 75cc variant of the rotary-valve, single-cylinder two-stroke engine that was now the mainstay of their range up to the 125cc YA5. However, the financial and management crisis led to it being put on hold for a year, finally arriving to market in both USA and Japan in March 1963. A scaled-down, pressed-steel frame from the YA5 housed the four-speed engine, generating 7bhp at 7,000rpm. It was the start of a bloodline that was to last well into the 1970s, with sports and trail-riding variants as well as several cosmetic makeovers. Once again it was in the right place at the right time, and America took to it in droves.

From this time, a myriad of small capacity sub-90cc model variations were built, to capitalize on the success of the YG1 and to keep the assembly lines as close to their production capacity as possible, to ensure the return on investment made on tooling up the factories. The YF1 was a 50cc version of the YG, which went through many cosmetic variations while retaining the original frame and engine. Ultimately it was to form the basis for the FS1E moped that took Europe by storm in the early 1970s. Naturally there was also a 60cc variation called the YJ1, as well as a YP1 with a 70cc tuned engine and sporty high-rise

exhaust, though this disappeared after 1965. The YGS1 engine was bored and stroked to 50 × 44mm to displace 86cc, and was renamed the H1.

During 1966, a new pressed-steel frame was developed and classified as the 'seven-bone', due to the shape of the main member, and this was adopted for all the sub-90cc capacity models in the Yamaha line-up. Thus the F-series engines displaced 50cc, the J-series 60cc, the G-series 73cc and the H-series 86cc. Still going strong into the 1970s, the models were rationalized and the confusing letter denomination replaced by displacements, leading to the YB60, YB90 and YB100, all still using the single-cylinder rotary-valve engine and 'seven-bone' frame. Although never challenging the huge success of the Honda 50cc Cub, Yamaha exported thousands of the bikes to export markets around the world, especially emerging markets, where there was heavy demand for this sort of simple and cheap transportation.

Racing Programmes

By the start of 1964, Yamaha had built themselves a decent bridgehead into the US and selected European markets. In total, between April and September 1963, Yamaha had exported almost 20,000 motorcycles with a capacity greater than 50cc, 25 per cent of their production run. In contrast Suzuki, who had been slow to move outside Japan, exported just 7 per cent of their bikes in this class, although they were still the number two manufacturer, thanks to the sub-50cc class. Even Honda, still dominating the market, had only exported 18 per cent of their larger capacity models. This was strong performance from Yamaha, and they were about to consolidate their lead in the export market through the racing programmes they had in place in both the GPs and US national racing.

After an unsuccessful short season of GP racing in 1961, Yamaha had spent 1962 weathering the crises in the company and developing their second generation of rotary-valved twin racer for the 250 class. The slow and bulky RD48 became the swift and agile RD56, and in 1963 it became clear that Honda had a serious challenger on their tail. A slightly lucky, but thoroughly deserved first and second place at the Belgian GP at Spa, the last of their planned GPs, was an enormous psychological boost to the Yamaha team. European riders were signed, and the initial planned short season for 1964 extended into a full-fledged challenge for the world title, which went to Phil Read and Yamaha at the cost of Jim Redman and Honda. The performance of the two-stroke twin against the four-stroke, 4-cylinder Honda made the headline in all motorcycle magazines. Yamaha's reputation had been made.

In the USA a similar process was at work, but then with the TD1, the production race bike that was available off the shelf to anyone with $600 and a racing habit. The TD1 had been built by Yamaha to beat Honda in the inaugural road race at Honda's new circuit at Suzuka in November 1962. The races had been for clubman racers – bikes with a street-bike pedigree – and Yamaha built and tuned a dozen bikes from YDS parts. The strategy was a great success, with TD1s taking the first two places in the 250, and even winning the 350 with a 255cc version of the TD1. Yamaha decided to market the racer, and started a bloodline of 250 production racers that led to the TZ 250 that is still produced today in 2009.

The TD1 was ideal for the US market, given the restrictions placed on racing factory prototypes. From 1963, TD1s started to appear in increasing numbers at the National and clubman roadraces, with practice for the Daytona 100-mile race in 1964, resulting in TD1 setting the top five times. Unfortunately the TD1s were a little low on stamina, finishing third and fourth in the 100-mile race. They were to return in 1965 and initiate a period of domination of 250 racing in the US, which was to last for years.

The US Yamaha marketing department played up on this to the full. When Cycle World was provided a YDS2 for a test, there just happened to be a TD1 also available, so the link was laid and of course the machines compared throughout the test report. When the YDS3 was released for road tests in July 1964, there just happened to be an RD56 on hand, together with Naitoh, the head of Yamaha engine design. Naturally there was full

coverage and comparison in the resulting article. Full-page ads recording Yamaha racing successes were also part of the campaign, with new media – namely television – and also running spots with race reports interspersed with sales pitch for the street machines. The message was hammered home, and booming sales were the result.

The YDS3

The YDS3 was released in mid-1964, and it carried a new feature that Yamaha had introduced to help widen the appeal of motorcycles, and two-strokes in particular. Labelled 'Autolube', it took the form of a separate pump and oil tank for the delivery of the two-stroke lubrication that had previously been supplied as a petroil mix from the fuel tank. The pump was driven off the mainshaft of the transmission, with plastic oil lines

○ Sensational Performance.! Acceleration 0 to 90 MPH Record Breaker.
○ Improved Port Timing With 2 Big Carburetors More HP less RPM.
○ ¼ Mile Drag Record Holder! 250 cc New Record Still Stands at 92 MPH plus W/Elapsed Time Less Than 14 sec.! 27 HP @7500 RPM.
○ Most Economical, Automatic Pump-feed Oiling System.
○ Separate Oil & Gas Tank. No Pre-mixng of Fuel.
○ Brand New 5-Speed Gear Box! Wider Teeth, Bigger Dogs & Wide Ratio.
○ Big, Powerful, Daytona Racer-Type Oversized Double Shoe Brakes.
○ Trophy Winner in Deluxe Style & Design With New Shiny Colors.
  ✲ Also available production road racer & scrambler with increased Hp.

Strengthening the sports link, the YDS3 was named after Yamaha's first international race on Catalina Island.

YAMAHA'S REVOLUTIONARY INJECTION SYSTEM

1965

SPECIAL FEATURES OF YAMAHA 250

250 WORLD CHAMPIONS

Yamaha's world grand prix racer proves the value of advanced engineering.

OIL INJECTION SYSTEM

No troublesome mixing required & no more plug fouls.

SENSATIONAL ACCELERATION

Standing 1/4 mile ········ 15.8 sec.

SPECIFICATION OF YDS-3

PERFORMANCE
Speed range ·························· 90—100mph
Fuel consumption on paved flat road ······· 80mi/gal
Climbing ability ························ 23°
Min. turning radius ··············· 88.0in. (2,200mm)
Brake distance ··40ft. (32mi/hr) =12.0m(50km/h) =

ENGINE
Model ·································· S 3
Type ························· 2 cycle gas engine
Lubrication system ····· Separate oil supply system
Displacement ················· 15cu. in. (246cc)
Bore & stroke ················· 2.21in × 1.97in
Fuel ······························· Gasoline

Compression ratio ···················· 7.5 : 1
Max. horsepower ···················· 27/7500
Max. torque ······················· 2.3/6000
Starting method ··············· Kick folding crank
Ignition system ················· Battery ignition

FUEL TANK CAPACITY ············· 4.1gal(14 ℓ)

OIL TANK CAPACITY ·············· 0.4gal(1.6ℓ)

SUSPENSION
Suspension front ···················· telescopic forks
Suspension rear ························ swing-arm
Damper front ·············· coil spring oil damper
Damper rear ·············· coil spring oil damper

Winner of the Auto & Motor Sport Magazine
Safety & Engineering Award.

YAMAHA
INTERNATIONAL CORPORATION

SINCE 1887

Technical innovation was starting to become important with the presentation of Autolube on the YDS3.

Mid-1960s and the demand for small bikes was exploding. Another batch of YF1 ready for shipping.

delivering the oil to feeds in the inlet manifold of the carburettor. The stroke of the oil pump was linked to throttle position, increasing delivery rates as the bike accelerated. It was another small enhancement that made life with a Yamaha two-stroke a little easier, and was soon adopted for the complete range, even finding its way on to the production racers late in the 1960s.

Another power increase was the result of the move from the YDS2 to the YDS3, with associated strengthening of the crank assembly and new cylinders, pistons and rings. Many of the improvements could be traced to the experience gained from the TD1 racers, where for instance there had been reports of the left-hand crankshaft snapping at the clutch mounting. 5mm thicker shafts were the answer. Carburettors had grown to 24mm (0.9in) to supply the extra charge need-

ed to generate the 24bhp now produced. The clutch was lifted from the YD3 with some detailed changes. The transmission was left unchanged, except the engine sprocket in the rear drive lost a tooth.

Sensitive to the criticism of the handling of the YDS2, some attention was paid to the frame and other chassis components. New front forks as well as updated rear shock absorbers, with adjustable spring pre-load, went some way to improve the steering. The resulting overall package was welcomed as an improvement over an already good 250 sports machine, and demand for the new 250 in both Europe and USA was heavy.

Too heavy in fact, as the motorcycle business had boomed from 1963 and Yamaha had underestimated the production capacity they would need to meet the orders flooding in. At the end of 1963

ABOVE: The early model 1964 YDS3 had the tuning fork logo on the tank.

BELOW: Second-generation YDS3 with Yamaha lettering on the tank.

Also known as the cross-country sport 305, the YM1 was justifiably popular in the USA.

Also known as the cross-country sport 305, the YM1 was justifiably popular in the USA.

Yamaha had increased their production levels to 20,000 per month in factories that were tooled for a level of 15,000 per month. While new factories were being built, double shifts were introduced and they managed to get production levels up to 22,000 units per month. Even so, they could only supply 70 per cent of the orders that were being placed. Of these, 8,000 were allocated to export, but the demand for the US alone was greater. Koike san, now managing director of Yamaha, went to the US to explain the difficulties, but returned with the sobering news that the extra capacity that would come on-line when the new factories were ready early in 1965 would still be inadequate. A crash programme was put in place to increase the capacity of the new factories to 35,000 units per month, and a prayer was offered that the potential customers would not turn to the competition.

From the very first bike that they built, Yamaha had adopted a principle of boring out the cylinder by a couple of millimetres and offering the same model in the next largest capacity class. There had been a YB1, a 127cc version of the Red

Dragonfly, and similarly, there had been 'E' versions of the YD and YDS series, with an engine displacing 255cc. Honda had produced the CR77 as a limited edition production racer in 1962 with a displacement of 305cc and enough power to give the tired old British 350 singles a run for their money. In 1964, a streetbike labelled the Super Hawk had come on the market with an almost identical silhouette to the 250 Hawk, but with the larger engine. It was a great success, and encouraged Honda to go a step further and work on their first large capacity bike, the CB450, which presaged the start of the end of the British motorcycle industry. Yamaha decided to join the chase.

The YM1

The 305 option was an easy way for Yamaha to move up a class, as the YDS engine design could remain unchanged, with simply a revised set of reciprocating parts to enable the bore and stroke to increase to 60 × 54mm. Transmission ratios were also slightly different, the most noticeable

The going's even greater with Yamaha in '65

Catalina 250 Twin (Model YDS3)
A hot one on the street, a winner on the track! Yamaha oil injection—dual cylinders—twin carburetors—5-speed constant mesh gearbox—$630, POE, Los Angeles.

Electra 250 Twin (Model YD-3)
A well-mannered twin for the open road. 4-speed constant mesh gearbox—19 HP, single carburetor—electric starter—big waterproof brakes—$549, POE, Los Angeles.

Riverside 55 (Model YJ1)
Safe and quiet—biggest bargain going in sportcycles! Big-bike styling and performance—4-speed gearbox —rotary valve engine— safety brakes—$249, POE, Los Angeles.

Santa Barbara 125 (Model YA6)
A zesty lightweight with rotary valve engine— electric starter—revolutionary oil injection. The Santa Barbara's nobly exciting ride makes you feel like a Samurai. $454, POE, Los Angeles.

Big Bear Scrambler 250 (Model YDS3-C)
Hottest and very newest in the Yamaha line! New oil injection—speedometer—tachometer—5-speed gearbox—knobby tires—twin carburetor engine—high pipes—$690, POE, Los Angeles.

Rotary Jet 80 (Model YG1-SK)
Fastest-selling sportcycle in America. Rotary jet—oil injection—big, dustproof, waterproof brakes—telescopic front and swing-arm rear— $350, POE, Los Angeles.

Trailmaster 80 (Model YG1-TK)
Extra climbing power for high-country trails! Rotary valve engine—new oil injection—knobby tires—quiet 4-speed gearbox—oversized rear sprocket—$365, POE, Los Angeles.

Omaha Trailmaster 80 (Model MG-1T)
A sure-footed trail bike for sportsmen! Rotary valve engine—4-speed transmission—knobby tires—electric starter—step-thru frame—$299, POE, Los Angeles.

YAMAHA
INTERNATIONAL CORPORATION
since 1887

Winner of the Auto and Motor Sport Magazine Safety and Engineering Award.

250cc World Grand Prix Champion

P. O. Box 54540, Los Angeles, California, 90054
Eastern Branch: U. S. Rte. 30, Bell Lane, Downingtown, Pa.
Canada: Pacific Seaboard Ltd., 1961 W. 4th Ave., Vancouver 9, B.C., Canada

Most of Yamaha's models could still fit on the back of a magazine at the end of 1964.

With the YGS1, even the small bikes were getting the sports treatment.

change being the closer gap between fourth and fifth gear. Displacement increased to 305cc and power went up a couple of bhp to 26bhp, but more useful was the increased torque produced by the engine. This helped to achieve quarter-mile times under 15sec, faster than many 500s and close to the 650 and 750 British street twins.

Cosmetically, the bike looked quite similar to the YDS3, with the clear distinction of white sidewall for the seat unit and the reintroduction of the full 'Yamaha' name on the tank, rather than the crossed tuning forks. The resulting bike, the YM1, was once again very popular in the USA, if you could get one, as production lines were still struggling to meet the demand. Perhaps this is the reason why the model was not offered for sale throughout Europe: Yamaha could sell every one they produced simply on the US market. Only Germany and the Netherlands were offered the YM1, and that was not before the start of 1966. This coincided with an update to the YDS3, with the same tank styling appearing, some engine porting adjustments and the YM1 gearbox ratios being passed down to the 250 model.

Ten Years of Yamaha

As the scales tipped to the second half of the 1960s, Yamaha could look back on their first ten years of motorcycle production with some amazement and pride: amazement that they had been able to achieve so much in such a short period of time, pride that it had been achieved in the face of massive competition from a domestic industry and a sceptical export market in a country that had been at war with Japan so few years before. Aided by the new social attitude of the youth of America, with increasing rejection of the conformity of earlier generations, it was the first post-war golden age of 'change', and Honda and Yamaha were able to exploit this. It was a classic example of being in the right place at the right time, but equally important, with the right product and image. Chastened by the mistakes of 1961/1962, the company had recovered well under the direction of Hisao Koike, Kawakami san's right-hand man, who had led the drive for success in the export market. The foundation had been built; guts and grit would secure the future.

3 Go West!

Yamaha had been quick to realize that their future lay outside Japan. Their determined push into the US market in particular during the early 1960s had resulted in strong sales, as the US interest in reliable, unintimidating and fun motorcycles went into overdrive. 1964 had been a testing year as demand heavily exceeded supply, but re-evaluation of the scale of the US market, and prompt steps to address the shortfall on production capacity, had set the company up to exploit the market to the full. As the company moved into the second decade of their existence they could justifiably claim to have the strongest outlook of all the Japanese motorcycle manufacturers. Although still lagging in third place in terms of the total number of bikes produced, for the first time in 1965 exports had exceeded domestic sales, with 63 per cent streaming into the USA. With markets in Europe still relatively untouched, but with the experience of establishing a large-scale export organization behind them, Yamaha were set to take on the world.

The first step to achieving their goals for domination of the export market was to deepen their product line with competitive products in each class. Until 1965, Yamaha had adopted a design philosophy that restricted sub-250cc capacity machines to a single cylinder. This in fact ran counter to a trend that was forming in the racing world, where even the smallest of engines were multi-cylinder in the drive to increase engine speed and obtain the associated extra power, albeit over an increasingly narrow powerband. By the end of the 1960s, as the Japanese withdrew from GP racing, this strategy had produced some amazing engines, culminating in the three-cylinder Suzuki 50cc RP68 that produced about 20bhp, but needed fourteen gears to keep it in the powerband. Yamaha themselves had raced 125 twins in 1964 and were working on the 125 and 250 V4 engines that they campaigned in the mid-1960s. It was logical therefore that the small featherweight street bikes would also adopt a multi-cylinder approach.

Discover the swinging world of YAMAHA

⊕ RECENTLY DEVELOPED AND DESIGNED ENGINE BASED ON THE YAMAHA GRAND PRIX ROAD RACER.

⊕ SENSATIONAL ACCELERATION AND REMARKABLE POWER RANGE WITH TWIN CYLINDER & TWIN CARBURETOR.

⊕ SEPARATE OIL AND GAS TANK. NO PREMIXING OF OIL WITH GASOLINE.

⊕ PERFECT WATER & DUSTPROOF DOUBLE SAFETY BRAKES.

Bit of a squeeze to get on the dual seat, but I don't think he's worried. YL1 for young lovers.

Phil Read on a YL1 at the foot of Mount Fuji? The deliberate blur suggests otherwise.

The YL1 Twin Jet

During 1965 it was decided to create a 90cc capacity model using a conventional piston-ported twin-cylinder engine. It was hung under the same pressed-steel frame as used by the YG derivatives with their rotary-valve, single-cylinder engine. The engine was typical Yamaha twin in design, although at last the clutch was moved from the crankshaft to the transmission mainshaft, a welcome change that was also to be adopted by the other twins in the line-up. Another improvement was that the drive for the Autolube, standard now on all of the Yamaha bikes, was tapped off the crankshaft instead of the main transmission shaft, so if the engine was running, the oil would flow. For the export mar-

ket a 100cc capacity engine was produced by boring out the cylinders from 36.5mm to 38mm, and the motorcycle was marketed in 1966 as the YL1 'Twin Jet'.

It must be said that the Yamaha range in the USA was getting quite crowded at the lower end, with nine of the twelve models offered at the time weighing in at under 125cc. Performance differences between, for instance, the YG1 series and the new YL1 were insignificant, and it was left to the marketing and sales departments to put a spin on the new model to catch the marketplace. It was pushed hard as a sports model, suggesting a strategy that would lead to 'twins' meaning 'sports' and 'singles' meaning utility and convenience. Also Honda had started to push the

One of the myriad of small capacity motorcycles Yamaha continued to build, the 1968 H3C.

Quite distinctive styling set the YAS1 apart from all the other export twins offered in 1968.

technology angle with an overhead cam version of their Super Cub 90, so the 'twin' was Yamaha's response. The Honda versus Yamaha wars were really hotting up in the USA.

The 'sportsbike' label would have been more credible if a tubular frame had been used to raise the sporting image, but the sales pitch went into overdrive with images of owners flat on the tank, and talk of hopped-up bikes taking you 'pretty close to the century mark'. In reality the bike would top out at around 60mph (96km/h), but a fairly sharp powerband did provide a modest 'kick in the pants', encouraging the impression of a sporty bike. With the big marketing push behind it the model sold well, and at the end of 1967 Yamaha owned up to what everyone had known all along. They fitted it out with an electric starter, and the sales pitch changed gear, emphasizing other qualities of the little twin. There was an attempt to retain a sports 90 bike, when the 90cc engine was slotted into a tubular frame to create the HS1, with a 100cc version labelled as the YLS1.

Interest in the ultra-small sub-125 class that had peaked in the USA in the 1960s was waning as the decade drew to a close, and never reached the same level of intensity in Europe. The YLS1 disappeared after a single year of sale; the HS1 derivatives were to continue in Asian markets for a couple of years, with cosmetic changes, before the twin-cylinder engine disappeared from this class at the end of 1972.

The 125cc YAS1

Sales crews now had a real sports bike to push in the featherweight class: the 125cc YAS1. The new machine took the twin engine from the AT90 and bored the cylinder to 43mm diameter. The engine was of a standard piston-port design, but reflected the latest technology that had been developed through the TD racers. There was a pair of transfer ports on either side of the cylinder, rather than the traditional single transfer port, making a total of five ports. On the TD race series, the extra ports, positioned to offer the best flow of fresh charge to flush out the spent exhaust gases after ignition, had produced a dramatic increase in power. The YAS1 offered 13bhp at 7,000rpm, but there was also the YAS1D available with a slightly tuned engine that produced 15bhp at 8,500rpm – and weighed 12kg (26lb) less. Guess which one was the most popular.

A spine frame was employed to hold the little twin, with a single large-diameter tubular beam dropping down from the top of the headstock and curving behind the engine to a fabricated box that held the rear engine mounting and swing-arm pivot point. A similar tube ran from the bottom of the headstock to the engine mounting point at the front of the engine. The crankcases were stressed members of the chassis. A lot of attention was paid to the styling, and a very smart machine was the result. The air filters were housed in vertical chromed covers and these dominated the side of the bike, becoming one of its key distinguishing features. The YAS1 came to market in November 1967 and was to be one of the best-selling models for the company in Europe, with good sales in the USA, especially of the 'scrambler' version with upswept exhausts that were very fashionable in the US at this time.

The YCS1 180 Twin

As the featherweight bikes had evolved, Yamaha had reintroduced another model that bridged the move from featherweight to lightweight. When the company had embarked on the motorcycle manufacturing path, their first expansion after the introduction of the YA1, 'Red Dragonfly', had been with the YC1, displacing 175cc. Now, ten years later, it was felt that there was a significant enough segment to reintroduce a stepping stone from the smallest twins to the mainstream 250s. The decision may also have been influenced by the arrival in 1966 of the Honda CB160, a bored-out version of the CB125 twin with ohc and a sporty image.

Yamaha responded with the YCS1 180 twin for the 1967 model year. Its production had not merely been a question of boring out the 125 twin or sleeving down the 250. The engine was a conventional three-port measuring 50 × 46mm, which produced 19bhp at 7,500rpm. Engine layout was conventional, with the vertically split crankcases following the design of the rest of the twins in the line-up. Autolube was, of course, a standard feature, as were the five-speed gearbox and the twin carburettors.

The very first YCS1 was fitted with 18mm Mikunis, but a year after the introduction of the new model, five-port cylinders were fitted and the throat diameter of the carburettors grew to 20mm. This resulted in a slight power increase, which was very welcome, as the YCS1 was no lightweight. There are reports of a weight of 131kg (289lb), which would have been gross, but others refer to a hefty 118kg (260lb), which was still a heavy bike.

Some of the extra weight was caused by the return of another feature that had disappeared a couple of years before. Yamaha were still undecided as to whether electric starters should or should not be provided on their twins, despite the ease with which they would kick-start. The company now entered a period of fitting a combined dynamo and start motor, along with 12volt electrics to power the starter.

Undergoing simultaneous development, both the YAS1 and the YCS1 used the same beam-type frame, with suitable geometry for the larger YCS1 engine. With the introduction of the five-port engine, the cosmetics had been altered, with a chequered flag on the side panels replacing the 'electric' and '180' epithets.

Although peak interest had past by the end of 1967, Yamaha were still pushing small bikes such as the YF5, hard.

The CS Series

Most of the YCS1s produced were earmarked for the US market, and it was to be 1969, with the arrival of the CS2, before Europe was exposed to the 180 twin. The CS2 was primarily a styling exercise with a few small detail changes to the five-port second-generation engine of the YCS1. It was well received in Europe, where there was still strong interest in the sub-250 class, mainly due to licensing laws allowing learners to ride bikes up to 250cc. For many new riders, the 250s were considered just a little too intimidating with their 14sec quarter-mile times and speeds close to 100mph (160km/h), and the 175 class was considered a good stepping stone. Both the CS series and the Honda CB175 were seen as popular alternatives.

The last of the 180 twins was to be found in the 1972 CS5, which again underwent a few changes on the engine with respect to its predecessor, linked to the increase in capacity to 197cc. The most significant upgrade was the adoption of a new frame for both the CS and AS series. The basic beam, which had been present from the start, remained, but the rails of the sub-frame extended up to the bottom of the steering head to provide far stronger support. A complete facelift brought the CS5 styling firmly in line with the rest of the twins that were marketed in the early 1970s, a range that emphasized the sports heritage and pedigree of the series.

The YDS3

With the YDS3, Yamaha were selling the best of the mid-1960s 250 sports models. They could sell as many as the factories in Japan could produce, and perhaps an air of complacency crept into the company. With the introduction in 1965 of the YDS3C, with the up-swept exhaust pipes and marketed as the Big Bear, they were able to maintain the image of an active 250 class development programme.

It is a little surprising that Yamaha didn't announce a new model at the end of 1966, as the YDS3 underwent enough changes to warrant it. The cylinder porting was adjusted, which, together with new heads, raised the power output to 26bhp. Gearbox ratios from the YM1 were fitted and the styling of the 305cc big brother adopted. A big splash model announcement would have helped to counter the new bikes coming out of Japan, which offered a serious performance challenge.

Halfway house to the 'big twins' was the 1967 YCS1.

Yamaha's most famous and celebrated moped, the FS1, was the legacy of a decade of small two-stroke motorcycles.

Paint it pink and add tassels to the seat and you've got a new bike to conquer the female segment.

Yamaha and the Japanese Export Market

The consolidation of the Japanese motorcycle industry was almost complete, with just seven manufacturers still active by the end of 1965. As well as Honda, Yamaha and Suzuki, there were Kawasaki, Bridgestone and Lilac/Marusho, all listed as manufacturers, with Fuji still producing the Rabbit scooter. The contrast between the top manufacturer Honda and the smallest, Lilac, was extreme. In the first six months of 1966, Honda built 756,956 machines, while Lilac produced ninety-four, ninety-two of which were exported to the USA. Unsurprisingly, Lilac was to fold later that year. The US market was still critical to the Japanese companies as it accounted for 70 per cent of their export sales.

Suzuki had for years been the second largest manufacturer in Japan behind Honda, but had been overtaken in the export market by Yamaha. In a desperate move to recoup this, they head-hunted Jack McCormack, the Honda America general manager who had established Honda's position in the US until 1964. He set about building Suzuki's position in the market, and with the arrival of the 1965 T20, known as the

X6 Hustler in the US, had the right weapon to do so. With a 15kg (33lb) weight advantage, six speeds and over 30bhp power output, this was a sports 250 to dethrone the YDS3.

Kawasaki had similar plans to extend their line-up beyond their four-stroke twin replicas of British bikes. They decided that a sports 250 would build a bridgehead in the US market. The result was the rotary twin A1 of 1966, again with 30bhp, but a similar weight to the YDS3. Noting the success of the TD1 derivative of the YDS series, Kawasaki also produced a production racer version of the 250, the A1R, with performance figures significantly better than the TD1B of the time. Yamaha's position as leading two-stroke manufacturer and challenger to Honda's four-stroke world, was under threat.

The YDS5E

At last, at the end of 1966, the YDS5E was announced, but it lacked the sparkle of the previous models. Yamaha chose to emphasize the electric start as the unique selling point, as indeed it was, but it was not the message needed when confronted by the Suzuki and Kawasaki rocket ships.

Yamaha also took a closer look at disc-valve street twins, as shown on this YDS5 prototype.

Amazingly, the new YDS5 was not as fast as the YDS3. Alloy barrels with cast-iron sleeves replaced the heavy all-iron items on the YDS3. At last the clutch was moved from the left-hand end of the crankshaft to the main shaft of the transmission, a major improvement for the TD series, with their persistent clutch problems, but also reducing the vibration produced by the heavy clutch spinning at engine speeds.

The Autolube oil pump was now driven off the crankshaft to ensure continuous delivery even when stationary. As on the YCS1, the electric starter was combined with the dynamo and powered by twelve-volt electrics. Carburettors grew to 26mm, with a redesign of the air filter housing to reduce intake roar.

It is quite possible that the new design, featuring a single air intake passage, was the cause of the rather lacklustre performance of the new bike. The frame was of the same design as the YDS3, but was built from heavier gauge alloy, with a slight change in steering geometry to cure a nervous front end over bumps. Rather conservative styling completed the bike, with the enlarged fuel tank dominating the front and the shrouded rear suspension appearing rather dated in comparison to the naked springs of the X6 Suzuki.

Yamaha needed to address the lack of poke on the new 250, and a year later a new version was released with 'GP technology' in the form of 'five-port technology' applied to the engine, with extra gulleys cut in the cylinder wall, acting as transfer ports through corresponding windows in the pistons. This matched the design of the new production racer, the TD1C, and helped improve engine scavenging as well as cooling the piston crown.

The 1968 YDS5E could give the Suzuki a run for its money.

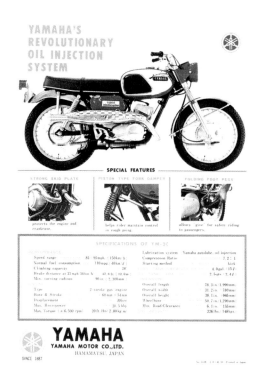

Hitting the showrooms at the peak of the street scrambler fashion, the YM2C sold very well.

Technology drive with the E for electric start and the five-port engine layout on the YDS5.

The 305cc YM2

Cosmetically identical to the YDS5E, the 305cc M2 was released on the market in early 1967, alongside the 250. As before there were many shared components between the two models, but the single most significant, and inexplicable, difference was the lack of electric starting on the YM2. Despite the larger capacity engine, the YM2 was just 2kg (4.4lb) heavier than its smaller brother, and with an extra 4bhp of power, offered the level of performance that the DS5 should have had.

This was the end of the line for the 305cc twin, although the YM2 continued to be sold until the end of 1968, with the street scrambler 'C' version proving especially popular. At last Yamaha had chosen to take the plunge and build a full-blown 350 to compete with the Honda 450cc Black Bomber and the increasing number of other Japanese mid-range motorcycles that

were appearing. The traditional British motorcycle industry, dominant in the large capacity classes, had scarcely five years to go; by the end of 1972 it was all but dead.

The YR1

Honda had announced the CB450, featuring a twin-cylinder double overhead cam engine, in the spring of 1965, offering it for sale in the USA from 1966. The technology they used had matured in their GP racing programme and they were able to apply mass production techniques to lower the overall unit costs for the production of the quite complex engine. Its sophistication with respect to the British 500 and 650 twins, with which it would compete, illustrated how well Japan had embraced mass-production techniques and how short-sighted the British industry had been in not following suit while it still could.

Model	AT90	YL1	YAS1
Year	1966	1966	1967
Capacity (cc)	89	97	124
Configuration	2-s 2 cyl	2-s 2 cyl	2-s 2 cyl
Induction	piston port	piston port	piston port
Bore × stroke (mm × mm)	36.5 × 43	38 × 43	43 × 43
Gearbox	4-speed	4-speed	5-speed
Final drive	chain	chain	chain
Frame	pressed steel	pressed steel	simplex spine
Wheelbase (mm, in)	1,145 (45.1)	1,127 (44.4)	1,200 (47.2)
Dry weight (kg, lb)	100 (221)	92 (203)	98 (216)
Power (bhp)	8 @ 8,000rpm	9.5 @ 8,500rpm	15 @ 9,500rpm
Torque (kgm)	0.73 @ 7,500rpm	0.83 @ 8,000rpm	1.3 @ 8,000rpm
Top speed (km/h, mph)	87 (54)	110 (68)	130 (81)

Model	YCS1	CS2	CS3
Year	1967	1969	1971
Capacity (cc)	181	181	195
Configuration	2-s 2 cyl	2-s 2 cyl	2-s 2 cyl
Induction	piston port	piston port	piston port
Bore × stroke (mm × mm)	50 × 46	50 × 46	52 × 46
Gearbox	5-speed	5-speed	5-speed
Final drive	chain	chain	chain
Frame	simplex spine	simplex spine	simplex spine
Wheelbase (mm, in)	1,245 (49)	1,245 (49)	1,245 (49)
Dry weight (kg, lb)	118 (260)	118 (260)	117 (258)
Power (bhp)	19.6 @ 7,500rpm	19.6 @ 7,500rpm	22 @ 7,500rpm
Torque (kgm)	1.91 @ 7,000rpm	1.91 @ 7,000rpm	2.17 @ 7,000rpm
Top speed (km/h, mph)	126 (78)	135 (84)	140 (87)

Model	YDS5	DS6	DS7
Year	1968	1969	1971
Capacity (cc)	246	246	247
Configuration	2-s 2 cyl	2-s 2 cyl	2-s 2 cyl
Induction	piston port	piston port	piston port
Bore × stroke (mm × mm)	56 × 50	56 × 50	54 × 54
Gearbox	5-speed	5-speed	5-speed
Final drive	chain	chain	chain
Frame	duplex cradle	duplex cradle	duplex cradle
Wheelbase (mm, in)	1,290 (50.8)	1,290 (50.8)	1,320 (52)
Dry weight (kg, lb)	145 (320)	138 (304)	138 (304)
Power (bhp)	27.5 @ 8,000rpm	27.5 @ 7,500rpm	30 @ 7,500rpm
Torque (kgm)	2.55 @ 7,500rpm	2.65 @ 7,000rpm	2.9 @ 7,000rpm
Top speed (km/h, mph)	148 (92)	145 (90)	150 (93)

(continued…)

Model	YM2C	YR1	YR2C
Year	1967	1967	1968
Capacity (cc)	305	348	348
Configuration	2-s 2 cyl	2-s 2 cyl	2-s 2 cyl
Induction	piston port	piston port	piston port
Bore × stroke (mm × mm)	60 × 54	61 × 59.6	61 × 59.6
Gearbox	5-speed	5-speed	5-speed
Final drive	chain	chain	chain
Frame	duplex cradle	duplex cradle	duplex cradle
Wheelbase (mm, in)	1,290 (50.8)	1,335 (52.6)	1,335 (52.6)
Dry weight (kg, lb)	148 (326)	155 (342)	155 (342)
Power (bhp)	31 @ 7,500rpm	34.1 @ 7,000rpm	36 @ 7,000rpm
Torque (kgm)	3.2 @ 6,500rpm	3.57 @ 6,500rpm	4.08 @ 6,500rpm
Top speed (km/h, mph)	153 (95)	160 (99)	160 (99)

Model	R3	R5
Year	1969	1970
Capacity (cc)	348	347
Configuration	2-s 2-cyl	2-s 2 cyl
Induction	piston port	piston port
Bore × stroke (mm × mm)	61 × 59.6	64 × 54
Gearbox	5-speed	5-speed
Final drive	chain	chain
Frame	duplex cradle	duplex cradle
Wheelbase (mm, in)	1,340 (52.8)	1,320 (52)
Dry weight (kg, lb)	155 (342)	141 (311)
Power (bhp)	34 @ 7,000rpm	36 @ 7,000rpm
Torque (kgm)	3.6 @ 6,500rpm	3.8 @ 6,500rpm
Top speed (km/h, mph)	160 (99)	170 (106)

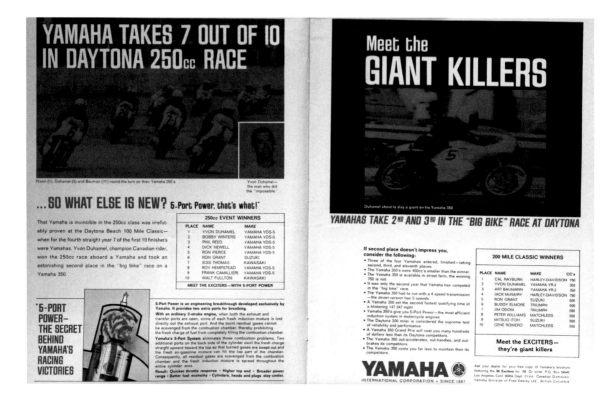

Links to racing as important as ever, with Daytona riders now on YDS5s rather than the actual TD1s.

Yamaha were slow to respond, just as they had been slow to introduce the YDS5E, their main development time in 1965 being spent on the tiny AT90 twin. But during 1966 the new model began to take shape, and it went on sale in the USA early in 1967, alongside the YDS5E and the YCS1.

The YR1 was a mixed bag. It was a milestone in that it was the first Yamaha two-stroke twin to adopt the horizontally split crankcases that would become common to the whole range. The engine layout followed the standard developing now for the twins, with the clutch on the right-hand end of the mainshaft, and the primary gear and Autolube pump on the right-hand end of the crankshaft, alloy barrels with cast-iron liners fed by two Mikuni carburettors of 28mm diameter on the 350. But in many ways it was also a massive disappointment. The cylinders were regular three-port, and performance was no better than adequate, just managing to break the magic ton of

top speed, and a quarter mile just under 15sec. Styling was very reserved, clearly aligned with the dreary styling applied to the YCS1 and YDS5.

This had been Yamaha's opportunity to stun the world with an outright fire-breathing race-bike for the street, reflecting their successes on the racetrack, but instead it seemed more like a steady tourer. Actually, it was in many ways a two-stroke equivalent of the CB450, so perhaps this was a deliberate choice. The chassis was essentially a larger version of the YDS5 frame with more powerful brakes, thanks to new drum linings. Suspension was quite firm, and steering neutral. The YR1 was a decent bike, but it could have been so much more.

Developing the Larger Bike

It was now critical that Yamaha establish a leading position in the larger bikes in their range, as there were strong signs that the US market was

ABOVE: *Early styling exercise for the new 350, code-named the YX03.*

BELOW: *The final version of the YR1, which launched Yamaha's legendary series of 350 two-stroke twins.*

The DS6 fitted with 'non-slip tires for safety' as the marketing blurb usefully points out.

Somehow the YR2 looked better on the tarmac than out in a field.

maturing, with growth tailing off, perhaps even shrinking. Honda had first noticed this during 1966, as demand for the smallest sub-50cc bikes seemed to evaporate overnight.

During 1967 it became clear that interest in the small capacity classes was waning, Bridgestone in particular suffering badly as they tried to crack the market with their 90cc rotary twin. A number of factors seemed to be at work. The rate of growth of the standard of living in the US peaked around 1965, so there was less money around for indulging in impulse purchases. The novelty of the zippy little bikes, buzzing around the town, was also wearing off. Interest in the smaller motorcycles had come largely from a new market segment of non-traditional motorcyclists who had bought themselves an inexpensive bike for fun, convenience, or on a whim, but were unlikely to become long-term motorcycle owners. Owners would either stick with the bike or, as the excitement faded, push it into a corner of the garage and forget about it. There was no natural evolution for many of these owners to larger Japanese motorcycles. The few that did become hardcore motorcyclists would move up through the 250, and now 350 classes and on to the large capacity Harleys, Triumphs and BSAs.

It was therefore important for all the Japanese manufacturers to expand their model line to capture this demand as it arose. At the close of the 1960s, the other big three – Honda, Suzuki and Kawasaki – in general did a better job than Yamaha in this area. Yamaha, however, were focused on opening up a new line of motorcycle business headed by their DT1, the dual sports off-road class.

The draft for the Vietnam War also put a dent in revenues. Not only were many potential customers fighting a war far from home, but also anyone drafted to Vietnam who had purchased a motorcycle on credit was entitled to defer payments until they returned. Sales growth flattened, with inventories growing, depressing Yamaha's financials in 1967 and 1968. It was at this time that Yamaha started to look more closely at the underdeveloped European market, and how best to serve it.

Model Upgrades

A year after their introduction, both the 250 and 350 underwent a mid-term upgrade to the engine with five-port cylinders intended to widen the powerband and raise peak power slightly. While the 250 continued to be called a

YAMAHA 250 STREET SCRAMBLER MODEL DS6-C

Now, the world's most complete 250cc street scrambler.
In the past, a lot of good scramblers—many of them Yamaha—have made scramble riding popular all over the world. But until the DS6-C, none has offered as much in performance and design refinements. Beginning with a powerful 30 bhp twin cylinder engine featuring Yamaha's 5-port super scavenging system and Autolube oil injection system, the DS6-C brings new performance standards to the 250cc class.

Custom features include twin upswept pipes, separate tachometer and speedometer, water and dust-proof brakes, large nonslip seat and sure-gripping universal tires.
Also new are GP type handle grips for fatigue-free riding.

The last of the line in street scramblers, now the real thing was available with the DT-1.

For one year the R3 would be Yamaha's top of the range, but the four-stroke XS1 was already on the drawing board.

GRAND PRIX 350 (R-3)
A brand new bike. 350ccs that have torn up the biggest of the big name tracks. (e.g. Daytona, Laconia, Mosport) An engine track-tested under every condition—consistently in the winner's circle. How does it perform on the street? Like a dream. A five-port power dream.

SPECIFICATIONS
Engine............................5-Port, Parallel Twin
Displacement.................348.2cc (21.23 cu.in.)
Max. horsepower........36BHP @ 7,000 rpm
Speed range............................100 mph plus
Transmission..................................5-Speed
Starting system...................................Kick
Weight..340 lbs.

DS5, the 350 became the YR2. In their search for performance the company had been desperate enough to consider using completely new disc-valve engines especially for the 350, needing to compete with the much more powerful Kawasaki and Bridgestone twins using this form of induction. In the end it was decided that restyling and the five-port cylinders would be adequate to remain competitive. It has to be said that the lines on the YR2 were a lot cleaner, the restyled teardrop tank doing a good job in giving the bike a much sleeker appearance.

Since February 1967, when the YCS1E, YDS5E, YM2 and YR1 release had coincided, the annual model upgrade for the 180, 250 and 350 occurred pretty much simultaneously. In January 1969, the last model update for the decade was announced. Externally it was clear that the 250 engine had been altered, thanks to the polished square-shaped cooling fins of the barrels. Internally the cylinders were quite new, with the next step in porting design that Yamaha had adopted primarily for their 250 TD racer, the TD2. The 'five-port' design of the past had involved the use

of two main transfer ports fed through passages in the cylinder wall from the crankcase, plus two auxiliary gulleys cut in the wall of the cylinder, fed through windows in the piston skirt.

The new design introduced full crankcase-fed auxiliary transfer ports, enabling the shape of the passages to influence the direction that the fresh charge would flow into the cylinder. Experimentation in this area, combined with exhaust pipe design, would for many years form the basis for improving the scavenging and resulting power output of racing two-stroke Yamahas.

There were a few other detail changes in the engine. Better lubrication for the big and little ends of the conrods was achieved by milling extra slots in the surface of the conrod eyes. A slightly different cush-drive was fitted to the clutch, and once again the air filters were reworked to find the best compromise between sufficient air flow and adequate damping of the intake roar. Again Yamaha changed their mind about the need for an electric start and it was removed from the DS6, never to appear again on a Yamaha 250 two-stroke twin.

The R3 could be pushed hard and handled well by contemporary 1969 standards.

Top US dealers were given the VIP treatment with a visit to Japan in November 1969.

Nothing significant changed on the chassis, which had shown itself to be quite satisfactory on the YDS5. The styling was a refined version of the YR2, with a long and flat tank, its shape emphasized with subtle striping along its profile. It suited the sports image well. The same styling was applied to the R3 and this was almost all that changed in the transition from YR2. The improved conrod design of the DS6 was also used, along with new cylinders and heads, exhaust pipes and cosmetic changes to the instruments, now featuring separate clocks for the speedo and tacho.

Although the model identifier was to continue, the DS6 really marked the end of the 250 series that had originated ten years earlier with the YDS1. It was arguably still the best of the 250s built in Japan, with a good balance between speed, handling and comfort. The engine was definitely stronger than the YDS5E, and much easier to use due to the fatter mid-range power delivery. While the YDS1 had set the standard for the 1960s for styling in the 250 class, the DS6 was more of a wolf in sheep's

clothing, looking a little boring but able to deliver the goods when needed.

Dramatic Expansion

By the end of the 1960s, the Yamaha motorcycle product line was starting to expand dramatically. In addition to the line of two-stroke street bikes on which Yamaha had built their success, the stunning success of the DT1, dual-purpose trail bike had the company working on this as a parallel line of models. At the Tokyo motorcycle show of 1969, Yamaha had showcased their new four-stroke 650cc twin, the XS1, responding to pressures related to anti-pollution regulations in the USA. With the strong segmentation of the marketplace that was developing, it was necessary for the company to define and manage separate product lines, the models within each product line aligned to the requirements for the targeted segment. Within each product line efficient practices would be needed to minimize design and development costs, and produce machines with a clear common image.

Redesigned and restyled, the R5 was the baseline for the iconic RD series of the 1970s.

Design Consolidation

Within the street two-strokes, the general rule of thumb had been to use piston-ported twin-cylinder engines for the sports models and the rotary valve single-cylinder engine for the small utility models. Yamaha had not initially attempted to link the models through styling, and any technically common features were more from pragmatism than design. This started to change with the models at the start of 1969, with the R3, DS6 and CS3 clearly sharing the same look, although the 125 YAS1 was quite different. Interestingly the 90cc HS1, the evolution of the AT90, did share some of the styling features of the larger sports twin series, such as the pin striping on the fuel tank. With the sports twin models that appeared in 1970, the link between the bikes strengthened cosmetically and also moved into the area of shared engine and chassis design. A single line of two-stroke sports twins was developing.

In consolidating the design of the bikes, it was possible to use the best of both worlds in setting the basic parameters for the engine. From the R series came the horizontally split crankcases, along with the general clutch and gearbox layout.

The DS series contributed the true five-port cylinders, with transfer passages to the crankcase for both main and auxiliary transfer ports. It was clear that the new engine was a baseline for the future, illustrated by the redesigned gears in the transmission. All of the gears were much narrower, resulting in a far compacter gear cluster and preparing for the moment, some time in the future, that an extra set of ratios would be added. For both models a new frame was used, bearing a strong resemblance to that used on the TD and TR production racers of the time. The frame design had a heritage dating back within Yamaha to the RD56 factory twin racer, which had been responsible for Yamaha's first racing successes. But the design had even deeper roots, going back to the 1950s, when Norton had used the Featherbed design to win world championships on the 500cc single-cylinder Manxs, against multi-cylinder Italian bikes from MV and Gilera.

The End of the First Generation

Reflecting the philosophy now present within the company, no attempt was made to increase the power produced by the new engines. Yamaha

Still anchored in the 1960s, the 1971 CS3 was brought in line with the other twins as the CS5.

were determined not to be dragged into a performance war with the new 500cc two-strokes from Kawasaki and Suzuki. Their intent was to produce balanced motorcycles whose handling and braking matched the performance of the engine, enabling the rider to get the best out of the bike. This contrasted dramatically with Kawasaki's philosophy, whose Mach 3 500cc triple was, for the time, blisteringly fast, but with such poor handling that it bordered on the dangerous. But it did put Kawasaki on the map as the producer of exciting high-performance motorcycles, on which it was able to capitalize as its model range expanded in the 1970s.

Yamaha relied on the racing successes, especially the TD2 and TR2, with strong links to the DS7 and R5, to retain the sporting image for the company. But for the diehard Yamaha enthusiast, the R5 did offer slightly better performance, helped by the loss of 14kg (31lb) of dry weight in the creation of the new bike. Thanks to this, the R5 was found to be 'the best 350 on sale in the USA' when *Cycle* magazine did their first shootout ever on the six different 350s available in the

US market. Not the best in any category, it was the best total package, justifying the development approach Yamaha had taken.

There was some confusion within the company on how to identify the new machines. They were clearly totally new models, and there was a school of thought that called for them to receive a new model tag. In Japan they were launched as the X series, becoming the DX250 and RX350 by the end of 1970. Outside Japan, it was considered better to retain the link with the past, so they were marketed as the R5 and DS7. Gradually, the rest of the twin clans lined up between the two models, the CS5 arriving at the start of 1971, with identical styling and a 200cc engine. The AS3 and pint-sized HS3 joined slightly later in the year.

By 1972, Yamaha had a five-piece two-stroke sports twin family, closely linked to race success and considered by many to be the best in class. It was to continue as the company's core motorcycle business, while other series were developed to address the evolution of the market, as world events shaped the marketplace of the future.

4 Saving the Planet

It could be argued that the history of the Japanese motorcycle industry has been dominated almost from the start by the rivalry between Yamaha and Honda. This was not so much in terms of size or volume of business, as, since the 1950s, Honda were never bested by any other manufacturer; rather, it was more in terms of prestige and profile that Yamaha strove to topple Honda from their throne. Yamaha's choice of two-stroke technology had positioned them well to challenge and beat four-stroke Hondas on the race-tracks of the world. In the GPs, there was glory gained by both factory teams, with Honda perhaps getting the edge in terms of the depth

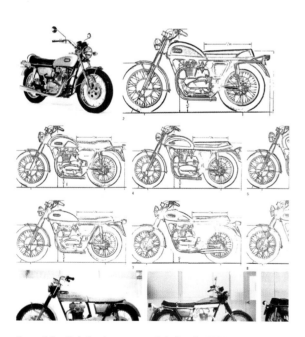

Lots of detailed sketches were made before the XS1 even got to mock-up stage.

and duration of their successful racing during the 1960s. The Yamaha TD1 production racer and its subsequent air-cooled descendants were undeniably the most successful of the racers for the common man, raising Yamaha's image as the supplier of the sports twins for the street.

But there was a fundamental flaw to the basis for Yamaha's success over the first sixteen years of their existence, and it was this same two-stroke technology. As the Western world came out of the darkness that followed World War II, and personal wealth stimulated the boom in motorcycling in the 1960s, other aspects of the human condition began to receive more attention from the baby boomers and their more enlightened elders. The post-war drive for industrial growth and expansion had been allowed to proceed unchallenged regardless of the effects it might have on the environment in which it occurred. The first murmurs of concern with 'pollution' emerged as a new phenomenon of smog enveloped London in the winter months during the early 1950s, and settled like a filthy blanket on the Los Angeles basin in October 1954.

Then in 1956 the introduction of the Clean Air Act in the UK introduced smokeless fuels in London, and the air quality improved dramatically. The US started its own investigation into the effects of pollution and the best way to tackle it, with one of the culprits quickly identified as the automobile and all sorts of internal combustion engines. Emission restrictions seemed to be the way to lower the levels of pollution in the air, and the two-stroke, with its reliance on an oil-petrol mix for lubrication, would find it tough to comply.

By 1965, the US government was drafting the regulations that would be applied to exhaust

Japanese test riders queuing up to give the new XS1 a spin.

emissions from 1968, with the state of California picking up an accelerated programme requiring automobile emissions to be reduced from model year 1966. The fight was on, intensifying with the US Clean Air Act of 1970, and despite a fierce rearguard action from the auto industry, by the end of the 1970s it was almost impossible to build a streetbike powered by a two-stroke engine that could meet Californian emission laws.

Developing the Big Bore Bike

By the late 1960s, it was clear to Yamaha that they would need to start to develop a four-stroke range of motorcycles to meet future emissions' regulations, forcing them to challenge Honda on their own territory. The Yamaha international office in the USA was also convinced that the downturn in the market, which had started in 1966, was not temporary, and indicated a fundamental change in buyer interest. As sales in light-weight twins dropped, interest in big-bore machines was picking up. Honda were able to exploit some of this with their CB450 that rivalled even the British 650 twins in terms of

performance. Unknown to Yamaha though, market research by Honda had found that few riders looking for large capacity twins chose the 450, despite the performance. More than anything it was engine size that was important; there was no substitute for 'cubes'.

Yamaha had nothing to offer in this segment. Early 1967 YIC management gave a strong pitch to build a new machine to address this buoyant market segment, but initially it was rejected by President Kawakami and the senior management. They felt the market should be left to the incumbents, the five remaining British manufacturers and their big bore twins. YIC aggressively defended their pitch, and ultimately brought the Yamaha management round. A project was started to build a big-bore four-stroke, known as Project 049 and managed by Daisuke Tanaka. The four-stroke project was officially started in August 1967, after a brief evaluation of a 650 two-stroke twin was rejected.

Interestingly, an almost parallel project was running at Honda, with a similar goal of entering the big bore market and competing head-on with the British manufacturers dominating the US market.

The XS1 might have been close to a Triumph, but the colour was very Japanese.

Honda's approach was bold and self-confident, not attempting to beat the competition by simply doing a better job, but building on their strengths to forge their own distinctive position in the market. They had spent ten years racing multi-cylinder engines in GPs, so this would form the base for their large capacity street bikes. Honda America had summarized their requirements as 'the bigger the better', and once Honda had learned of Triumph's plans to build a 3-cylinder 750, it was clear to them that a 650 would not be acceptable.

Within a year, the CB750 had reached a level of development that it could appear at the October 1968 Tokyo motorcycle show. Its imminent appearance was rumoured throughout 1968, but the impact it made when it appeared at the show was huge. In some ways similar to the influence of the 1959 YDS1 on lightweight sports bikes, the CB750 set a benchmark that established the direction of motorcycle design for the next ten years and beyond.

Yamaha's approach was different and, in hindsight, flawed. They fell back on the principle that had got the company started, which was to identify the best of the class, and improve on it. It set them on a path that deviated from the mainstream 4-cylinder four-stroke design principle

that became the Universal Japanese Machine standard for many years. Perhaps this was intentional, given its origins with Honda. But throughout this period, Yamaha struggled to find a design principle that would bring them the popularity enjoyed by Honda and others with their 4-cylinder machines. It resulted in many original, innovative and interesting designs, but the technical and design originality was not reflected in overwhelming commercial success. Ironically, the two-stroke twin remained in many ways the iconic flagship of the company.

In discussions with the YIC team in Los Angeles, it was decided that the market they wished to address was characterized by the mature rider who wanted a motorcycle that offered a good balance between performance and ease of use, handling and comfort, design and practicality. The bike that came closest to manifesting these qualities was the Triumph Bonneville 650, and this was chosen as the yardstick against which the new motorcycle would be measured. Triumph had sold about 20,000 of the bikes in the USA in 1967, taking the lion's share of the British export market to the USA, so it was clear that there was sufficient demand in the marketplace. The development team got to work.

Working with Toyota

Yamaha had established themselves as the foremost two-stroke manufacturer in the world, but they were not without some insights into the four-stroke engine. In 1960 they had established a sports car research group within the nascent Yamaha Technical Laboratories and had produced a rudimentary 4-cylinder, water-cooled, dohc 2-litre engine, which continued development until the project was stopped early in 1962 at the height of the financial crisis of the company. Two years later, Yamaha were approached by Toyota to consider co-operation in producing a sports version of the 6-cylinder, 2-litre, four-stroke engine fitted to the Toyota Crown model. From 1965, they worked on producing a dohc version of the engine, and later co-operated in the development of the rest of the car that was to become the Toyota 2000GT. The car was to remain a hand-built special with ultimately just 337 being produced, of which 115 were exported by the end of production in October 1970.

Having cut their eye teeth on the Toyota, this was the first source that the design team turned to when starting engine development for the new motorcycle. Two cylinders from the 2000GT, with its 75 × 75mm dimensions and with the stroke reduced by 1mm, gave a displacement of 654cc and this was adopted as the basic engine configuration. Rejecting the dohc design as too complex for their initial manufacturing process, new cams were developed for the sohc design, but the valve train was essentially lifted from the Toyota engine, with 2 valves per cylinder. Cam design on the 2000GT engine had been done by Toyota so Yamaha went back to scratch, using the Yamaha Musical Instrument computer at night as they had no computer of their own at that time.

The bottom of the engine was not so different from that found on the YR1 350 two-stroke twin that the company had launched in 1967, with horizontally split crankcases and the drive for the ohc being taken off the centre of the pressed-up, 360-degree crankshaft. The design and any transmission components were taken from the YR1 to lower production costs. Wet sump lubrication was used with an oil pump driven off the right-hand end of the crankshaft. For the first time, a Yamaha came with constant velocity (CV) carburettors, in which the throttle position controls a butterfly valve in the inlet tract of the carburettor. Vacuum in the engine acts on a diaphragm to raise a needle and supply the required air-fuel mix. Yamaha's in-house carburettor supplier Mikuni built them under licence from Solex, and they worked well, with reports of good clean throttle response.

Initial mock-ups of the new motorcycle had made use of the YR1 frame, but ultimately it received its own design. This combined the double-loop cradle of the DS and R series with the single, large diameter tube from the top of the headstock bending round the back of the engine down to the rear engine mounting brackets, as found on the AS and CS ranges. There had been extensive dialogue between Japan and Los Angeles on the best styling to adopt, with Japan pushing designs that linked into the rest of the Yamaha range, but the US rejecting this, wanting to push the look closer to the contemporary British twins. The final motorcycle was quite similar to the Bonneville, with the exception of the exhaust pipes, with Yamaha adopting a straight, slightly tapered conventional design rather than the midsection bulge of the British bike.

The XS1

The development programme was long and tortuous, with many false steps and redesigns needed. Numerous prototypes were built and rejected, leading in total to a file containing 2,500 pages reflecting design modifications undertaken during the project. At last, in October 1969, at the Tokyo motorcycle show, the final prototype of the XS1 appeared, a year later than Honda's CB750, whose development had started at the same time. Finished in a distinctive green and white livery, contrasting with the dour candy-red colours used by Triumph, it provoked much interest from the industry and the public as Yamaha's first four-stroke production motorcycle.

YAMAHA TIME

Quarterly Issue

No. 2-1970

Were Yamaha really targeting the outlaw biker with the XS1, or was this a stamp of approval?

Shipment to the USA began in early 1970, with only token numbers going to Europe for evaluation. The bike had been created for the US market, and the sales push was clearly focused on America. Road tests confirmed that this was the best 650 twin on the market, although the exhausts were perhaps too loud, and the vibrations through the handlebar and footrests were bad enough to numb hands and tire the rider. Handling was reasonable although the rear shocks were too soft, with the bike wallowing in bumpy corners. Starting with the kick-start was quick and easy, with the carburetion spot on, the cold choke setting working well. The greatest asset was the oil-tight engine, the weeping crankcases of the British twins being legendary, engendering a pre-conception in many non-owners that all bikes were cursed in this way. Most reviewers felt the styling was a little bland, identifying too much with the standard silhouette of a parallel twin; but given all the other improvements of the breed, a bright future seemed to lie ahead for the bike.

Initially it seemed that no one had correctly read the mood of the market, and the XS1 wouldn't make the impression Yamaha had expected it to. The parallel twin had been selling well in the US for maybe twenty years, and there was no reason to believe that this would not continue. Undoubtedly there was still a market for parallel twins, but the customers in this segment were not inclined to exchange their traditional British bike for a Japanese clone. They rode British parallel twins, and would continue to do so, despite the oil puddles on the garage floor, the continuous maintenance schedule and the 'Prince of Darkness' Lucas lighting. The closer the British industry slipped towards extinction, the more fanatical they became in their support for the dying breed. Yamaha would find few buyers here.

Furthermore other, less xenophobic riders looking for big bore 'superbikes' were much more interested in the multi-cylinder technological masterpiece of the CB750, or the quirky two-stroke twins and triples that Suzuki and Kawasaki continued to produce. For them the XS1 was simply too bland. Had Yamaha built a motorcycle that no one wanted?

Fortunately not, because the bike in fact carved out a new market segment. Owners seemed indeed to be a mature version of the baby boomers who a few years before had flocked to the featherweight scootarounds they had used at college and locally as a mixture of fun and practical mobility. Now a few years older, they still felt a lingering sense of fun in cycle riding, and had no desire for the extreme of long-distance touring or timed rides through the canyons. All they wanted was just simple, hassle-free, short blasts on a distinctive bike that would get the job done, blow out the cobwebs and bring the rider home with a smile on his face. For these people, the XS was perfect.

The XS1B

The bike magazines never really seemed to fully comprehend the appeal of the XS, using traditional yardsticks to measure its qualities. It came up short in many of them, and testers found it difficult to look past the flaws and appreciate the character. Road tests were generally quite critical, while bike sales' numbers remained buoyant. As a measure of the importance of the bike and the sensitivity of Yamaha to the negative comments they had received, the XS1B was available by the end of 1970, arriving also in Europe a few months later. There were detail changes to move the rear brake pedal and kick-start further away from the engine cases to give owners better room to place their feet. The rubber sleeves on the front forks were dropped, and the candy-green colour scheme became candy orange.

Within the engine there had been a few updates as well, the carburettors being tweaked to help cold starts and idle running, but the bike still had a tendency to a lumpy run at idle speeds. During the XS1B production runs, different pistons were fitted to lower the compression ratio, and this had a more significant effect. Yamaha had rightly chosen to keep a distinctive sound to the bike, but the XS1 had

The engine was pretty much a standard parallel twin, but no shame in that.

been a little too noisy for some people's tastes, so new double-walled pipes were fitted with different baffles to take the edge off.

All these modifications contributed to a slightly better bike, although performance did seem down compared to its predecessor. What was not fixed, however, was the severe vibration and marginal handling, and these traits had the company scrambling to issue yet another new version in August 1971.

The XS2

This new version appeared as the XS2, the most obvious changes being colour – candy orange was replaced by brilliant red – and a disc brake mounted on the front wheel. The CB750 had first introduced this new technology, and it was spreading rapidly down from the big bore bikes to the smaller models. Yamaha's version seemed to work especially well, in contrast to some of the other early designs.

An electric starter found its way on to the 650 twin, a Bendix-type starter engaging with teeth cut into the surface of the outer web of the right-hand cylinder. A special lever was positioned on the handlebar to raise the exhaust valve on the left-hand cylinder as the electric motor was engaged. It was quite an ingenious system, but unfortunately it transpired that the start motor delivered so much torque that it could twist the crank out of alignment and worsen the engine vibration.

Nevertheless the vibration on the XS2 seemed to be less than previous models. Pulling away from idle had been tricky, and it was hoped that a slightly lower first gear would help. In fact the gearing across the range seemed to be too high, with top speed reached well before the red line of 7,500rpm, possibly to make the vibration as unobtrusive as possible.

By 1972 the XS2 was the best seller in the Yamaha US range, helped by a bargain basement price. In Europe, the 650 was introduced to the

XS1·B

The XS1B appeared within a year of the launch of the XS1, correcting a few flaws. It was still very colourful.

Model	TX500	XS500B	XS500C
Year	1973	1975	1976
Capacity (cc)	499	499	499
Configuration	4-s 2 cyl	4-s 2 cyl	4-s 2 cyl
Induction	8-valve dohc	8-valve dohc	8-valve dohc
Bore × stroke (mm × mm)	73 × 59.6	73 × 59.6	73 × 59.6
Gearbox	5-speed	5-speed	5-speed
Final drive	chain	chain	chain
Frame	duplex cradle	duplex cradle	duplex cradle
Wheelbase (mm, in)	1,410 (55.5)	1,410 (55.5)	1,410 (55.5)
Dry weight (kg, lb)	199 (439)	198 (437)	198 (437)
Power (bhp)	48 @ 8,500rpm	48 @ 8,500rpm	48 @ 8,500rpm
Torque (kgm)	4.4 @ 6,500rpm	4.5 @ 6,500rpm	4.5 @ 6,500rpm
Top speed (km/h, mph)	155 (96)	155 (96)	155 (96)

Model	XS500D	XS500E	XS1
Year	1977	1978	1970
Capacity (cc)	499	499	654
Configuration	4-s 2 cyl	4-s 2 cyl	4-s 2 cyl
Induction	8-valve dohc	8-valve dohc	4-valve sohc
Bore × stroke (mm × mm)	73 × 59.6	73 × 59.6	75 × 74
Gearbox	5-speed	5-speed	5-speed
Final drive	chain	chain	chain
Frame	duplex cradle	duplex cradle	duplex cradle
Wheelbase (mm, in)	1,410 (55.5)	1,410 (55.5)	1,410 (55.5)
Dry weight (kg, lb)	198 (437)	198 (437)	185 (408)
Power (bhp)	48 @ 8,500rpm	48 @ 8,500rpm	53 @ 7,000rpm
Torque (kgm)	4.5 @ 6,500rpm	4.5 @ 6,500rpm	5.5 @ 6,000rpm
Top speed (km/h, mph)	155 (96)	155 (96)	185 (115)

Model	XS1B	XS2	TX650
Year	1971	1971	1973
Capacity (cc)	654	653	653
Configuration	4-s 2 cyl	4-s 2 cyl	4-s 2 cyl
Induction	4-valve sohc	4-valve sohc	4-valve sohc
Bore × stroke (mm × mm)	75 × 74	75 × 74	75 × 74
Gearbox	5-speed	5-speed	5-speed
Final drive	chain	chain	chain
Frame	duplex cradle	duplex cradle	duplex cradle
Wheelbase (mm, in)	1,410 (55.5)	1,410 (55.5)	1,435 (56.5)
Dry weight (kg, lb)	185 (408)	194 (428)	212 (467)
Power (bhp)	53 @ 7,000rpm	53 @ 7,000rpm	53 @ 7,000rpm
Torque (kgm)	5.5 @ 6,000rpm	5.5 @ 6,000rpm	5.5 @ 6,000rpm
Top speed (km/h, mph)	185 (115)	185 (115)	185 (115)

(continued…)

Model	XS650	XS650B	XS650C
Year	1974	1975	1976
Capacity (cc)	653	653	653
Configuration	4-s 2 cyl	4-s 2 cyl	4-s 2 cyl
Induction	4-valve sohc	4-valve sohc	4-valve sohc
Bore × stroke (mm × mm)	75 × 74	75 × 74	75 × 74
Gearbox	5-speed	5-speed	5-speed
Final drive	chain	chain	chain
Frame	duplex cradle	duplex cradle	duplex cradle
Wheelbase (mm, in)	1,435 (56.5)	1,435 (56.5)	1,435 (56.5)
Dry weight (kg, lb)	212 (467)	212 (467)	212 (467)
Power (bhp)	53 @ 7,000rpm	53 @ 7,000rpm	53 @ 7,000rpm
Torque (kgm)	5.5 @ 6,000rpm	5.5 @ 6,000rpm	5.5 @ 6,000rpm
Top speed (km/h, mph)	185 (115)	185 (115)	185 (115)

Model	XS650D	TX750
Year	1977	1972
Capacity (cc)	653	743
Configuration	4-s 2 cyl	4-s 2 cyl
Induction	4-valve sohc	4-valve sohc
Bore × stroke (mm × mm)	75 × 74	80 × 74
Gearbox	5-speed	5-speed
Final drive	chain	chain
Frame	duplex cradle	duplex cradle
Wheelbase (mm, in)	1,435 (56.5)	1,455 (57.3)
Dry weight (kg, lb)	212 (467)	225 (496)
Power (bhp)	53 @ 7,000rpm	63 @ 6,500rpm
Torque (kgm)	5.5 @ 6,000rpm	7 @ 6,000rpm
Top speed (km/h, mph)	185 (115)	190 (118)

UK for the first time, with predictable comments in the road tests about the vibration; but in general it was well received.

Developing the 750 Twin

Having established a quite successful big bore four-stroke in the marketplace, Yamaha were intent on spreading their wings into the 750cc market and build a new bike that would take the basic twin concept and demonstrate that it could rival the performance of the multi-cylinder bikes that Honda were producing. Yamaha was adopting the twin as their trademark across the range, two-stroke and four-stroke, and they were convinced that with a slim design, careful weight control and a compact, moderately tuned engine, they could rival the CB750 in terms of performance.

But to be able to truly challenge the Honda flagship, they also needed to conquer once and for all the vibration caused by a 360-degree vertical twin, matching the smoothness of the four-cylinder power plant. Yamaha achieved this with their omni-phase balancing system, involving a pair of contra-rotating weights located underneath the crankshaft with a chain drive taken off a sprocket next to the cam-chain sprocket. The

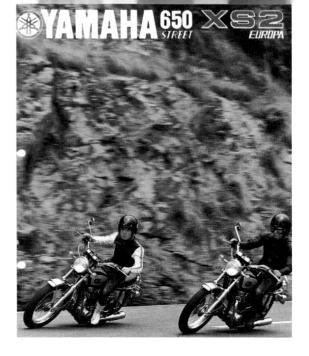

There doesn't seem too much wrong with the handling, but in reality the XS2 was far from perfect.

weights ran on shafts mounted in the lower crankcase and were accessible via a plate underneath the engine. Although not the first of its kind in the internal combustion engine, it was the first time it had been applied to a motorcycle engine. It worked very well, and the smoothness of the engine was considered remarkable in contrast to the XS650, and as effective as the Norton

Following on thick and fast, the addition of an electric start turned the 650 into the XS2.

Building the twin series with the ill-fated 1972 TX750.

Commando 750 twin that had used Isolastic rubber engine mounts to cure the problem.

With this fixed, the rest of the engine design was focused on raising performance levels. The XS2 had a claimed power output of 53bhp, with the CB750 pushing out 67bhp. Power levels close to the Honda would be needed to be able to wear the 'sports' tag with pride. A rather optimistic 63bhp was quoted in the sales literature, with all testers estimating it to be substantially lower. Indeed the quite conservative engine design would also suggest that high performance had not been the most important in the list of development requirements. It was a sohc, with two valves per cylinder, with a very rugged bottom end of the engine. The one-piece forged crankshaft, as well as the big and little end of the conrod, ran in plain bearings, albeit with a special copper plating for the piston gudgeon pin.

The penalty paid for this design simplicity was the need for a high-pressure oil feed to the bearings. A single pump was used to feed the engine bottom and top end, with a scavenging function to return the oil to the tank behind the right-hand side cover via the transmission, clutch and balance weights. Compression ratio was a modest 8.4 to 1, and with the valve seats made from a special hard alloy, the engine would run happily on lead-free petrol, acknowledging the squeeze coming in the US to reduce emissions.

Convenience necessitated the adoption of an electric start, with the 750 fitted with a conventional electric starter assembly mounted on the front of the engine, chain-driving the crank when engaged.

There was more innovation in the form of a chromed balancer pipe between the exhaust, ribbed for extra cooling. This was intended to quieten the exhaust note that had been so raucous on the 650 twin. Taking another bow to the anti-emission lobby, Yamaha also fitted positive crankcase ventilation to recycle fuel-rich fumes that entered the crankcase as piston blow-by: via a reed valve the fumes were directed back into the air-filter box to join fresh air entering the engine.

There was less innovation present in the chassis, where a traditional double loop cradle frame, similar in design to the RD series of two-strokes, supported the massive engine. While the frame design seemed just fine, the suspension was poorly set up with inadequate damping and a front spring rate that was far too soft. Brakes were shared with the XS650 and were good, although the weight of the bike took the edge off their performance. Weighing in at 225kg (496lb), 30kg (66lb) heavier than the 650, the sheer mass of the TX750 left it struggling to match its rival the CB750. Most testers concluded that its best use was as a long distance tourer, despite the heavy fuel consumption, awkward handlebars and very soft seat.

There were other little niggling points such as the clutch, whose engagement point would vary with oil temperature, as well as the harsh engagement of first gear on some bikes. There had been a change of design for the tensioner of the chain driving the counterweights under the engine, as it had a tendency to stretch and unless adjusted would gradually creep out of phase with the engine, resulting in steadily worsening vibration.

The TX750

The TX750 was an innovative motorcycle that was above average in most things but didn't really excel in anything. But what good is innovation if, on top of the little imperfections clearly present, the bike fails in the most critical way? This is what happened to the earliest owners of the TX750.

The first model, produced from July 1972, was sold on the domestic market. Export sales to Holland, Germany, France, Australia and the USA started in early 1973 and were strong, and the model seemed to be a success until in Europe, reports started arriving of partial and in some cases complete engine seizure. In the US, Yamaha had admitted that they had measured extremely high oil temperatures during extended rides through the desert, and tests in the European HQ in The

Netherlands confirmed that some oils would froth badly, seemingly originating from the balance weights spinning under the engine. They initiated a model recall to fit an engine oil cooler, but the real fix involved a deeper crankcase sump with extra baffles. This was fitted standard to the second generation TX750 that was offered for sale from April 1974, with a host of other improvements garnered from a troubled first year of existence.

There had been enough problems with the new bike and many of its innovative features, with the result that it was withdrawn from production in 1974, going into history with a reputation as a brave but ultimately unsuccessful attempt to challenge the 4-cylinders' increasing domination of the big bore market.

The TX500

Before the TX750 finally bit the dust, it did spawn a smaller brother, the TX500. In fact it was Yamaha's intent at the time to build a complete set of TX twins, with some speculation that the original 750 was designed with the intention of also creating a 900cc or even 1000cc larger version. As it was, the XS2 was renamed the TX650, with no significant changes to the design, and a new 500cc twin was released in April 1973. It is strange that, in many ways, Yamaha had forced the two-stroke twin series into the cosmetically and technically aligned RD series, while the TX series of three models featured three totally different designs. The common factor was that they all featured vertical twin engines, nothing more. Perhaps Yamaha were really simply trying to find their way in this strange new four-stroke world, as the third twin they developed rejected many of the design principles of both of its predecessors.

Weight and mass had been a problem for the 750, so the omni-phase contra-rotating balance weights were replaced by a contra-rotating balance shaft located above the engine. The 650 and 750 had featured 360-degree cranks, but the 500 had the conrods separated by 180 degrees, the cylinders firing unevenly. In contrast to the tunnel situated between the cylinders on the other big twins, on the 500 the cam-chain drive was on

From above, it's clear how slim the TX750 is, compared to the Honda and Kawasaki 4-cylinder bikes.

You wouldn't want to push the TX750 much harder before the poor suspension became apparent.

A chip off the old block? No, almost all the innards of the TX500 were of a different design to its big brothers.

The TX series wasn't working out, so this TX350 never made it into production.

The best XS so far had some input from ex-Triumph testers, with tangible results.

the right-hand side of the engine, with a geared-down indirect pickup from the crankshaft to enable smaller gears to be fitted to the camshafts in the cylinder head.

This was a dohc engine with 4 valves per cylinder. The smaller valves would enable the engine to run higher engine speeds safely and breathe better when it got there, but in reality the claimed peak power of 48bhp at 8,500rpm was just 38bhp when measured at the rear wheel, and an engine speed of 7,500rpm. This was comparable to the twenty-year-old Triumph Daytona, about to leave the world stage for good, equipped with pushrod activation of the 2 valves in each cylinder head. The TX500 did therefore share the same slightly disappointing performance of the other twins in the series.

The rest of the engine was conventional, with the frame and chassis much like that of the 750.

The end result was a good bike, far more polished than either of its larger capacity siblings and an interesting alternative to the Honda CB500 4-cylinder. It was, however, still quite dull, in a world awed by the crackerjack performance of the Kawasaki two- and four-stroke firebrands and the smooth, confident rush of the multi-cylinder Hondas. As one road tester poignantly stated, 'at least Yamaha is still king of the two-strokes'.

With the demise of the TX750, Yamaha seemed to have a crisis of confidence, as their strategy of using the twin design to build a charismatic series of large capacity four-strokes was not working. A TX350 was created as a mock-up, but never went into production. The 500 and 650 continued in production, but there was no superbike to lead the Yamaha range. The GL750 had appeared at the Tokyo Show in 1971, the 4-cylinder two-stroke 750 machine turning the show on its head. It never went into production, perhaps serving as a base for the TZ750 racebike that appeared in 1974. A year later they did it again, with the twin-rotor Wankel-engined RZ201, but it, too, disappeared without trace. Yamaha badly needed a flagship product, but would have to rely on the 650 and 500 twins as well as the ever-popular RD two-stroke series, until it appeared.

Continuing as the XS500 from 1975, the XS500C had a wider, less peaky powerband.

Improvements to the 650

Determined to fix the 650's handling problems once and for all, ex-Triumph test rider Percy Tait was commissioned in Europe to get the bike sorted. He recommended a number of changes, and these went into production on the 1974 TX650A. The swing arm was lengthened, and extra gusseting added to the critical areas of headstock and engine mounting plates. The engine was moved forwards and slightly lower, and the headstock itself lengthened. New suspension was fitted front and rear; initially it was too stiff, but it softened out after a couple of thousand miles, providing a better ride. But despite the altered engine position, the bike still felt top heavy, although in general it seemed to corner better than previous models.

Tackling the still intrusive vibration without resorting to a total redesign to incorporate the 500's balance-shaft was tricky. Some tweaking of the compression ratio, and reduction of the reciprocating mass through lighter pistons and conrods, helped a little. Every release of the bike was a little better than the previous one, although it still came up short in some areas. Inadvertently Yamaha seemed to have picked up on the essence of a charismatic bike, as displayed by the British twins that it emulated. A relationship needed to be developed between owner and machine, and the well reported shortcomings of the 650 seemed to

give it the character that at least some owners sought. Sales continued to be strong, helped no doubt by Kenny Roberts' success racing XS-based twins in the US TT and dirt racing events.

After the difficulties encountered by the TX series, Yamaha were anxious to drop the model identifier. From 1975, the survivors became the XS500B and XS650B. It was primarily a rebadging exercise, although the 500B was set up with very poor low-speed throttle response, which, combined with the continued drive-train backlash, made the bike difficult to drive at low engine speeds. There were small changes in the coming years, with the 1976 C models featuring shared exhausts between the two models, repositioning of the front brake calliper behind the disc, and linkage between the two carburettors to aid synchronization.

Invisible, but noticeable, were the substantial changes to the 500cc engine, which featured a revised cylinder head containing a different combustion chamber shape and reworked valve passages. The XS series had always featured quite light flywheels on the crankshaft, this being one of the most noticeable differences with respect to the British twins. This aided acceleration, but

Yamaha's superbike for the '70s that was not to be – the GL750.

LEFT: *Given the history of Wankel technology, Yamaha were right not to turn the 1972 prototype RZ660 into a production model.*

BELOW LEFT: *By 1978, the specials had arrived and a new breed of street cruisers was born.*

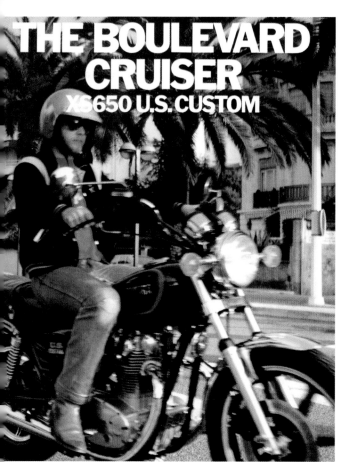

THE BOULEVARD CRUISER
XS650 U.S. CUSTOM

made it tough to keep it in any powerband that might be present. The TX500 had actually quite a peaky power delivery, and the new cylinder head on the XS500C, combined with a heavier crank, flattened and widened the powerband.

The Kayaba forks that had previously been fitted on the 500 and 650 were replaced by Showa units, which were a little soft but handled bumpy roads well without ruining stability in the corners.

Marking time as the XS500D in 1977, the last year of the 500 was to be 1978, with the 500E gaining a slight performance increase thanks to new pistons increasing the compression ratio. The evolution over the years had resulted in a good 500cc twin, regarded as the best of the half-litre twins in existence, but the class was overshadowed by the increasing number of 4-cylinder 550 and 650 models, with the general consensus that four-stroke twins were best left to the mid-range 360 and 400 class, which Yamaha had also cultivated. It was time for the 4-valve 500 to pass into history.

The 650 Special

The final upgrade for the 650 vertical twin with which Yamaha had staked their claim in the four-stroke market, came with the 1977 XS650D. There

The 650 twin was rejuvenated by the new line of specials, and the XS650SE looked fantastic.

were a few small updates to the brakes and suspension, and so it was to remain for the 1978 and 1979 models that remained available. Worldwide sales had dropped to about 20,000 units by 1976.

Yamaha decided to use the 650 as the basis for their first 'Special' model, as the fashion for customization started to develop in the USA. In 1977 Kawasaki had launched their KZ1000 LTD custom, based on their enormously popular 4-cylinder sportsbike, and it had proved very successful. From 1978 SE versions of the 650 were

marketed with a styling exercise employing shorter exhausts, cast wheels, a 16in rear wheel with an extra fat tyre, and swept-back handlebars. It was a masterstroke, and sales picked up dramatically, leading to new, restyled versions each year until finally it disappeared from the market in 1983. Fittingly, at the end, just like at the beginning, it was only available in the US, and after a production run of fourteen years, it can only be described, in hindsight, to have been an overwhelming success, warts and all.

5 Mission Accomplished

Throughout the world, the 1970s were a turbulent period in history. It was to become a decade heavily influenced by the increasing wealth and political muscle of the Arab nations, with oil crises in 1973 and 1978 that paralyzed Western economies, introducing a new factor of uncertainty into the capitalist economic system. Another less spectacular, but equally significant event was the unilateral announcement by President Nixon of the USA on 15 August 1971 that the US government would no longer honour the fixed dollar value of gold that had been agreed and maintained since 1944. Until this time, the exchange rates of members of the International Monetary Fund had been fixed, but now their value against the dollar was free to fluctuate as the market demanded.

For the Japanese manufacturers this was a disaster, as the yen increased in value, making their products more expensive in their export markets. Yamaha tackled this by introducing a buffer of inventory that enabled them to smooth out currency fluctuations and prevent them having immediate effect on the showroom prices. On the downside were the large numbers of unsold motorcycles on their books; in the US, for example, these reached 200,000 units at one stage. The fallout from the first oil crisis in 1973, coupled with the large inventories on their books, resulted in the rate of growth for the big four in Japan slowing dramatically in 1974, with a drop in overall sales for Yamaha in 1975.

The 1976 XS750 was Yamaha's attempt to challenge the 4-cylinder hegemony of their rivals.

The shaft drive added weight and absorbed power, so the 1977 model was rushed out to correct this.

The Company Reorganizes

It was a difficult period in the company's history, and for Genichi Kawakami, who had been company president since July 1955, it was an appropriate moment to step down and pass the keys to Hisao Koike. Koike had been responsible for steering the company to recovery during its misfortunes in 1962, when bankruptcy had threatened and he had overseen the spectacular growth in export markets during the 1960s. He was therefore well placed to guide the company through this new storm. His presidential message on survival in a low-growth market was clear: stimulate demand through technological innovation, and lower costs through workflow innovation.

Yamaha had always felt the need for technological innovation, but there had been less of a focus on costs in the euphoria of a demand-pull market. From the mid-1970s continuous evaluation and refinement of production and business processes were to become mainstream activities within the company.

The 1974 downturn in the industry and Yamaha's financial results coincided with the realization that the four-stroke line-up that had been created – the TX750, 650 and 500 – was not the success the company had intended. Fortunately other models in their range were doing well, especially the rebranded two-stroke twins now grouped under the RD banner. The complex TX750 model was dropped completely, and the 650 and 500 were given a facelift to buy time while a new flagship for the XS series was created.

With the difficult birth and development of the first XS model series, Yamaha decided to reorganize their development process before proceeding. A new design division was set up, staffed with both motorcycle and automotive engineers, and charged to focus solely on four-stroke machines. After the failures of the past, Yamaha could not afford to get it wrong a second time.

The power and smoothness of a four, but the compactness of a twin. The perfect compromise?

Developing a Flagship Superbike: the XS750

It was decided that the company should adopt the format that was now becoming universal within the Japanese manufacturers, namely a four-stroke, 4-valve, 1000cc superbike. It would be based on the XS500 twin. Honda had started the trend with the CB750, extended it with 500cc and 350cc models, and had been joined by the ground-breaking Kawasaki Z1 in 1972. The performance levels obtained by the 900cc Kawasaki had created a new class of sports superbikes, which established the company as the leader in the field of the visceral, adrenalin-charged motorcycle experience. With Suzuki entering the multi-cylinder market with its GS550, only Yamaha continued to neglect this trend.

The secret of a successful manufacturer, however, lies not only in getting it right, but in acknowledging when you get it wrong and rectifying this. Yamaha decided that 1975 would be the year that they would join the 4-cylinder multi-club.

Yamaha USA, however, disagreed. They were still a major influence on basic product and design decisions, just as they had been when the XS1 was conceived. Yamaha USA felt it would be wrong to go head-on with the other manufacturers, and saw an opportunity to develop a high profile, charismatic flagship without copying the opposition. It would be a triple – that is, a 3-cylinder engine – with the possibility to build a modular line of twins, triples and eventually 4-cylinder bikes as the series expanded in capacity. True, there was still the 3-cylinder Triumph Trident in production, but the great British marque was struggling to survive and was expected to fold within the year.

The central design team were not convinced this was the right approach, but the Yamaha USA product planning team were adamant this was the right strategy. In the end, when it was found that the production line tooling for the now defunct TX750 twin could be adapted to build a 3-cylinder 750, it was agreed that the XS750 would be a triple.

Resolving the Faults and Weaknesses

Most important was that it should break with the legacy of faults and weaknesses of its predecessors, beginning with the buzz. Like all triples before it, the crank configuration had the three conrods mounted at 120-degree intervals, which would not be conducive to a smooth, vibration-free ride. However, rather than complicate the engine with yet another version of the omniphase balance weights, the design team found a way to mount the engine in the frame that dramatically reduced the transfer of the vibrations to the chassis. There was still some buzziness at certain engine speeds, but not sufficient to be considered really intrusive. This was innovation of a new sort, not complex engineering, but careful analysis and isolation of the problem.

One down, two to go: the poor suspension and handling of the twins was next to be dealt with. The double cradle frame was of conventional design with a massive backbone pipe and heavy gusseting at the headstock and swingarm pivot.

Showa suspension was fitted with far better low-friction fork travel and the right balance of spring rate and damping. The XS750 handled well, soaking up bumps, free of the tingling footrests and handlebars.

This was looking good, but the last weakness was still not properly fixed on the new XS, which continued to be afflicted by a sudden transition from idle to take-up that had the bike lurching away from a stationary position. In addition there was significant play in the transmission, which, combined with the off-idle throttle problems, caused the bike to jerk and buck on take-up or slow-down. So just two of the three major problems on the old generation XS series had been solved.

Technological Innovation

There was not a lot of technological innovation to be found on the XS750, but what there was had a large visual impact. With long-distance touring in mind, a drive shaft was fitted as the

By 1980, the 750 had grown 100cc but was strangled by emission restrictions.

final drive to the rear wheel, with the shaft also acting as half of the swingarm. Rather than invest heavily in this design, initially Yamaha licensed it from BMW; however, they found that it was necessary to make such substantial changes in order to link it to a laterally fitted crankshaft and transmission that in the end they developed their own version.

There was, however, a weight penalty to be paid for the fuss-free final drive, resulting in the production version of the XS750 tipping the scales at 230kg (507lb). This was comparable to other bikes in this class, but by the time the engine power had found its way to the rear wheel through at least three power-sapping geared drives, there was just 52bhp available. Disappointingly, the bike covered the quarter mile in just under 14sec – over a second slower than the Suzuki and Honda competition. Clearly, the dragstrip was not the XS750's home territory; rather the wide open spaces and blacktop stretching into the distance were its world.....

But why not cater for both? The Kawasaki 900 flagship had shown that it was possible to build a performance bike that was a capable tourer, could be dressed to reflect the owner's personality, was happy with one up or two, and was as good as any at carving its way through the canyons.... a Jack of all trades and master of most. In contrast, the XS750 was the sensible man's superbike, competent, but a little uninspiring. The slight criticism there was on the qualities of the bike referred to the still-imperfect throttle response and gear lash, with the disappointing performance also mentioned.

The XS750 Series Models

The performance difference was so significant that Yamaha rushed out a new version of the 750 early in 1977. It was labelled the 750-2D, as the initial 750 had arrived so late in the 1976 season that it had been given the 1977 'D' letter suffix. The most visible change was the use of two exhaust pipes, coupled with a balance pipe under the rear of the engine, the system giving better mid-range power delivery and restoring the bike's visual balance.

The 750D, with its three-into-one pipe, had been stylistically ahead of its time, something that Honda interestingly chose to emulate on their CB750 in 1977, just as Yamaha returned to the symmetry of an exhaust pipe on both sides. At the same time, the exhaust plumbing was raised to give better ground clearance; this had previously been limited on the right-hand side of the bike. There was a little tuning to the suspension with larger diameter front forks, single-rate springs and longer rear shock travel, added to the increase in trail to improve straight-line stability. Performance was tweaked through a different cam profile, which knocked half a second off the dragstrip quarter miles.

It is quite strange that Yamaha didn't go the whole way and immediately make the changes in 1977 that came with the 1978 XS750E. Once again the cam timing pushed for performance, along with higher compression in the engine, a larger airbox and wider carburettor throat, coupled to a new set of gearbox ratios. In this tuned form, the XS leaped through the quarter mile well under the 13sec mark, turning it into the fastest 750 on the market – though not at the expense of the other qualities of the bike, which had it selling well as a tourer. The only other changes were the pre-load adjustment on the forks and a new point-less ignition system.

The 1979 XS750F was virtually identical, with some new transmission components, but no change of spec or performance. With the success of the Custom 650s, these model variants were also offered on the 750 from 1978, essentially just a styling exercise for those looking for a little more flash.

1979 was to be the last year for the XS750, but the same bike appeared for the following season bored out by 3.5mm to give a displacement of 826cc and calling itself the XS850G. There were detail changes throughout the bike, but it shared the same design philosophy as its smaller predecessor. Hitachi were asked to build a CV carburettor that worked and managed a far better off-idle response, but gave very poor full throttle performance. It was an indication of the restrictions that were now beginning to bite hard in the emissions'

Model	XS250	XS360	XS400
Year	1978	1976	1977
Capacity (cc)	248	353	391
Configuration	4–s 2 cyl	4–s 2 cyl	4–s 2 cyl
Induction	4–valve sohc	4–valve sohc	4–valve sohc
Bore × stroke (mm × mm)	55 × 52.4	66 × 52.4	69 × 52.4
Gearbox	6–speed	6–speed	6–speed
Final drive	chain	chain	chain
Frame	spine cradle	spine cradle	spine cradle
Wheelbase (mm, in)	1,335 (52.6)	1,335 (52.6)	1,335 (52.6)
Dry weight (kg, lb)	168 (370)	168 (370)	169 (373)
Power (bhp)	25 @ 9,500rpm	34 @ 8,900rpm	37 @ 8,800rpm
Torque (kgm)	1.9 @ 8,500rpm	3.2 @ 8,000rpm	
Top speed (km/h, mph)	130 (81)	140 (87)	150 (93)

Model	XS750D	XS750-2D	XS750E
Year	1976	1977	1978
Capacity (cc)	747	747	747
Configuration	4–s 3 cyl	4–s 3 cyl	4–s 3 cyl
Induction	6–valve sohc	6–valve sohc	6–valve sohc
Bore × stroke (mm × mm)	68 × 68.6	68 × 68.6	68 × 68.6
Gearbox	5–speed	5–speed	5–speed
Final drive	shaft	shaft	shaft
Frame	duplex cradle	duplex cradle	duplex cradle
Wheelbase (mm, in)	1,465 (57.7)	1,465 (57.7)	1,465 (57.7)
Dry weight (kg, lb)	230 (507)	230 (507)	230 (507)
Power (bhp)	60 @ 7,500rpm	67 @ 8,000rpm	66 @ 8,000rpm
Torque (kgm)	6 @ 6,500rpm	6.4 @ 6,500rpm	6.3 @ 6,500rpm
Top speed (km/h, mph)	175 (109)	175 (109)	175 (109)

Model	XS850G	XS1100E	
Year	1980	1978	
Capacity (cc)	826	1102	
Configuration	4–s 3 cyl	4–s 4 cyl	
Induction	6–valve sohc	8–valve dohc	
Bore × stroke (mm × mm)	71.5 × 68.6	71.5 × 68.6	
Gearbox	5–speed	5–speed	
Final drive	shaft	shaft	
Frame	duplex cradle	duplex cradle	
Wheelbase (mm, in)	1,465 (57.7)	1,545 (60.8)	
Dry weight (kg, lb)	236 (520)	255 (562)	
Power (bhp)	79 @ 8,500rpm	95 @ 8,000rpm	
Torque (kgm)	7.1 @ 7,500rpm	9.2 @ 6,500rpm	
Top speed (km/h, mph)	190 (118)	210 (130)	

regulations imposed by the EPA in the USA. The performance of the 850 was worse than the 750 before it, almost certainly because of the need to pacify the Environment Agencies in the US, with Europe still some years behind. Fortunately the 850 was no longer the four-stroke flagship of the range, because an XS1100 had taken over in 1978.

At Last: the 1100cc Superbike!

Already early in 1977 at the Las Vegas dealer show, Yamaha had reported that a 1000cc 4-cylinder rocket ship in the XS mould was undergoing construction back in Japan. Tired of the constant reproaches that the top-of-the-range Yamaha four-stroke was no performance match for the other three Japanese manufacturers, the company talked of producing a bike that would not be beaten on the drag strip. It would be the undisputed, tyre-smoking, eye-popping, shoulder-wrenching king of the traffic-light drag.

Dealers were in need of some motivational words, and a response to their continuous complaint of the need for a model that would knock the Kawasaki Z1000, the King, off its pedestal. There was rumour

of a phenomenal 6-cylinder Honda in the wings, and Suzuki's successful GS750 had a larger brother coming together in the development department. One more year and the dealers would be rewarded with a bike truly worthy of the flagship epithet. During the year, an artist's impression appeared with a large XS1000 emblem on the side cover.

In short, the world was waiting for the 1000cc monster to appear. It finally broke cover at the dealer convention in New Orleans late in 1977, after a spectacular introduction film showing the bike roaring away from the lights at a drag strip, on tyres that were smoking from a pre-run burnout. The XS1000 had arrived, and it was an 1100! Displacing 1101cc, Yamaha had applied a little subterfuge to ensure that none of the other manufacturers trumped them on their moment of glory.

The dealers loved it, of course: at last a four-stroke superbike to compliment their class-leading two-stroke twin RD streetbikes, as well as the Yamaha two-stroke TZ track bikes that had ruled open class racing for several years. The superbike was claimed to cut the quarter-mile lights at just under 12sec, making it the quickest motorcycle in production. Such claims by manufacturers were often far too

If you can't beat them, join them. Top-of-the-range 1978 XS1100.

optimistic, achievable only by an under-sized rider with a tail-wind on a specially scrubbed and cleaned track. But road tests showed that even quicker times were possible, besting the Z1R by a quarter of a second. Yamaha had fulfilled their promise: this was the fastest streetbike you could buy.

But it didn't stop there, because it was a very comfortable bike to ride long distances, with soft compliant suspension, endless power available, and no significant vibrations getting through to the rider. This had all been achieved with essentially the same design as the XS750, although there were some detail changes in the way the engine power was delivered through the transmission. The 1100's heritage was most noticeable in the age-old problem that had plagued the series for several years: the off-idle carb-induced lurch as well as the drive-train lash. It was a lot better than the 750, despite using the same design of shaft-drive linkages, but it should have been fixed before the bike went to market. Inconceivably, given the flaws of the rest of the XS series, if the drive train had been sorted, the XS might, by contemporary standards, have been considered perfect.

Performance was excellent, and it also handled surprisingly well for a 255kg (562lb) motorcycle,

The technology within Yamaha's first 4-cylinder revealed.

only really getting out of shape when pushed hard in corners.

The final piece in the makeup of a perfect motorcycle lies with the styling, the visual appeal of the machine. The XS1100 was physically heavy and the styling emphasized rather than masked this, giving the bike a bulky, massive look. Possibly this was intentional, to command a presence in this way. For some, this would appeal to their emotions; others would find the package ugly.

Limited edition, full dress Martini tourer.

Styling changes kept the XS1100 looking good in 1981.

The 'Specials' Market

Sales were good in both the USA and Europe. A very distinctive, full touring faired version was offered as a limited edition to 500 riders in Europe, sporting Martini Racing colours. In the USA, the market for 'special' versions of the big bore bikes had exploded, with the XS650 Special selling 25,000 units in 1978 and big brother the 750, adding another 18,000. For the 650 it was enough to keep the model going for another six years. Inevitably, the XS1100 underwent the same metamorphosis for 1979, turning into the XS11 Special.

In these early days of the Cruiser market, only a handful of changes were needed to produce a special. Starting at the tail, there was the fat rear tyre, the flared open exhausts, the two-step seat, the pull-back bars and cast wheels front and rear. The rest of the conversion from tourer to vaguely bad-boy chopper was achieved with lots of chrome and, the cherry on the cake, the flowing,

teardrop-shaped fuel tank. From a styling perspective, the XS11 SE was a stunning success, and backed up as it was by the superb powerplant all but unchanged from the previous year, it was the best four-stroke bike Yamaha had marketed to date. Both of the 1979 US versions of the XS11 had lost just a little of their performance as the jetting was leaned out again to meet emission regulations.

For 1980, the engine underwent some more vigorous changes to stay one step ahead of the annually harsher emission requirements in the USA. Larger valves and a new shape for the combustion chamber, coupled to a flatter piston crown, recaptured some of the power lost in the move towards lower-octane petrol. The kickstart was finally dropped altogether, after being carried on the 1979 model in a little compartment behind the engine, for emergencies. Cosmetics were the cause of the rest of the changes: new year, new styling, especially for the special.

The Midnight Specials

With all the manufacturers piling into the specials market in the USA, Yamaha needed to distinguish themselves with a special amongst the specials. The result was the black and gold Midnight Special editions, a spectacular dark and glitzy makeover that set the standard for Japanese innovation in this market segment. Black chrome was found everywhere, with gold plated highlights on what was positioned as a limited edition for 1980. They were gone in a flash, so another batch was produced for 1981. Slowly but surely Yamaha were finding their way in the four-stroke market, not only in engineering, but with a smart approach to the marketplace.

By 1980, Yamaha had decided that it was time for a new series of four-strokes, but before they really emerged, a final full model year for the XS11 was announced. The standard model was joined as usual by the L Limited edition in the USA. In Europe a sports version was also marketed with a small headlight fairing and numerous cosmetic changes to project a different look to the regular version. With black-chromed exhausts, black engine finish and gold-highlight-ed, curve-spoked wheels, taken from the RD sports two-stroke series, the overall effect was striking, although it exuded none of the racetrack aura normally associated with sports models. The XS1100 was still available in 1982, but the XS series was fading rapidly, replaced by the ubiquitous XJ model range.

The XS Series is Phased Out

The last survivors of the XS series were to be the twins, not only the 650 that had started the whole range of four-strokes, but the 400cc twin that had first been sold in 1977, after a 360 twin had appeared on the market in 1976. At the time it was Yamaha's response to the boom in the mid-capacity class, as accidental motorcyclists, many riding simply because it was a convenient form of transport, migrated from the smaller two-strokes to competent, but unexciting mid-range four-strokes. The Honda CB350 had led the field for a couple of years, but the other Japanese manufacturers soon joined, and by 1976 they all offered a 360cc four-stroke twin. In fact they all offered two versions of their twins, a stripped down basic model and a slightly more luxurious version.

The 1978 XS400 was as good as any of the mid-range twins produced by the Japanese manufacturers.

The smallest of the XS series was the 250, which arrived in 1977.

Typical of the special editions that swept the market from the late 1970s is this 1980 XS400SE.

For Yamaha, the eco-model introduced in 1977 saved about 20 per cent on the list price by having a drum brake instead of disc on the front wheel, no electric start, no self-cancelling indicators and no centre stand. The rest of the bikes were identical, having a 180-degree twin cylinder engine, with single overhead cam driving 2 valves per cylinder, six-speed gearbox to a final drive chain. Yes, it had 34mm CV carburettors that were sensitive off idle, and yes, there was plenty of drive-train lash, stamping it a proud member of the XS family. The frame was a half-double cradle, the twin loops at the front of the engine being replaced by a large-diameter downtube. Suspension and handling were adequate, and if anything, better than the competition.

1977 was a transition year for the middleweight twins with the two 360cc versions available as well as the 400, which was an over-bored 360 displacing 392cc. The following year the 360s had disappeared; the standard and economy versions of the 400 continued for two years. By 1980, Yamaha had discovered that there was more to be gained from a special version of the 400, so the pairing of standard and S model continued to be available until the XS series was suspended at the end of the 1983 season.

The passage of the XS series marked the end of an era in which Yamaha had cut their teeth on four-stroke motorcycle design, deliberately choosing a different design ethos to their great rivals Honda. Ultimately proven wrong, and not helped by flawed attempts to innovate with twin-cylinder engine design, they had managed to re-establish themselves as suppliers of competent, reliable, comfortable, high performance, large capacity motorcycles.

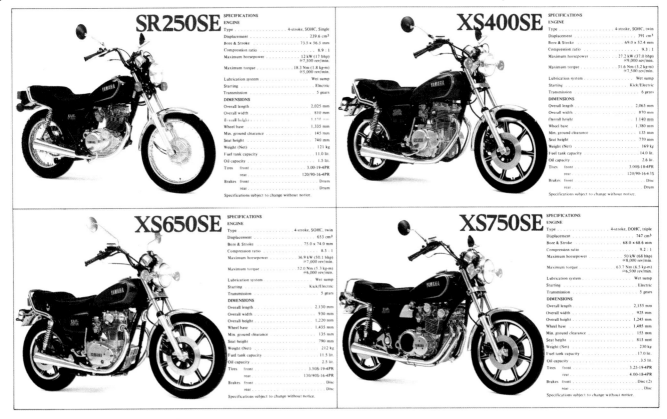

YAMAHA MOTOR N. V.
Postbus 7829 PROF. E. M. Meyerslaan 3
Amstelveen (Amsterdam), Holland
LIT-3MC-0107405-80E/54.12 × 7 ½ Printed in Japan (B.S)

Europe plugged into the specials rage with the 1980 US Custom series.

But there had been no Eureka moments in the history of the XS, no instant recognition of a fundamentally different, yet intrinsically right, new motorcycle. The YDS1 had brought them this glory on the edge of the 1960s, but it had been Honda with the CB750 and Kawasaki with the Z1 900 in 1972 that had changed the world of motorcycling in subsequent years. Despite this, the XS series had been deeply important to Yamaha, as a learning school for the four-stroke future that lay ahead for the company.

6 Two-Stroke Bedrock

Yamaha's growth and expansion into the Western world had been built on two-stroke engine technology. It had been the heart of their racing programme, elevating simple race-track competition into a bitter feud between rival Japanese manufacturers, with Honda, champion of the four-stroke, their greatest adversary. Through a concentrated drive to link racing success with their streetbikes, they had built the cachet of two-strokes as fast, high-performance motorcycles. With some innovative features for the street models, they had succeeded in creating mainstream confidence in the two-stroke engine and its acceptance as simple, reliable and user-friendly. Based on these two widespread perceptions, the two-stroke twin had become an icon for Yamaha throughout the world.

As the Japanese motorcycle industry spread globally, Yamaha were especially effective at establishing and exploiting bridgeheads into new markets, the two-stroke twins leading the drive forwards. Export successes strengthened their position as a major threat to Honda, and as the second half of the 1960s broke, Yamaha could look back on ten years of extraordinary company financial performance, with the prospect of continued exponential growth.

However, scratching the surface of the financial reports would reveal some rather risky aspects of the commercial miracle. There was a huge dependency on the US market, just as there was for Honda and Suzuki. The slowdown in the mid-1960s in the US had a direct effect on the bottom line for all three companies, although Yamaha came off best as it was less reliant than Honda on the ultra-small capacity motorcycles. It was, however, a direct incentive for Yamaha to pursue a more aggressive policy towards the European market, which had been subjected to a piecemeal approach, country by country. This initiative gained even more focus as the implications of the impending targets on pollution reduction within the USA became clear. The technology on which they had built the company and had expected to build their future would be excluded from use in the USA.

It was almost as if the company had to start from scratch, designing, developing and marketing four-stroke motorcycles, whereas Europe, with a less vigorous time-table towards emission restrictions, could act as the cash cow, funding the effort to build for the future. And it would be the two-stroke twins that would be the rock on which the company would grow.

The 1973 RD Series

The consolidation of the series of twins had started with the last models of each of the different capacities. The 1970 DS7 250 and R5 350 had not only looked very similar, but had started to share many engine components. The 200cc CS5 and 125cc AS3 followed suit, so that by 1972 there was a family of two-stroke twins ranging in capacity from 125cc to 350cc. For 1973, the union was formalized, with the release of the 1973 RD series.

Although cosmetically now clearly one family, there was still a split in terms of the engine design, carried over from the pre-RD series heritage. The 250 and 350 continued with a horizontally split crankcase sharing a stroke of 54mm and driving an identical six-speed gearbox, fed by the same 28mm Mikuni carburettors. The 125

RD250

and 200 continued to use vertically split crankcases, and no attempts were made to rationalize and share more engine components. The single unifying technical feature of the RD series was the adoption of reed valve induction throughout the complete range. Yamaha, continuing their development of two-stroke technology, especially for their off-road and road-racing programmes, had decided to make use of a unidirectional valve in the inlet tract of their two-stroke engines.

In 1971, Yamaha had initially applied the reed valves to their off-road machines, and had christened the system 'torque induction'. The name referred to the boost that the valves gave to the mid-range of the two-stroke engine, resulting in a stronger and wider powerband at the expense of all-out top-end power. It was this disadvantage that prevented the reed valve being applied to the road-racing TZ 250 and 350 series, as the obstruction formed by the valve mounting cage in the inlet tract compromised top-end power.

Sunrise on the start of the most famous two-stroke model series, the RD.

Torque induction had turned the DS7 into the RD250. Reed valves had arrived on Yamaha's streetbikes. This is the 1974 incarnation.

Spot the difference. The 1975 RD350 was cosmetically identical to its 250 brother.

For larger capacity road-racing engines, the reed's advantages were felt to outweigh their disadvantages and they were fitted to the 500cc factory machines that were campaigned in GPs from 1973 until 1976. They also appeared on the new TZ750 4-cylinder production racer that was released in 1974.

With the introduction of the reed valves, all the twin series needed new cylinders as well as the components needed to mount the valves on the cylinder inlet tract. Carburettors on the 250 and 350 had grown from 26mm diameter to 28mm, and a new air-filter design helped make the most of the new induction method.

There were six speeds in the gearbox, but initially sixth gear was blanked off on the RD250 and 350. This strange restriction was related to the origins of the extra speed in the transmission. In the USA, road-racing regulations called for the bikes to have a streetbike heritage. Yamaha had started to compete very successfully against 750cc racing versions of the last of the British BSA and Triumph 3-cylinder four-strokes, with the occasional Harley Davidson thrown in. To be competitive they needed to be tuned for peak power, resulting in a narrower powerband over which good power was available. With a five-speed gearbox, it was very difficult to keep the bike in the powerband, and this resulted in many close finishes, in second place, the bike struggling to get in the powerband in the drive from the last corner. The problem was fixed with an extra gear in the streetbike gearbox, and the TD3 and water-cooled TZ350 started winning open class events such as Daytona. Fortunately it was quite simple to remove the restriction, although it did involve splitting the crankcases to get to the gear selection drum.

There were very few changes to the chassis, the same frame design as the DS7/R5 remaining in use. Yamaha had started to introduce front disc brakes on the twins before the RDs were launched, but now they came as standard on the 250 and 350. The 125 and 200 models appeared slightly later in the year, with the same styling as their big brothers, dominated by the matt-black crankcase covers with the contrasting polished strip identifying the bike as a Yamaha. All the bikes had benefited from the adoption of reed valves, which had been combined with a mild engine tune to sharpen up the performance of the range. It was at this point that the RD250 and 350 really started to dominate the sporting middleweight class in Europe, with good sales for the 350 also reported in the US.

For the next couple of years, with the series selling well, little attention was paid to the further development of the twins. In 1975, the B series was released with a few small changes, most significant being revised ratios for the top three gears, as well as a styling face-lift. Disc brakes were fitted to both the RD125 and 200, bringing them even closer to the styling of the larger bikes.

The RD400C

In Japan, a gradual move away from the 350 capacity had started with the Honda and Kawasaki 400s in 1974, and for the 1976 model year, the stroke of the engine was increased by 8mm, resulting in a displacement of 398cc – and the RD400C was born. The opportunity was taken to strengthen the crankshaft to accompany the new cylinder, conrods and pistons.

Some slight changes were made to the chassis to move the engine forwards by 20mm (3/4in), but the steering geometry was not altered. Cast wheels were standard on the 250 and 400, with disc brakes at front and rear. European styling was super sharp, with a black engine complemented by speed stripes on the square tank and side panel. In contrast, the US retained the polished cooling fins of the 350B and these, together with the unbroken horizontal stripes on the tank and side cover, resulted in a much blander appearance.

The 400 was even more of a tiger than the 350, effortlessly hoisting the front wheel when the throttle was snapped open at low revs in first gear. It was really the start of a love affair for the sports rider looking for a bike that would flatter his image with some mildly anti-social behaviour: mono-wheeling away from the lights, grinding the footrests over the blacktop in the corners, chirping the tires with full snatch braking and rider grinning from ear to ear.

Engine
The unique design of the RD250 two-stroke engine, developed by YAMAHA, utilizes the exciting seven-port Torque Induction system. The important seventh port functions both as an intake and scavening port, increasing vital engine breathing. With this superb system, the throttle responds instantly over the low and medium rpm ranges as well as at high rpm. Like the outstanding YAMAHA GRAND PRIX machines, the instant throttle response of the RD250 gives you faster acceleration for a quick get-away.

The V-type reed valve
The RD250 V-type reed valve is just one more key development supporting YAMAHA's remarkable Torque-Induction system. Two special stainless-steel reed valves provide an instant response to negative pressure from the cylinder, eliminating blow back to the carburetor at low speeds.

Autolube
YAMAHA's two-stroke engines are lubricated by a separate, unique system called Autolube. With Autolube, the amount of oil fed into the high performance RD250 engine, is regulated by throttle action. This precision, engineered system saves you oil and lengthens the life of your engine.

Transmission
The RD250 uses a five-speed, constant mesh transmission which effectively utilizes engine power at all speeds. Gears two, three four and five are close ratio for consistent high performance. The sport gear-change should be the short stroke of the RD250's five-speed transmission makes fast shifting simple and easy.

Front forks and rear shock absorbers
Exciting telescopic, oil damped front-forks are standard equipment on the RD250. The spring and oil damper are specially combined to smooth out all road shocks and bumps. The rear suspension consists of a swing-arm combined with adjustable, hydraulic shock absorbers. These three-step, adjustable shock absorbers allow the rider to choose the best spring tension relative to road conditions and rear weight. The race-proven, rear suspension provides maximum stability on the open highway or along twisting country roads.

Frame
Built around the RD250's high performance engine is a specially designed, double-cradle frame. Light in weight and constructed from high-tensile tubular steel, it's the same kind of frame used on YAMAHA's winning GRAND PRIX machines. Its sturdy design gives you outstanding all around road-holding under any conditions.

Speedometer and Tachometer
YAMAHA's conveniently mounted speedometer and tachometer allow the RD250 rider to read these important instruments at a glance, day or night. The precision speedometer and tachometer are specially designed to utilize indirect lighting, eliminating glare for night riding.

Brakes
Braking at a tough is easy, and at high speed safe, with the RD250 special double-piston hydraulic, front disc brake. The RD250's tough rear brake is a single-leading shoe which provides guaranteed stopping power. For your own personal comfort on the RD250, the front brake lever is adjustable to fit your hand and the rear

Yamaha were keen to push the RD technology and its links to racing.

RDs for Europe

The RD250C was a European motorcycle, no longer available on the US market. It sold in huge numbers in 1976 and 1977, the model remaining unchanged. For 1978, both the 250 and 400 for the European market underwent some improvements to engine and chassis. CDI electronic ignition was fitted to provide a strong, reliable spark. There were some adjustments to the cylinder porting to cure a partial throttle stutter that the bikes had experienced. In the US, the 400C had come with 2mm wide passages drilled from above the exhaust port down to the exhaust tract, meaning that post-ignition pressure in the combustion chamber would be eased slightly before the main exhaust port opened as the piston descended on its power stroke. In addition there had been slots cut into the exhaust-side piston skirts, resulting in the exhaust port being opened to the crankcase as the piston reached top dead centre. All rather unorthodox practices in the world of two-strokes, but it had fixed the surge that had been present on the 350B.

The imminent demise of the two-strokes in the US meant that for once, the European market received the most significant updates; on the E models in Europe, the footpegs were bolted straight on the frame, while in the US they were still slung under the frame to drag through corners. The front forks were the new 35mm-diameter units with special anti-stiction bushings that had proved so successful on the XS four-stroke series. The European 1979 RD250 and 400 had a few very small changes, and were discontinued at the end of the year – but something special would take on where the air-cooled RDs left off.

The RD400 Daytona Special

It was thought by many that the RD400E would be the last of the air-cooled twins in the US. Strict emissions regulations came into force in January 1978, and the E just managed to become homologated before the bill took effect. It seemed as if the two-stroke twin had passed on for good, twenty years after first appearing in the US as the YDS1. Miraculously though, Yamaha weren't ready to let the bike that had built them their success in the USA pass away so quietly. Digging deep into their rich history of developing two-stroke engines, they found a way to produce a version of the RD400 that could pass the EPA emissions measurements and still preserve the whippersnapper characteristics of the RD series.

It was a last gasp effort, intended to commemorate the achievements of their two-stroke twins, and it proudly bore the name of the place Yamaha had experienced its most glorious racing successes over the previous two decades. It was the Daytona special. The whole bike was essentially the RD400E that had been available in Europe, with trick adjustments to meet the emissions controls. Yamaha had managed to beat the emissions regulation through the use of butterfly valves fitted between the exhaust tract in the cylinder and the exhaust pipe. At low engine speeds, the valves were kept shut to prevent unburnt hydrocarbons escaping to the atmosphere, and, of course, the EPA emissions measurement sensors. It worked well, and for one final glorious year, US riders could enjoy the unique excitement of the air-cooled RD400 twin. From 1980 it was gone.

The 1978 RD400 was the ultimate air-cooled Yamaha two-stroke twin.

LCs for Europe

While the US riders addicted to lightweight rocket ship two-strokes were left to manage their habit by any means at their disposal, European riders of the same ilk were treated to the LCs. Development of the new range of twins had been passed to the Yamaha headquarters in the Netherlands, as the bikes were to be focused sharply on the European market.

The foundations for the new design were laid down over a period from 1977 up to their release in 1980, the team responsible given the mandate to capture the link with racing that had gradually disappeared from the RD line. Whereas Yamaha's air-cooled production racers had literally had many parts interchangeable with the DS and R series of streetbikes, the adoption of first water-cooling in 1973 and then Monoshock suspension in 1976 had broken the links between the TZ race bikes and the RD series. In addition, US racing regulations had scrapped the link with streetbikes that had kept the two so close, instead adopting homologation of a minimum number of

units available for purchase. This, coupled with claiming rules enabling bikes to be purchased for a fixed amount at the end of each race, discouraged factories from entering expensive highly modified specials. All the same, it was not the intention to re-adopt the shared components of the past; it would be sufficient to style and promote the bikes as race replicas. It was a wildly successful approach.

Needing to link into the GP classes, the top of the range was once again a 350, joined by a 250, and much later a 125cc and 80cc version. The first LCs had the same cylinder dimensions as the TZs, a common stroke of 54mm and a bore of 54mm for the 250 and 64mm on the 350. Reed valves were retained on the new series, feeding into the same seven-port layout cylinder now wrapped in a light alloy, water-cooled jacket. Oil pump and water pump were both driven by a gear on the right-hand end of the crankshaft next to the primary transmission gear. Both models had the same transmission ratios, although the 350 had two less teeth on the rear wheel sprocket, raising the gearing.

The street variant of the Monoshock suspension chassis that had been introduced on the TZs

The second generation of the RD series, the water-cooled LC models, appeared in 1980.

Studio work to emphasize the link between the new RD and its TZ 350 cousin.

Out of the studio and on to the racetrack, into its element.

The dream of 'wannabe' racers everywhere.

in 1976 was derived from the 1979 season TZ, which was itself the second generation Mono-shock chassis. The most significant difference between the two was the use on the LC of a short conventional rear shock absorber anchored at the top to a mounting plate where the rear sub-frame joins the apex of the double-looped cradle holding the engine. In contrast, the TZs used a very long, nitrogen-charged decarbon damping unit that stretched up to a mounting point under and behind the headstock. The lower mounting point of the rear suspension was quite similar between LC and TZ, although the U-shaped upper swingarm on the TZ was much stronger, with extensive extra gusseting support.

Rather than just slap on the conventional straight-spoked, cast wheels that were becoming standard on most sports bikes, very distinctive curved-spoke wheels were developed, for many Europeans the trademark of the LC series. The RD350LC was equipped with double disks up front and a single rear, while the 250 had to make do with a single front disk; this was the most immediate feature distinguishing the two, other than the decals on the side cover.

To say that the new model range made an impact on the market would be an understate-ment. In the UK, the bikes were massively suc-cessful, the 250 benefiting from the contem-porary regulations allowing riders to ride the 250 with a provisional licence, ostensibly in preparation for taking and passing their test. But given that the magic 'ton' of 100mph (160km/h) could be reached without too much difficulty, especially with the help of a few of the numerous after-market go-fast accessories, there was really no rush to get a full licence.

It was, however, a victim of its own success, as inevitably there were claims that it was dan-gerous to allow inexperienced riders on to such a fast machine, and laws were introduced to lower the maximum capacity of learner machines to 125cc. Almost 20,000 units of the RD250LC were sold in Europe for the two full years before this restriction was introduced. For 1982, with the law coming into force in Octo-ber, just 2,000 units were sold. The 250 class was almost dead in the UK.

Model	RD125	RD125LC	RD200
Year	1974	1982	1974
Capacity (cc)	124	124	196
Configuration	2-s 2 cyl	2-s 2 cyl	2-s 2 cyl
Induction	reed valve	reed valve	reed valve
Bore × stroke (mm × mm)	43 × 43	56 × 50	52 × 46
Gearbox	5-speed	5-speed	5-speed
Final drive	chain	chain	chain
Frame	spine	duplex cradle	spine
Wheelbase (mm, in)	1,240 (48.8)	1,300 (51.2)	1,245 (49)
Dry weight (kg, lb)	120 (265)	113 (249)	133 (293)
Power (bhp)	16 @ 9,500rpm	20 @ 9,500rpm	22 @ 7,500rpm
Torque (kgm)	1.3 @ 8,500rpm	1.5 @ 9,250rpm	2.17 @ 7,000rpm
Top speed (km/h, mph)	130 (81)	125 (78)	140 (87)

Model	RD250	RD250C	RD250LC
Year	1973	1976	1980
Capacity (cc)	247	247	247
Configuration	2-s 2 cyl	2-s 2 cyl	2-s 2 cyl watercool
Induction	reed valve	reed valve	reed valve
Bore × stroke (mm × mm)	54 × 54	54 × 54	54 × 54
Gearbox	6-speed	6-speed	6-speed
Final drive	chain	chain	chain
Frame	duplex cradle	duplex cradle	duplex cradle
Wheelbase (mm, in)	1,320 (52)	1,320 (52)	1,380 (54.3)
Dry weight (kg, lb)	144 (317)	148 (326)	141 (311)
Power (bhp)	30 @ 7,500rpm	30 @ 7,500rpm	35 @ 8,500rpm
Torque (kgm)	2.92 @ 7,000rpm	3 @ 7,000rpm	3 @ 8,000rpm
Top speed (km/h, mph)	160 (99)	160 (99)	160 (99)

Model	TZR250	TDR250	R1-Z 250
Year	1987	1988	1991
Capacity (cc)	249	249	249
Configuration	2-s 2 cyl watercool	2-s 2 cyl watercool	2-s 2 cyl watercool
Induction	reed valve, YPVS	reed valve, YPVS	reed valve, YPVS
Bore × stroke (mm × mm)	56 × 50	56 × 50	56 × 50
Gearbox	6-speed	6-speed	6-speed
Final drive	chain	chain	chain
Frame	deltabox	duplex cradle	trellis
Wheelbase (mm, in)	1,375 (54.1)	1,375 (54.1)	1,380 (54.3)
Dry weight (kg, lb)	126 (278)	134 (295)	133 (293)
Power (bhp)	45 @ 9,500rpm	45 @ 9,500rpm	45 @ 9,500rpm
Torque (kgm)	3.5 @ 9,000rpm	3.6 @ 9,000rpm	3.7 @ 8,500rpm
Top speed (km/h, mph)	185 (115)	170 (106)	160 (99)

Model	TZR250R	RD350	RD350LC
Year	1991	1973	1980
Capacity (cc)	249	347	347
Configuration	2-s 2 cyl watercool	2-s 2 cyl	2-s 2 cyl
Induction	reed valve,	YPVS	reed valve reed valve
Bore × stroke (mm × mm)	56 × 50	64 × 54	64 × 54
Gearbox	6-speed	6-speed	6-speed *(continued…)*

Final drive	chain	chain	chain
Frame	deltabox	duplex cradle	duplex cradle
Wheelbase (mm, in)	1,340 (52.8)	1,320 (52)	1,380 (54)
Dry weight (kg, lb)	126 (278)	149 (328)	143 (315)
Power (bhp)	45 @ 9,500rpm	39 @ 7,500rpm	47 @ 8,500rpm
Torque (kgm)	3.8 @ 8,000rpm	3.8 @ 7,000rpm	3.8 @ 8,000rpm
Top speed (km/h, mph)	185 (115)	170 (106)	180 (112)
Model	**RD350 YPVS**	**RZ350**	**RD350F2**
Year	1983	1983	1983
Capacity (cc)	347	347	347
Configuration	2-s 2 cyl	2-s 2 cyl	2-s 2 cyl
Induction	reed valve, YPVS	reed valve, YPVS	reed valve, YPVS
Bore × stroke (mm × mm)	64 × 54	64 × 54	64 × 54
Gearbox	6-speed	6-speed	6-speed
Final drive	chain	chain	chain
Frame	duplex cradle	duplex cradle	duplex cradle
Wheelbase (mm, in)	1,385 (54.5)	1,385 (54.5)	1,385 (54.5)
Dry weight (kg, lb)	145 (320)	163 (360)	141 (311)
Power (bhp)	59 @ 9,000rpm	59 @ 9,000rpm	63 @ 9,000rpm
Torque (kgm)	4.4 @ 9,000rpm	4.4 @ 9,000rpm	4.4 @ 9,000rpm
Top speed (km/h, mph)	185 (115)	180 (112)	195 (121)
Model	**RD400C**	**RD400E**	**RD400F**
Year	1976	1978	1979
Capacity (cc)	399	399	399
Configuration	2-s 2 cyl	2-s 2 cyl	2-s 2 cyl
Induction	reed valve	reed valve	reed valve
Bore × stroke (mm × mm)	64 × 62	64 × 62	64 × 62
Gearbox	6-speed	6-speed	6-speed
Final drive	chain	chain	chain
Frame	duplex cradle	duplex cradle	duplex cradle
Wheelbase (mm, in)	1,315 (51.8)	1,315 (51.8)	1,315 (51.8)
Dry weight (kg, lb)	157 (346)	161 (355)	161 (355)
Power (bhp)	38 @ 7,000rpm	40 @ 8,000rpm	40 @ 8,000rpm
Torque (kgm)	3.9 @ 6,500rpm	3.8 @ 7,500rpm	3.8 @ 7,500rpm
Top speed (km/h, mph)	170 (106)	170 (106)	170 (106)
Model	**RD500**		
Year	1983		
Capacity (cc)	499		
Configuration	2-s 4 cyl		
Induction	reed valve, YPVS		
Bore × stroke (mm × mm)	56 × 50		
Gearbox	6-speed		
Final drive	chain		
Frame	duplex cradle		
Wheelbase (mm, in)	1,375 (54,1)		
Dry weight (kg, lb)	180 (397)		
Power (bhp)	87 @ 9,500rpm		
Torque (kgm)	6.9 @ 8,500rpm		
Top speed (km/h, mph)	220 (137)		

New technology with the powervalve and styling to link to racing: the 1983 RD350LC.

The 350LC

Not so the 350. The new LC was even more popular than the 250, pushed by a strong marketing campaign driving home the link with sporting heroes such as Barry Sheene and Kenny Roberts. Although its existence had been announced at the end of 1979, it was to be another six months before shipments started to arrive in Europe. Even the delay had not been long enough to ensure that it performed well out of the crate. The first units had an enormous mid-range hole, caused by a carburettor glitch that was fixed by new main jets and replacement reed boxes under warranty.

With the bike running as designed, riders were ecstatic about its sublime package of speed, acceleration, handling and comfort, all wrapped in the beautiful white-dominated styling set against the matt black engine and exhausts. No major changes were made to the 350 in 1981 and 1982, with the single-cylinder RD125LC coming on to the line-up to cater for the new UK regulations limiting provisional licence holders to machines under 125cc capacity. It would continue to be offered for many years to come in markets such as the UK, undergoing cosmetic changes to keep it identifiable as one of the RD family, but with no significant changes to the engine or chassis. There was even a midget RD80, fitted out in the same colours and styling and available from 1982.

Since much effort had been put into linking the LC series with the production racer, Yamaha needed to ensure that they didn't drift apart as they had done with the air-cooled RD series. The 1981 TZ250H had undergone major engine redesign, employing for the first time a cylindrical valve in the exhaust tract of the cylinder, with a cutaway section that would line up with the roof of the exhaust when the throttle was fully open. In this position it offered no obstruction to the spent gases as they were scavenged from the cylinder. On partial throttle positions, the cylinder cutaway projected below the roof of the exhaust tract, effectively lowering the exhaust

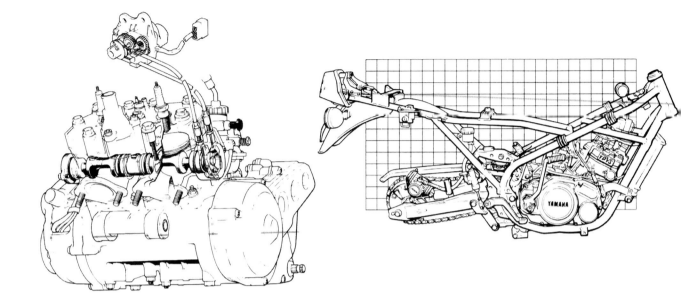

Variable height exhaust ports made possible through the rotating powervalve.

A new frame design could also be found on the 1983 series, in some ways leapfrogging TZ design.

port height. This variable exhaust-port timing was coined the Yamaha power valve system (YPVS) and enabled the engine to be tuned not only for peak power, but also to return a decent mid-range. For 1983, YPVS found its way to the LC series. The rest of the engine was largely unchanged, but an all-new chassis was, surprisingly, one step ahead of its racing cousin, the TZ.

Yamaha had been promoting their monoshock suspension for many years, since its introduction on their motocross models in 1973. Its main benefit came from the increased rear-wheel travel that was possible with this design, enabling softer springs to be fitted and drive improved through the rear tyre. Kawasaki had taken the design a stage further with their Unitrack system that not only provided good rear-wheel travel, but also applied a rising rate of resistance to further compression of the rear suspension. It took Yamaha several years to accept that the advantages of such a design outweighed the benefit of the corporate branding linked to the monoshock moniker. By 1982, it

was starting to be introduced on the motocross models, but the first design was not good, being too soft at the start and too hard at the end of the rear wheel travel. For 1983, Yamaha were confident enough to bring the design to the LC series, while the TZs would have to wait another three years before it appeared on the TZ250S.

Since a new frame was needed anyway for the rear suspension, some alterations were made to the structure, with slightly quicker steering geometry, although it was still a double-looped cradle holding the engine. The italic wheels were replaced by three-spoke blocked cast wheels, fitted with floating calliper double discs at the front and a single twin-piston calliper on the rear. Braking performance was excellent as a result. Once again, the aura of the bike would be determined by its bold styling, with a white version with red frame and blue and red stripes sweeping up from the belly-pan fairing, and continuing along the plastics to the rear of the bike. A small bikini fairing completed the sports image.

For 1985, the naked RD350N, stripped of all fairings.

The RZ350

The YPVS models came on the market in Europe in April 1983. With a claimed 59bhp at 9,000rpm, it looked as if it would leave the first generation 350LC in a cloud of blue smoke. True, it was faster, but not dramatically, and it seemed less spectacular to ride as the mid-range was a lot fatter in contrast to the sharper adrenalin-kick powerband on the first LC. They still proved popular with the punters, and sales were strong. A miracle was seen to unfurl in the USA when the 1984 Yamaha streetbike series was found to include the RZ350, rising like a Phoenix from the ashes of the RD series that had expired four years earlier. It was a development welcomed by enthusiasts everywhere in the USA, as it brought a touch of sparkle to a world that had fallen into the rut of middleweight 4-cylinder clones from all the manufacturers, classified with some disdain as the 'Universal Japanese Motorcycle'.

Ironically California – home of US road-racing talent, the hunting grounds of the canyon carvers, with an attitude closest to the cult groups in Europe who were running RDs, and birthplace of Yamaha America – was excluded. Even with the catalytic converter technology fitted to the YPVS RD, the emission rules in California could not be met. The other forty-nine states partied, while California mourned, observed by the greatest Californian of them all, Kenny Roberts, staring out from the double-page fold-out ads for the black and yellow RZ350. Yamaha USA did an amazing job of getting the twin two-stroke through the emissions restrictions, thanks to some leaning out of the carburetion and a lot of extra kit to clean up the exhaust gases. Catalytic converters were fitted within the exhausts, burning off the residual fuel mix on the gauze filters coated with a platinum catalyst. This was helped by a small bleed system that would allow fresh air to be sucked into the exhaust pipe to aid in the post-ignition combustion of the remaining charge. Admittedly the system sapped about 10 per cent of the power, down now to 52bhp, and it added another 20kg (44lb) to the weight of the bike, but it lived. It was a figurative breath of fresh air in the rather bland choices otherwise available to US riders.

So for two marvellous years the RD once again could be found scratching around the roads of the US, helping thousands of new owners discover the joy of the cut and thrust of a middleweight two-stroke twin. But from 1986 the dream was over, the two-stroke street twin gone from the USA, this time for good.

Enthusiasts in the rest of the world were a little more fortunate. Both the 250 and 350 continued to be sold in Europe and underwent some small chassis changes in 1985. The forks were now claimed to have variable damping valves that would change both bump and rebound damping, depending on the compression position of the forks. A new swingarm was fitted, with needle bearings at the frame pivot. There was an option for a fully faired F version of the unfaired N version. Thanks to the improved handling, it was generally agreed that these models were significantly better than the previous YPVS LC, despite the lack of attention to the engine to breathe a little more fire into the powerplant. This was addressed by the 350 N2 and 350 F2 models that were offered from 1986, the RD250 dropped from the line-up.

There was substantial work done on the engine to give the bike more zest, resulting in a 4bhp increase to 63bhp at 9,000rpm. This was not just the result of cylinder port timing, but the combustion chamber shape was altered and new exhausts fitted, along with an engine-wide makeover to strengthen the most heavily loaded components. Nothing substantial changed on the chassis, and the traditional white/red, black/red and white/blue colours were available.

A full fairing turned the RD350 into a comfortable sportsbike at the expense of a few extra kilograms.

The end of an illustrious line: the RD350R produced to a tight budget in Brazil.

As the 350 drifted away from its race origins, the 1987 TZR250 took a step closer.

Stripped of the street gear, the TZR250 looked every inch a racer.

The LCs are Laid to Rest

In truth though, the RD350 was over the top. There had been a surge of true GP replica two-stroke 250 twins coming out of Japan, much more cutting-edge than the LC, with razor-sharp power-bands and feather-light handling. The LC had all the qualities that didn't appeal to this type of rider, and the F2's over-faired, roomy riding position lent itself more for comparison with 500cc four-stroke utilitarian bikes, than the sharp cut and thrust of the smaller twins. It was a bike for the conservative two-stroke twin sports rider, but there weren't any. From 1988, only the F2 was available and continued to be offered for sale in the UK and a few other markets until 1995. Production was moved from Japan to Brazil in 1991, with a corresponding drop in build quality, and the whole package seemed to lose its sharpness. It was with a relief that the 1996 Yamaha catalogue no longer carried an LC in its line-up: the old dog, once a champion of the road, had finally been laid to rest.

But Yamaha had not yet passed up on the strong link between road and racetrack. In 1983 Suzuki had released the RG250 streetbike, prompting the other three manufacturers to follow suit with race replicas. Yamaha's response was the TZR250 that appeared in Japan in 1985. It was a new parallel twin engine slotted into an aluminium Deltabox twin-spar frame, bringing this revolutionary new technology, perfected in the GP500 class, to the street, before even the TZ production-series racers could benefit from the lighter, stiffer frame the following year. There were no components common to the pukka TZ250 racer of the era, but the impression it created was if it had just rolled off the same assembly line before being fitted with the minimum bits and pieces to make it street legal.

This was to be the start of an increasingly radical set of 250 twins that grew closer to the TZ series over the next seven years. Arriving first in Japan, it was exported from 1986 to 1989 to Europe and Australia, even touching down in Canada for a couple of years. In the 1980s a class of streetbike-based racing had developed for Formula 1, 2 and 3 classes. The 250 two-stroke

Only available for a couple of years, the 1988 TDR250 with the two-stroke twin engine in a Super Motard chassis.

twin was eligible for Formula 3 racing against four-stroke 400s, so Yamaha supplied tune-up kits for the 250 that would push standard 50bhp levels up well over the 60bhp, with a red line at 12,000rpm.

The engine served as a base for a few other Yamaha models, such as the TDR250 Motard replica. The Motard fashion had developed in France, where motocross bikes were fitted with 16in or 17in slick tire-shod wheels and ridden on part tarmac, part dirt tracks. In 1989, Yamaha offered the TZR250 engine in a traditional double loop cradle frame, with high-rise exhausts and a styling exercise to evoke the sports connection, but retaining 18in front and 17in rear tyres. It was popular in UK and Germany, with a 240cc version available for the French market. In 1990, the R1-Z 250 appeared in Japan, with a trellis frame and a low-slung parallel twin engine, with both exhausts exiting low at the right-hand side of the bike. It was essentially a styling exercise, perhaps influencing Ducati's enormously successful Monster series that was released a couple of years later.

For 1989, Yamaha modified the parallel twin engine to reflect the reversed cylinder engines used on the 1988 TZ 250U production racer, but kept these jewel-like little machines available solely to the Japanese market. The design was an exact replica of the TZ, complete with carburettors feeding the eight-petal reed valves straight into the crankcases at the front of the engine. The transmission consisted of a cassette-style gear cluster that could be slid from the side of the engine as a complete unit, reflecting cutting-edge GP technology. The chassis was no different, with massive deltabox frame, swingarm graced with an extra fork under the main arms, and bell and crank rising rate suspension. There had never been a closer link between the streetbike and the racer.

Yamaha had won the 250cc world title in 1990 on a special factory V-twin racer, and in 1991 both the production racer TZ250 and the streetbike TZR250R were replicas of this world championship machine. In a move reminiscent of the very first 1962 TD1 production racer, the TZ and the TZR shared the same crankcases. The layout of the 90-degree V-twin was identical on both machines, with simply a difference between strength and tolerances depending on the application of the two machines. Inside the cylinder the port timing was similar, although the 1992 TZ250 showcased the first seven-port layout on the TZ series, while the TZR made do with just five ports. Once again only Japan was blessed with these models, which continued to be built until 1999.

The two-stroke twin as a design icon. The Japanese market R1-Z.

The release of the 1984 RD500 GP replica corrected the error of fourteen years before, with the GL750.

The Ultimate Yamaha Two-Stroke: the RD500

The TZR 250R can be considered the ultimate Yamaha two-stroke twin, epitomizing the link between track and street that was Yamaha's credo when they started to build their first sports twins. Arguably though, it was not the greatest of all of Yamaha's two-stroke road bikes: this accolade should go to the RD500 LC that was announced late in 1983. The 1983 500cc GP season had been a tense Honda versus Yamaha battle between Freddie Spencer and Kenny Roberts, with the title finally going to Spencer on his 500 two-stroke triple.

It was a bitter pill for the company to swallow. Honda had been able to master road-racing two-stroke technology in two short years, based on their ten-year-old work on two-stroke motocross bikes. Now Yamaha would not be able to release the replica of their GP 500 machine as a championship-winning homage to Kenny Roberts, but everything else was in place to create the most eagerly awaited bike launch of 1984. Yamaha had been battling initially Suzuki and then latterly Honda in the 500cc GPs for almost ten years. Since 1982 Yamaha had settled on a trademark V4 configuration contrasting with the Suzuki RG square-four engine and the Honda NS triple. There was never any doubt that the RD500 would be a water-cooled V4, with the reed valves used throughout the RD series.

Much of the design followed that of the 1983 OW70 factory bike, with the upper pair of cylinders reversed so that the exhausts passed straight to the back of the engine. With the two pairs of cylinders angled at 50 degrees, the front pair was canted forwards and the exhausts ran down under and to the side of the bike. There was insufficient room to mount the four carburettors between the cylinder pairs, so a pair was bolted to each side of the engine with the inlet tracts turning 90 degrees to be able to feed the reed cages into the crankcase. Each cylinder pair was served by a separate crankshaft, the two crankshafts driving the primary gear on the clutch through a spring-loaded split gear. A side-loading transmission was needed to fit the design of the V4 crankcases.

Gearbox ratios were chosen to supply long first and second gears, with the top three gears very

Although it wasn't a true racer, the RD500 still looked good on a track.

close to keep the engine on the boil at high engine speeds. A small balance shaft was needed to cancel out the vibes from the 50-degree V, driven along with the water pump from the front crankshaft. All told, this was the most sophisticated two-stroke engine ever seen in a road bike.

The chassis was sophisticated as well. Although conventional in being a cradle rather than the very latest beam frame that the factory 500 had used in 1983, it used box-section tubing, mild steel in most markets, but aluminium in the Japanese market RZ500R. Rear suspension was unorthodox in its use of a horizontally placed rear shock lying along the longitudinal axis of the bike operated by a rocker arm. This was a time when all the Japanese factories were experimenting with weight distribution and the rolling inertia of race bikes to obtain the best steering characteristics as the bike is turned into a corner. This was also the reason for the small 16in front wheel while a conventional 18in rear wheel was fitted.

Following in the footsteps of the 1983 RD350, the 500 was finished in the same white

and red colours, the Japanese RZV 500R version breaking the swatch of red on the side plastics with white stripes to create the speed block effect synonymous with Yamaha in the USA. It was an impressive bike, in presence, technology and performance.

Suzuki and Honda rushed to put out their own versions of their GP 500s, with the RG500 and NS400 arriving in 1985. Back to back, there wasn't a lot of difference between the three, but it was clear that excessive weight and slow steering left the Yamaha trailing the other two machines. For all three companies, these bikes represented the pinnacle of their two-stroke streetbikes. Given Yamaha's heritage, the RD500 was an important testimonial to the two-stroke technology that had formed the bedrock of the company for more than two decades. With Yamaha's future linked totally to their prowess in developing four-stroke streetbikes, the RD500 would pass into history as a monument to everything they had achieved with the two-stroke.

7 Call of the Wild

Throughout the 1960s and well into the 1970s, the US market remained the most important to Yamaha as well as to all the Japanese manufacturers; the success or failure of a model in the USA had a direct influence on the company's financial performance. By 1965, 63 per cent of Yamaha's exports went to the USA. If the US economy caught a cold, the sneezes started in Japan. The company had quickly understood the need for a direct link into the market, and had acted promptly to secure control over their distribution network and build a local team that would provide critical input into product planning. Yamaha International Corporation had been established in June 1960 and, with the sales network functioning well by 1964, expanded with a large office in Montebello, California, developing the marketing and product planning teams on the instructions of Yamaha Japan. These teams were responsible for Yamaha's enormous growth over the next ten years.

Developing the Trail Bike

The direction that the US market had taken from the early 1960s was quite unique. On the wave of the prosperity brought by the pre-Vietnam war economic boom, they had embraced the small capacity run-around two-wheelers in great numbers, fuelling most notably Honda and Yamaha's export drive. Mobility was at the heart of the interest in tourism and recreation, which had expanded dramatically after World War II as personal transportation came within the reach of many family budgets.

In the US, tourism and recreation were closely linked with the passion for the Great Outdoors, the desire to escape the urban and suburban sprawl to discover the true America at the frontiers of the inhabited world. It was a phenomenon that was unique to the USA, and was quickly identified by the Japanese motorcycle manufacturers, with an increasing number of small capacity 'trail' models appearing in the model catalogues. In addition, it sparked the styling efforts to capture some of the aura of off-road riding with the minimum of changes to a standard road bike. The SS or street scrambler variants of the standard road bike were produced and sold in large numbers, usually equipped with nothing more than up-swept exhausts, a slightly detuned engine, dual-purpose tires and a bash-plate under the engine. Anyone attempting to do serious off-road riding on these heavy, slow-steering and under-powered bikes would have been severely disappointed.

The Bultacos

But there were bikes on the market that truly lived up to the 'trail' tag that this class of machine had been given. Most of them came from Spain, and the best of the Spanish bikes were the Bultacos. This was a family concern headed by 'Paco' Bultó, who had broken from Montessa in the late 1950s to create his own company. Specializing in single-cylinder two-strokes, the firm produced a bewildering number of models ranging from 125cc to 250cc, for all forms of off-road riding, as well as streetbikes and road racing.

By 1965, Bultaco had an annual production run of about 20,000 units, with 60 per cent of these going to the USA. But these numbers were split between as many as ten or more models in a single year, with the associated logistical nightmare of managing such a dis-

The first of its kind and a true revolution: the 1968 DT1.

parate set of machines and their spares. All the same, there were Bultacos built that did come close to providing the right balance between street and off-road functionality, most notably the Bultaco Matador that appeared in early 1966 as a 250, after a year on the market as a 200. It had the right packaging, offering good suspension, with plenty of travel, comfortable riding position and seat, good power and drive as a 250, and light yet stable handling. It was to serve as a blueprint for Yamaha in their decision to target this market segment.

Yamaha's Off-Road Bike: the DT1

Yamaha's product planning process involved frequent meetings between the team in Los Angeles and the development group in Japan. Coming together early in 1966, there were some worried faces round the table as the first signs had appeared of the slowdown that was to strike hard at sales over the next couple of years. Feedback from US dealers and sales staff was always con-

sidered important, and legend has it that the Yamaha salesman responsible for Denver, Colorado, had written stating: 'Models that can be ridden freely, not only on public roads, but also in the meadows or in the mountains, are popular, but road sports models aren't selling in Denver. Why doesn't Yamaha try building an off-road bike?'

The argument was supported by Jack Hoel working in the YIC product planning group, who had himself been observing the phenomenon in South California and was convinced that such a model would be successful. There was some scepticism and incomprehension expressed by the Japanese developers, but the need to expand the product line beyond the sports twins and runaround utility models meant that Japan was willing to take the risk. Coincidentally, they had been developing a 250 single-cylinder two-stroke engine for the motocross programme that they intended to run in the Japanese 1967 championships, and this would be a suitable starting point for the trail bike.

Riding on the success of the DT1, the series quickly grew to include the CT1 in 1969.

SINGLE ENDURO 175 (CT-1)
Is the 250 Enduro too much machine? Then we've got just the one for you. 175ccs will take you over any terrain with the ease only 5-port power can supply. The lightweight perfect mate to the DT-1B. And notice the styling. Those front forks (Enduro specials) take all the punishment, all the pounding, and bounce back for more. Standard features include adjustable rear shocks and separate DT-1B Enduro speedometer and tacho-meter.

SPECIFICATIONS
Engine .... 5-Port, Single
Displacement .... 171cc (10.44 cu. in.)
Max. horsepower ...... 15.6 BHP @ 7,000 rpm
Speed range .... 65 mph plus
Transmission 5-Speed
Starting system .... Primary Kick
Weight .... 212 lbs.

To ensure a solid understanding of the goal of the project, key members of the design team spent several weeks in the US. A Matador was acquired. It was ridden and analyzed by the design team, and guidelines for the project drawn up and jointly reviewed. The most critical design objective was to meet a weight target of just 100kg (220.5lb), almost half the weight of the YDS3 250 twin. It was quickly decided that the only way to achieve this was to start with the YX26 prototype 250 cross bike that later made its debut in May 1967 in the Japanese championship with a race victory. This stripped-down competition machine weighed in at 86kg (190lb), so even this needed to be revamped to meet the 100kg target with full street-legal equipment, as was required. In the end, the team missed the mark by just 5kg (11lb), but they had produced an off-road bike that was to set an industry standard for years to come: the Yamaha DT1.

The heart of the DT1 was the single-cylinder two-stroke engine measuring 70 × 64mm and displacing 246cc. Peak power of 21bhp was delivered at just 6,000rpm, with a wide, flat delivery curve and plenty of torque that made the bike easy to ride along fire roads and off-road trails. The engine itself was quite conventional, at least by Yamaha's two-stroke standards. The cylinder was a full 'five-port' design, with a pair of both main and auxiliary transfer ports. Yamaha had developed the use of the extra pair of transfer ports on their road-racing engines, and this design was starting to find its way into the rest of the two-stroke range. Needle bearings supported the pins at both ends of the crankshaft, and true to the rather lazy nature of the engine, heavy thick flywheels were used to assist in the bike's ability to lug through off-road terrain.

Everything in the engine and transmission was built for strength and durability, despite the directive to meet the 100kg (220.5lb) target. A five-speed gearbox was fitted, mandatory for street use but in fact a novelty for the Spanish dual-purpose machines that had gone before. The exhaust wrapped up and around the right-hand side of the bike, nicely tucked away so as not to compromise the riding position, secured to the cylinder with a pair of springs, in true road-racing fashion. Naturally the practicalities of Autolube were provided, the oil tank under

YAMAHA TRAIL

YAMAHA TRAIL 125/AT-1

A new 125 for the roughest country. 5-port single engine for remark performance. Special front forks absorb the roughest terrain. Adjust rear shock absorbers. Separate speedometer and tachometer. Exclu Yamaha Autolube injection system.

YAMAHA TRAIL 175/CT-1

175 cc of power to take you over any terrain with ease. 5-port single eng for dynamic power. Sturdy front forks designed to absorb the toug punishment. Yamaha's proven Autolube injection system. Other spe features include adjustable rear shock abosrbers and separate speedom and tachometer.

YAMAHA 80/YG5-T

A rugged trail model, designed to conquer the roughest trails and also give smooth performance on city streets. Double sprocket construction and Rotary Valve single cylinder with the Autolube injection system engine are the secret.

YAMAHA TRAIL 250/DT-1

Engineered especially for expert rough country riders. Extra strong for Famous 5-port single engine delivers exciting power. New tapped head a plug for compression release. Adjustable rear shocks. Separate speedome and tachometer. Exclusive Yamaha injection system.

100/L2C-A

The outdoorsman's dream. Built to take all of the tough punishment of trail riding. Long front fork, special engine guard, 'seven-bone' frame de- sign, sturdier springs and a special rear arm to absorb vibration. Scrambler tires for better traction. Two-step change over trailmatic transmission system. Electric starter. Upswept muffler. Plus all of the regular Yamaha extras like the exclusive Autolube injection for reduced engine wear.

The complete trail line-up for 1970.

YAMAHA 360
ENDURO RT1·B

It's a better machine

The 1971 360cc trail bike had a very healthy 30bhp available to the rider.

the seat and the oil pump driven off the right-hand end of the crankshaft. A VM26SH Mikuni carburettor and magneto ignition on the left-hand end of the crankshaft completed the simple, yet effective package.

Primary kick-starting, which allowed the bike to be started in gear with the clutch disengaged, showed the thought that had been put into the functionality of the machine. There were other little touches, such as the sparkplug angled off-centre to make it easier to remove, and the main jet mounted on the side of the carb body, for the same reason. It was clear that the bike had been designed by a team that understood the ergonomics of off-road riding.

Equally simple and no less effective was the chassis. The frame was a double loop cradle with a large diameter central tube running from the top of the headstock to the point where the rear sub-frame met the main cradle, just above the rear of the engine. A box-section swingarm, running in plain bushes, held the 18in rear wheel, with two conventional oil-damped rear shocks offering three-way adjustment of the spring preload. The traditionally sized 19in front wheel was held by Ceriani-style forks with drum brakes front and rear. A sturdy bash-plate was mounted under the front of the engine, wrapped around the curve of the frame loop.

Especially conspicuous was the big, wide and thick seat to keep the rider comfortable for hours out on the trail. Fitted with everything needed for street use, yet designed to be used off-road, the DT1 was ideal for the nascent market for dual-purpose machines: unintimidating for the novice, but capable enough for the more experienced rider. And not least, it looked right. For the first time since the creation of the YDS1 in 1959, Yamaha had built a motorcycle that was to define all the others of its kind that were to follow.

Sales were spectacular when it appeared in the US showrooms in April 1968. Production plans had been laid for a maximum of 12,000 units per year, with YIC claiming that 20,000 units per year could be reached. The first batch of 8,000 that arrived in the US were sold within three months, and the production lines were stretched to work

flat out with 2,500 DT1s rolling out of the factory each month by the end of the year.

The AT1

For Yamaha, the DT1 sparked the recovery from the mid-1960s slump, and all the manufacturers rushed to address the new market segment the company had uncovered. Determined to exploit their success to the full, Yamaha were quick off the mark in extending their range, and a 125 was available before the end of the year. The AT1 was very close in design to the DT, with just a handful of detail differences in the clutch and gear selectors. Frame design was a little different, bearing a strong resemblance to the large diameter, single tube backbone design of the 125cc and smaller streetbikes. Producing 11bhp at 7,500rpm, power was sufficient for the 94kg (207lb) lightweight.

Towards the end of 1969, the 175cc displacement CT1 arrived, with an AT1 engine bored out to 66mm. No other substantial changes had been made to produce the bike, representing a very low development cost to bring yet another model into the series.

The T Series Evolves

The DT1 was selling so well through 1969 and 1970, there was no need to invest in anything more than a new point job in the evolution through to the 1971 DT1E. Heading the range from 1970 was the 360cc RT1, 10kg (22lb) heavier but with some of the small, niggling problems of the DT1 fixed, and almost ten extra bhp to play with.

The T series had grown to dominate the Yamaha line-up by this time. Eleven of the eighteen models available from the company in 1971 were Ts, including their full off-road MX variants. Inevitably the Japanese competition had struck back, and in particular Suzuki had been able to produce a very effective set of two-stroke, dual-purpose and full-on competition machines. The Yamaha MX models that were available were really just stripped-down versions of dual-

Even the 90cc HT1 could look good speeding through the rough stuff.

purpose bikes and could not compete with the motocross bikes that Suzuki were producing. Realizing that a harder edge competition series was needed, it was at this stage that development started on the full motocross YZ range that became available from 1973. Until then, Yamaha riders had to stick to the MX series and invest in a lot of aftermarket accessories.

Torque Induction: the Application of Reed Valves

Yamaha had always placed great store in the use of new technology, both to improve the performance of the machines, but also to raise their innovation profile. To that end, it was felt appropriate to adopt a refinement to the two-stroke engine that Yamaha named 'torque induction', but which was more commonly known as the 'application of reed valves'. Not that two-stroke engines fitted with reed valves were very common in the early 1970s, certainly not in the motorcycle world.

Reed valves had been first developed almost forty years before by DKW, pioneers of the two-stroke. The valves had been adopted for use on piston-ported engines to provide a physical barrier to blowback from the crankcase as the piston falls after the ignition of the charge in the combustion chamber. Without the valve, blowback had been controlled by the piston skirt on the inlet side of the engine, covering the inlet port as it started to compress the charge in the crankcase. But the same skirt, ideally long to close the port as soon as pressure compression started, needed to be short to allow as much fresh charge as possible to be drawn into the crankcase as the piston rose. With a unidirectional valve, the problem would be solved, as the valve would snap open as a vacuum developed under the rising piston and snap shut as the piston began its descent, driving the fresh charge through the transfer ports to scavenge the engine.

In addition, great strides had been made in the 1950s with reed valve design on the back of the power lawnmower boom of the 1950s in the US. Jacobsen Manufacturing was one of the largest suppliers of power mowers in the USA, and they had spent considerable effort in redesigning the reed valves on their engines. Interest in reed valve induction had developed around a desire to be able to supply fresh charge straight into the crankcase rather than into the cylinder, freeing the engine design to place the carburettor wherever this was convenient.

Jacobsen had discovered that the use of the valve had resulted in the need to add more oil to the pre-mix, resulting in very smoky engines. They developed double-petal reeds with stops to limit the degree the reed would open. With the reeds mounted in the crankcase, they could direct fresh charge towards the big-end bearings to provide the necessary lubrication, even with lower levels of oil in the fuel mix. They also discovered that a wedge-shaped pair of double-petal reed valves would be even more effective at high speeds, though this wasn't relevant for the power mowers they marketed.

It was relevant to the karting community, however, who were pulling two-stroke engines from mowers and mounting them in low-slung, light

As Yamaha embraced reed valves, all off-roads were soon equipped with this technology, including the DT400.

chassis to create go-karts. Reed-valve development became linked to go-kart development, and under go-kart rules, single speed transmissions were required. They needed flat, wide powerbands, and that's what they were able to get with multi-petal reed valves fitted to their engines. Flat, wide powerbands are useful in off-road riding as well, so it was natural that Yamaha should look at the reed valve for their development programme. It wasn't the first time Yamaha had turned to the karting world for development of their two-stroke engines: it has always been rumoured that the five-port engines that first appeared on their TD1C racer came from some ideas being used to great effect in the two-stroke kart engines.

Torque Induction for the T Series
Mid-year in 1971, torque induction arrived on the AT, DT and RT series, the CT following later in the year. This was big enough news to crank up the series identifier to two, and the new series models all benefited from a stronger, gutsier mid-range engine. The opportunity was also taken to strengthen the frame, with thicker walled tubing and extra gussets – though in the process this added weight, for instance 7kg (15lb) to the 250,

which was not good for an off-road bike.

But was this really an off-road bike? Scarcely, as Yamaha were edging gradually towards a split between streetbikes with an off-road pedigree – the T series – and the true off-road YZ for competition, and the MX series for fun. All the same, they were not to let the Ts get too far away from the rough stuff, following the trend by fitting 21in front wheels for the 1973 DT3 and RT3. The extra rolling leverage over rocks and obstacles was useful in the dirt, but it did make the bikes a little twitchy on the street, because it essentially tightened up the steering, as the frame was left unchanged.

From 1973, across the complete Yamaha line-up of streetbikes, the letter capacity designation made way for a model identifier with the capacity in the name. Thus the complete T series became DTs, varying between the DT90 and the DT360.

The DT Series

From this time there were two separate evolution lines in the DT series. Most serious attention was paid to the development of the 250 and 360, while the 100, 125 and 175 only came in for minor changes until the major rework in 1978, when the 125 and 175 received the YZ-derived full monoshock chassis. At this time, the fashionable radial-finned cylinder heads were fitted, although engine power characteristics were essentially unchanged. The extra gear in the transmission was useful though, and this generation of lightweight DTs was still considered the best-in-class by many roadtesters. In fact the IT175 Enduro bike Yamaha had started to build in 1976 went on to be considered class leader for many years in the late 1970s and early 1980s. The 125 and 175 survived in the Yamaha line-up until 1981, with just the utilitarian twin-shock DT100 available a couple of years longer.

More care and attention had been applied to the 250 and 360 during the remainder of the 1970s. After just a single year of torque induction, the twin-petal reeds were replaced by three-petal reeds. The most noticeable improvement as a result was the dramatic drop in oil consumption, Yamaha seeming to follow in the footsteps of the Jacobsen power mowers twenty years before. The frames were also adjusted to compensate for the 21in wheel that had been fitted to the DT3 and RT3. With a longer wheelbase and slightly less steep steering, the stability that had been missing now returned.

For some strange reason, only the 360 was equipped with solid state CDI ignition, the 250 making do with a magneto until it too was eventually upgraded in the DT250's last year of existence.

For 1975, the top of the range became a 400, with the cylinder bored out by 5mm to give a capacity of 397cc. Clearly distinguished by the new radial-finned cylinder head, and unchanged for 1976, this was the calm before the storm, when, a year later, the DT250D and DT400D were fitted with a completely new monoshock chassis, along the design lines of the YZ motocross bikes. All the theoretical advantages of this single-shock design were relevant to the DTs, with increased wheel travel enabling softer springs to be fitted and allowing the rear wheel to better track the rutted surfaces on which the DT might be run. The physical dimensions of the bike and steering geometry were not changed, and a couple of kilograms were usefully lopped off the weight. In the engine Yamaha went mad and introduced eight-petal reeds on both models, perhaps again in a quest to improve the lubrication of the engine; this enabled oil delivery to be cut back to improve emissions, since EPA was starting to look very closely at motorcycle exhaust gases.

Meeting EPS Standards

The 400's days were numbered, with competition elsewhere within the Yamaha motorcycle line-up, and from 1979 it was only available outside the USA. It was this year that Yamaha flexed their muscles in a final attempt to bolt on some trick equipment to reduce emissions to meet the latest EPS standards. The DT250F was able to achieve this through the use of a small airbox tapped into the exhaust tract of the cylinder and controlled by a small reed valve. Fresh air would be drawn into the exhaust manifold, resulting in the oxidization of some of the unburnt hydrocarbons in the exhaust gases. It was enough for 1979, but not a long-term viable solution, so like the 400, from 1980 the 250 was only available outside the USA.

The XT500

By this time the two-stroke was effectively dead in Yamaha's streetbike line-up, and they had been working throughout the 1970s to find four-strokes that would keep them in business when things became really tough with the EPA. Some of these attempts disappeared into obscurity, but there were a couple that were so spectacularly successful that they were to become classics, not only of the era, but of Yamaha's complete history. One of these was the XT500.

Ultimately in Europe alone over 70,000 XT500s were sold, and worldwide maybe double this number. Following on from the class-creating DT series, the XT repeated the job for the four-stroke, launching a dual-purpose family of streetbikes that could, at the weekend, take a left turn and cut some tracks through the woods, blow out the cobwebs, spark a little adrenalin, get closer to nature, live. And isn't that what motorcycling's all about?

The XT500 appeared in 1976 and was to become yet another legendary dual-purpose legend.

On a mountain somewhere, Yamaha's complete 1976 range of dual-purpose machines.

Model	AT1	AT2	DT125
Year	1969	1972	1973
Capacity (cc)	123	123	123
Configuration	2-s 1 cyl	2-s 1 cyl	2-s 1 cyl
Induction	piston port	reed valve	reed valve
Bore × stroke (mm × mm)	56 × 50	56 × 50	56 × 50
Gearbox	5-speed	5-speed	5-speed
Final drive	chain	chain	chain
Frame	duplex cradle	duplex cradle	duplex cradle
Wheelbase (mm, in)	1,285 (50.6)	1,280 (50.4)	1,280 (50.4)
Dry weight (kg, lb)	94 (207)	100 (220)	100 (220)
Power (bhp)	11.5 @ 7,500rpm	13 @ 7,000rpm	13 @ 7,000rpm
Torque (kgm)	1.17 @ 6,000rpm	1.38 @ 6,000rpm	1.38 @ 6,000rpm
Top speed (km/h, mph)	90 (56)	90 (56)	90 (56)

Model	CT1	CT2	DT175
Year	1970	1972	1973
Capacity (cc)	171	171	171
Configuration	2-s 1 cyl	2-s 1 cyl	2-s 1 cyl
Induction	piston port	reed valve	reed valve
Bore × stroke (mm × mm)	66 × 50	66 × 50	66 × 50
Gearbox	5-speed	5-speed	5-speed
Final drive	chain	chain	chain
Frame	duplex cradle	duplex cradle	duplex cradle
Wheelbase (mm, in)	1,290 (50.8)	1,290 (50.8)	1,290 (50.8)
Dry weight (kg, lb)	96 (212)	98 (216)	99 (218)
Power (bhp)	15 @ 7,000rpm	16 @ 7,000rpm	16 @ 7,000rpm
Torque (kgm)	1.64 @ 5,500rpm	1 64 @ 5,500rpm	1.64 @ 5,500rpm
Top speed (km/h, mph)	110 (68)	115 (71)	115 (71)

Model	DT1	DT2	DT250
Year	1968	1972	1975
Capacity (cc)	246	246	246
Configuration	2-s 1 cyl	2-s 1 cyl	2-s 1 cyl
Induction	piston port	reed valve	reed valve
Bore × stroke (mm × mm)	70 × 64	70 × 64	70 × 64
Gearbox	5-speed	5-speed	5-speed
Final drive	chain	chain	chain
Frame	duplex cradle	duplex cradle	duplex cradle
Wheelbase (mm, in)	1,366 (53.8)	1,330 (52.4)	1,410 (55.5)
Dry weight (kg, lb)	105 (232)	105 (232)	112 (247)
Power (bhp)	21 @ 6,000rpm	24 @ 7,000rpm	24 @ 7,000rpm
Torque (kgm)	2.5 @ 5,000rpm	2.5 @ 6,000rpm	2.5 @ 6,000rpm
Top speed (km/h, mph)	120 (75)	125 (78)	125 (78)

Model	XT250	XT250	RT1
Year	1980	1984	1970
Capacity (cc)	249	249	351
Configuration	4-s 1 cyl	4-s 1 cyl	2-s 1 cyl
Induction	2-valve sohc	4-valve dohc	piston port
Bore × stroke (mm × mm)	75 × 56.5	73 × 59.6	80 × 70
Gearbox	5-speed	5-speed	5-speed

(continued…)

Final drive	chain	chain	chain
Frame	duplex cradle	duplex cradle	duplex cradle
Wheelbase (mm, in)	1,395 (55)	1,420 (56)	1,400 (55.1)
Dry weight (kg, lb)	113 (249)	113 (249)	117 (258)
Power (bhp)	21 @ 8,000rpm	23 @ 8,000rpm	30 @ 6,000rpm
Torque (kgm)	2.0 @ 6,500rpm	2.15 @ 6,500rpm	3.6 @ 5,500rpm
Top speed (km/h, mph)	125 (78)	130 (81)	130 (81)
Model	**RT2**	**DT360**	**XT350**
Year	1972	1974	1985
Capacity (cc)	351	351	346
Configuration	2-s 1 cyl	2-s 1 cyl	4-s 1 cyl
Induction	reed valve	reed valve	4-valve dohc
Bore × stroke (mm × mm)	80 × 70	80 × 70	86 × 59.6
Gearbox	5-speed	5-speed	6-speed
Final drive	chain	chain	chain
Frame	duplex cradle	duplex cradle	duplex cradle
Wheelbase (mm, in)	1,385 (54.5)	1,425 (56.1)	1,420 (56)
Dry weight (kg, lb)	119 (262)	125 (276)	119 (262)
Power (bhp)	32 @ 6,000rpm	32 @ 6,000rpm	31 @ 7,500rpm
Torque (kgm)	3.82 @ 5,500rpm	3.82 @ 5,500rpm	2.15 @ 6,500rpm
Top speed (km/h, mph)	130 (81)	130 (81)	130 (81)
Model	**DT400**	**XT500**	**XT550**
Year	1975	1976	1981
Capacity (cc)	397	499	558
Configuration	2-s 1 cyl	4-s 1 cyl	4-s 1 cyl
Induction	reed valve 2-	valve sohc	4-valve sohc
Bore × stroke (mm × mm)	85 × 70	87 × 84	92 × 84
Gearbox	5-speed	5-speed	5-speed
Final drive	chain	chain	chain
Frame	duplex cradle	spine simplex cradle	spine simplex cradle
Wheelbase (mm)	1,410 (55.5)	1,420 (56)	1,400 (55.1)
Dry weight (kg)	124 (273)	139 (306)	137 (302)
Power (bhp)	27 @ 5,000rpm	28 @ 5,500rpm	33 @ 7,100rpm
Torque (kgm)	3.82 @ 5,000rpm	3.6 @ 5,000rpm	4.5 @ 5,000rpm
Top speed (kph)	125 (78)	135 (84)	140 (87)
Model	**XT600**	**XTZ660**	**XT660R**
Year	1984	1991	2004
Capacity (cc)	595	659	659
Configuration	4-s 1 cyl	4-s 1 cyl	4-s 1 cyl
Induction	4-valve sohc	5-valve sohc	4-valve sohc
Bore × stroke (mm × mm)	95 × 84	100 × 84	100 × 84
Gearbox	5-speed	5-speed	5-speed
Final drive	chain	chain	chain
Frame	spine simplex cradle	spine simplex cradle	duplex cradle
Wheelbase (mm, in)	1,435 (56.5)	1,490 (58.7)	1,500 (59)
Dry weight (kg, lb)	136 (300)	169 (373)	165 (364)
Power (bhp)	44 @ 6,500rpm	48 @ 6,250rpm	48 @ 6,250rpm
Torque (kgm)	5.0 @ 5,000rpm	5.8 @ 5,250rpm	5.8 @ 5,250rpm
Top speed (km/h, mph)	150 (93)	145 (90)	165 (103)

Yamaha reinvented the big single, but there was nothing so very new to it at all.

It's strange that this all worked for Yamaha, rather than Honda, who back in 1972 had produced a competent little XL250, along with their first two-stroke motocross bike, the Elsinore. A couple of years later it was joined by a competent little 350 – and still the world slept on, ignorant of the fun they were missing, for the XL350 could be fun in the dirt, albeit in a quiet unassuming way. It would get you places you'd otherwise not see – though there might not be a lot of adrenalin in your blood once you got there.

Yamaha, on the other hand, had seen the grins on the faces of their DT400 owners, and knew that fun was a crucial ingredient in a successful off-road package. The reed valve on the DTs had given them the wide, flat power that worked so well off-road, and the idea was to produce this on the new four-stroke – but then more of it, a lot more.

There had always been something charismatic about the big British BSA Victor and Matchless G85 off-road bikes, and Yamaha came close to capturing that with the XT. Lots of engine was the key ingredient, so there was little hesitation in going for a full 500, especially as the slot was vacant at the time. Yamaha adopted the shorter stroke engine similar to the Matchless, rather than the long stroke

BSA, focusing on a compact engine with small flywheels and a dry sump. They resisted the temptation to put too much innovation into the XT, adopting just a 2-valve cylinder head in contrast to the 4-valve ohc Honda engine. Wisely, a compression-release mechanism lifted the exhaust valve through a lever on the handlebar to assist kick-starting the hefty cylinder. Following in the footsteps of the four-stroke XS series, a small valve was fitted to provide positive crankcase ventilation to vent any pressure build-up in the crankcase, and recycle the oily fumes through the engine.

The rest of the engine was quite conventional, although a separate oil tank was dispensed with, the oil being stored in the large-diameter backbone element of the frame. Two oil pumps were fitted, one to scavenge oil from the sump and the other to pump oil to the crankshaft and camshaft. Access to the oil reservoir in the frame was through a small plug just behind the headstock. The frame itself was semi-double cradle, with the oil-carrying front downtube and backbone member.

Yamaha were on the brink of introducing the monoshock design into their off-road range, but this was complicated by the tall engine and dual-purpose frame, so traditional twin-shock suspension was fitted. Some increased wheel travel could be obtained by mounting the shocks in a laid-down position. Standard dual-purpose equipment – including a 21in front wheel, bash-plate, trials universal-type tyres and cleated footrests – followed DT standard practices. The strangest design error, apparently insisted on by Japan, was to route the exhaust pipe down and under the right-hand side of the engine, leaving it very exposed to any immovable objects and unprotected.

The bike was warmly welcomed, and commonly acknowledged to be the best of the dual-purpose bikes offered on the marketplace, displacing the DT400 in the process. It had a powerful, meaty engine that could dig in and drag the bike through loose surfaces, supple long-travel suspension for off-road riding and a comfortable riding position. On the blacktop there was enough power and handling to offer reasonable streetbike performance, resulting in the best compromise that is always the lot of a dual-purpose machine.

The XT500 was to have a long lifeline, with few changes over the years. This is 1988.

Yamaha had done it again, and unwittingly created a Japanese classic in the process. Right from the start the XT sold well, as did its brother, the TT, only available in the USA and stripped of all the lights and equipment for the street. There were few criticisms levied at the bikes, although the exhaust was clearly in the wrong place and very easily damaged on the rough stuff. Also the small flywheels on the crankshaft helped the bike to rev easily, but also made it easy to stall, especially as the rear brake was a little fierce and could lock up the engine.

The light flywheels were something XT500 owners had to learn to live with, as this wasn't fixed on the 1977 D model. But there were some improvements. The chassis underwent a few changes, with fork internals from the full-on IT Enduro series and a slightly sharper steering-head angle. The bash-plate on the C had been too short, but now it extended back under the complete length of the engine, giving good protection. The exhaust was also moved out of harm's way, snaking along the cylinder over the engine casings, between the loops of the frame and out to the rear of the bike.

Kick-starting the C had been tricky for some owners, so assistance came on the D in the form of a small inspection window on the cylinder head. When the engine was turned over with the compression-release lever pulled, a silver disc would appear in the window at the optimum moment to engage compression and heft a kick to the engine. This made things really easy.

The XT Series

For 1978 the D became the E, with just some minor changes, and the E became the F with no changes at all – and still the XT was the best of the dual-purpose machines on the market: but only just. Both Honda with the XL500 and Suzuki with the DR400 were snapping at its heels, and the XT was sorely in need of a serious makeover, enough to slash 15kg (33lb) or more, to remain the top of the heap.

It didn't come, and by 1980 the G was second-best in the class it had created. The steering had been quickened yet again, but this didn't compensate for the bulk and mass of the bike, making it a handful in the dirt, especially on loose sandy surfaces. In the USA, 1981 saw the XT500H available to the buying public, proudly

Never really intended for off-road riding, the 1981 XT550 could still look good when trucked to the top of a mountain.

There were a lot of design changes in the evolution of the XT500 to XT550.

*Chip off the old block. The
XT250 joined the line-up
in 1980.*

*The XT350 arrived in
1985 and was to remain in
the line-up for fifteen years.*

flawed and unchanged from the G of the previous year. It was to be its last year of sales in the USA, although it continued to be available throughout the 1980s in Europe. It sold in large numbers especially in Germany and France, and was unchanged other than styling cosmetics, except for the switch to 12–volt electrics in 1986.

But the XT had spawned a complete family of smaller bikes, from 125 to 350. First to arrive was the 250G, replacing the last of the DT two-strokes in 1980. It was a totally different bike from the 500. Needing to adopt the mono-shock design of the DTs, the XT500 oil-filled frame would not be possible. This in turn, meant that the engine would either need to have a separate oil-tank somewhere or change to wet-sump lubrication.

Thanks to the smaller engine, enough ground clearance could be achieved even with the deeper wet-sump crankcase, especially when it formed a stressed member of the frame, replacing the under-engine cradle members. The other change of design philosophy lay in the adoption of a counterweight to suppress the engine vibrations. The XT500 had used rubber engine mountings, but the new generation XTs had the counterweight driven directly off the crankshaft. Despite this, the 250 did buzz quite badly, much worse than the other Japanese competition.

It was also a difficult starter, despite an internal automatic compression release mechanism, simplifying the starting procedure.

All told though, the XT was a worthy replacement of the DT250, as good as, if not better than its rivals from Honda and Kawasaki. It was to remain in the US model range until it was dropped in favour of the XT350 in 1985, though it continued to be produced for other markets around the world. From 1984 it had undergone a conversion to a 4-valve head, with complimentary lightening of the crankshaft and flywheels to allow the engine to spin faster. It was this legacy that the XT350 inherited and retained in the years ahead.

For a couple of years, 1982 and 1983, there were also 125 and 200 versions available, sharing many components and built as clones of the 250. These models fell victim to the big shakeout in the wake of Yamaha's financial and business crisis of 1982/1983 and were dropped for the rest of the 1980s, though they lived on in a few other parts of the world.

The XT350

From 1985, the XT350 was Yamaha's main offering in the lightweight dual purpose, or 'all-road' class as it was increasingly being referred to. Many components remained unaltered from the 250 that preceded it, but the overall package benefited enormously from the extra grunt from the bigger engine. Larger throat carburettors delivered more charge to the engine through valves that were unchanged from the 250. The crankshaft and transmission were modified to strength-

Bringing the desert to the XT350 was far easier than the other way round.

ABOVE: Form was more important than function by now, and the 1988 Ténéré looked fantastic.

BELOW: Image was important to cultivate, so desert rallies featured regularly in XT marketing material.

en and match the increased power level, with extra oil lines ensuring efficient lubrication.

On the chassis, the steering was quickened and a disc brake supplied on the front wheel to replace the poor performance of the drum brakes on the 250. It proved to be a good combination of power delivery, low weight and sharp handling, and it remained in the Yamaha catalogue until 2000, essentially unchanged, a testimonial to the qualities of the original design.

The XT550

The disappearance of the XT500 from the USA corresponded to the appearance of a new flagship dual-purpose dirtbike, the XT550. Although it was a totally new design of both chassis and engine, it did retain a couple of the cornerstones of the XT500 design principles, with a dry sump and oil reservoir in the frame. Unwilling to make the engine any taller, the extra capacity was obtained by increasing the bore of the engine and this, coupled to the new 4-valve head, increased the power output by about 5bhp.

The XT series had been low on acronyms, but for the 550, the Yamaha dual-intake system was applied. YDIS took the form of a double carburettor, with a slide carb supplying charge for the first half of throttle operation, and a constant velocity carb taking over for the rest. Feeding the engine through its own slightly offset inlet tracts, it was claimed that the engine burnt more efficiently and lowered fuel consumption.

In general, the engine seemed a lot more powerful than the old 500, but there were problems with starting, and reports of some testers experiencing mid-range stumble as the CV carb started to kick in. It had been decided to add a balancer weight to keep down the vibrations, but as on the 250 this was only partially successful. Long rides were not comfortable, with the buzz contributing to the poor riding position. The frame was a hybrid between the XT250 monoshock design and the original XT500. Oil was stored in a shorter but thicker backbone frame member and front downtube, but the engine was also a stressed frame member, eliminating the need for the tubes to

loop under the engine. The triangulated steel rear swingarm was box section, with a short rear shock linking the apex of the upper arm to the bottom of the oil-carrying backbone member. Ground clearance increased by 2cm (¾in).

The XT600

The overall package was a lot better than the XT500, but it was not intended to be used in anger in the dirt. Fast riding on stable ground was fine, but sand or loose surfaces had the bike tied in knots. Suzuki and Honda had very comparable 500 dual-purpose bikes in their line-up, and it was debatable which of the three was the best. In fact the 550 was to be quite short-lived, as in Europe an XT600 Ténéré was available already in 1983, with a TT600 pure off-road model also being available in the USA from that year.

The new XT600 featured not only the larger engine, but also a move to the rising rate monocross chassis, tidying up the rear end of the bike, increasing rear-wheel travel and making enough space available for an oil tank behind the engine. The frame was now just a frame. For the first time a disc brake was fitted on the front wheel, a development that was just starting to find its way on to dirt bikes.

In Europe the Ténéré was primarily a styling exercise, but underneath all the plastic was a significantly improved XT that was to form the basis for a fresh start to the series in 1984. It was just as well that the base was quite competent, other than the over-soft suspension, as the model was scarcely changed over the next six years. It was to be 1990 before any dramatic changes were made to the design of the 600. It was selling very well in Europe, the new focus for the XT series, so there was little drive to evolve. The pimped-up Ténéré continued to be sold in Europe, and from 1986 was fitted with an electric starter, in keeping with the styling exercise that this was.

For 1990, the XT600 underwent the last of the design changes for the series. It would seem that Yamaha finally adopted the street scrambler philosophy for the XT, keeping the styling in line with the aura of exploration and off-road riding,

Sluggish, with an uncomfortable seat, many riders were spotted like this with their XT660Z.

Nothing much except styling had changed on the XT600, but the 1998 XT600E still looked good.

Back to basics, with almost thirty years of single-cylinder design going into the XT660R.

The perfect environment for the XT660R, an unhurried run through the backroads.

Gently does it, and the XT660R could handle a little off-road action.

The 2008 version of the Ténéré was once again firmly in the styling tradition of the series.

while building a bike that would not function well away from tarmac. Once again the frame was chosen to double up as oil reservoir, enabling the separate oil tank to be dumped. Frame design itself was essentially unchanged, although suspension travel was 30mm (1.2in) less front and rear, to lower the seat height. Suspension components were much lower spec, with steel swingarm, forks without air caps and rear shock without bump and rebound damping adjusters. Alloy wheel rims made way for steel. The Ténéré's electric starter was fitted, the piston lightened, and the big-end eye on the conrod widened a little.

The new XT, a streetbike with off-road styling, weighed in heavier than its predecessor. But just as had been the case in the 1960s, this didn't seem to be important to potential buyers, who continued to snap up the XT600 until it was finally laid to rest in 2003.

The XTZ660

Coinciding with the last redesign of the XT600, a decision was taken to split off the European Ténéré series from the mainstream XT series. In the mid-1980s, Yamaha had decided to embrace 5-valve four-stroke technology, and this formed the basis for their line of sportsbikes. To mark the Ténéré as something special, this technology was applied to the engine along with another displacement delta and water-cooling. The XTZ660 was born.

Basic design philosophy was unchanged, with similar oil-carrying frame layout and a dry sump engine. Few attempts were made to make this suitable for off-road riding, and the weight of the resulting bike was an intimidating 169kg (373lb). With just a couple of bhp extra generated by the engine, the bike was sluggish and slow, with poor brake performance. This, coupled with what was claimed as being the most uncomfortable seat on any bike available in the early 1990s, emphasized that the design had been a gratuitous application of styling and technology, with little regard to functionality or purpose. It remained available in the catalogue through to the end of the millennium, selling well in certain markets like France, but poorly in the UK.

A New XT660

During the 1980s, Yamaha had set the pace for Adventure bikes such as the XT series, but this waned through the 1990s. European manufacturers such as BMW and Aprilia were taking the initiative in styling and configuration, with twin cylinders becoming the most common base for big trail bikes. Yamaha decided that they needed to have a presence in this sector, and in 2004 relaunched the XT series with a totally new XT660 machine.

Rejecting the move towards twin-cylinder bikes, Yamaha developed a new 4-valve, water-cooled, single-cylinder engine, sharing the 100 × 84mm bore and stroke of the old air-cooled unit. The dry sump with oil tank in the frame was a characteristic, also retained from the old models. The new bike was equipped as a base for the next generation of singles.

Two versions were introduced simultaneously, styled for different market segments. The XT660R was the traditional off-road version with a 21in front wheel, while the XT660X was a Supermotard version with a 17in front wheel fitted with a 320mm diameter disc brake and larger fuel tank. As far as singles go, the XTs were good, despite the non-adjustable damping for the suspension, but the single-cylinder engine with its 43bhp left it at a serious disadvantage with respect to the twins, even with the positive weight differential.

Having marketed the new generation XT for four years, Yamaha felt it was the right moment to resurrect the Ténéré series, and launched the bike for the 2008 model year. They chose not to grasp the moment to add an extra cylinder, using the same spec engine as the rest of the series. Gaining 10kg (22lb) in the transformation to Ténéré, even with the new aluminium swingarm, meant that the 660 was still sluggish on the road – but true to Ténéré tradition of old, this was primarily a styling exercise, and from that perspective it was an undoubted success. The larger tank and handlebar fairing, coupled to the khaki green and grey styling, made the bike look as if it had just escaped from a 'special ops' mission in Iraq.

There was every reason to believe that the Ténéré would be a worthy successor to the XT500 that had launched the Adventure bike segment over thirty years before.

8 Beauty or Beast?

Much of the pleasure experienced in riding motorcycles comes from the change of reality that occurs when the bike is rolled out, fired up and driven off. Different muscles come into play for machine control, thought processes must guard against the dangers of a persona exposed to the greater risks of nature, the elements and unfocused drivers sharing the streets. Survival is driven by a self-awareness of your presence on the bike on the road and an image is built of yourself in the eyes of the others on the road. This image will be a projection of the character of the rider, the emotions that led to the ride, the senses to be stimulated, the urges to be pacified. For some, it's the thrill of challenging the laws of physics as bikes are hustled along a twisty road. For others, it's the need to express individuality by breaking out from the hum–drum, safe, regimented life so many of us lead, and to feed the alter ego with perceived peer respect for the rejection of the status quo.

For this group of motorcycle owners, a massive industry segment was to evolve. By 1982, over 40 per cent of all motorcycles sold in the USA could be labelled as 'cruisers'. The art of individuality had become mainstream.

There had been an undercurrent of image-building present in the US market from the 1960s, when this had focused primarily on the off-road styling exercises known as street scramblers. Despite the fact that the bikes were often a lot worse than the original, their huge success underlined the importance the market attached to form over function. Ironically, the origins of custom bikes were the reverse. It had been the drive to strip the bikes of unnecessary, heavy components that had led to specialized shops 'chopping' the skirts off the large front and rear mudguards. It moved on to other parts of the bike, where often everything was junked in the drive for a lighter weight, and a focus on the engine as heart of the bike. Smaller-than-stock fuel tanks, seats, indicators and lights were fitted, until the bike had been turned into a minimalist replica of the standard model.

Easy Rider

At this stage, the drive for low weight changed into a drive for cool styling. The headstock was chopped from the frame and fitted to extended front forks, giving an extreme rake angle and wheelbase length. Straight line stability was good, but it took a lot of effort to push the bike into a turn. But who cared, it looked cool, and the coolness was immortalized in the radical 'Captain America' chopper built by Cliff Vaughs and Ben Hardy for Peter Fonda in the *Easy Rider* film of 1969.

The Easy Rider choppers had been built around Panhead Harley Davidson engines, and for 1971 the factory took the first small steps into factory custom bikes with the Super Glide, with forks from the XLH Sportster mated to the FLH frame and rear suspension. But it was not a successful model, and it was left to Kawasaki to start the custom rush with their LTD series in 1976. Yamaha were close behind with the rejuvenated XS650SE of 1978. Soon all the Japanese manufacturers were offering custom versions of their standard 2- and 4-cylinder bikes – but they all steered clear of competing head on with the Godfather of the chopper craze, Harley Davidson. It was a golden period for Japanese manufacturers, as the low production costs ensured very healthy margins on large unit volume sales.

A V-twin was needed, that was certain, but how about styling? A pre-TR1 drawing.

V-Twin Streetbikes

Yamaha decided that this market segment was so successful that it warranted its own individual range of motorcycles. They decided that they would build a series of streetbikes based on the V-twin design principle that until that time had been the domain of Harley Davidson and Ducati. At the time it seemed to herald the final onslaught on the remaining large volume non-Japanese motorcycle manufacturers. If successful, it would leave just BMW, with their eccentric, but highly regarded boxer twin as an alternative to what was becoming known as the Universal Japanese Motorcycle.

The Virago and the TR1

Given that the target for the new bikes were not the other three Japanese manufacturers, Yamaha felt able to continue in the line of their design principles of the 1970s. This meant that the new bikes would not need to be blisteringly fast or to have the sharpest of handlers, but they would need to be the best all-round package for the market segment they would address. For 1981, the XV750H Virago would complement the Specials that had been offered, based on the parallel twins, and the XV920RH, known as the TR1 in Europe, would offer an alternative to the ubiquitous multi-cylinder large displacement sports bikes offered by all Japanese manufacturers.

Yamaha needed to compromise on the ideal 90-degree V-twin configuration they would have liked to use to achieve perfect natural cancellation of crankshaft imbalances. A 75-degree angle kept the engine compact enough, without excessive vibration. A single crankshaft ran both conrods, resulting in a slight offset of the cylinders. The rear cylinder was reversed, with the carburettors nestling in the space between, fed from an air filter located in the space between the sides of the pressed-steel monocoque frame. With space around the engine at a premium, it functioned as a stressed member of the frame. The bike was fitted with a sophisticated rear suspension unit offering twenty-position rebound damping as well as air-controlled spring rates.

The 750 and 920 had the same design and shared many components. The most significant differences, other than engine capacity, was the shaft drive found on the XV750 in contrast to the enclosed final drive chain on the 920. Also the Virago was styled as a custom cruiser, with lower-stepped seat, pulled-back handlebars and forward-mounted footrests. The more conventionally styled 920 was a lot more comfortable to ride.

The overall packaging of the two bikes was good, despite the suspension where it was difficult to find a compromise between soft ride and adequate ride height to prevent the exhaust and footrest dragging on the right-hand side. Both bikes also suffered from

The first V-twin, the TR1 or XV920 as it was known in the USA.

some of the driveline snatch that Yamaha had been struggling with on the XS series. All the same, the new V-twins were good enough and sold well enough for Honda, Suzuki and Kawasaki all to embark on development programmes for similar models, prompting the V-twin cruiser wars that were to rage throughout the 1980s.

On-going Rivalry with Honda

But all was not well with Yamaha. While appearing to be thriving, it was in fact sitting on an increasingly critical level of debt that would once again threaten the future of the company. This originated from, as always, the bitter rivalry with Honda and the intense focus on taking the position as largest Japanese and hence worldwide motorcycle manufacturer. In the domestic market at the end of the 1970s a 'soft motorcycle' war had developed between the two to target the female light user with a small unintimidating scooter, in the tradition of the step-throughs that had been produced in the 1960s. Honda had their RoadPal series and Yamaha had the Passol, with design and cosmetics the primary selling points, rather than performance or technology.

It was a total programme for Yamaha, with a whole culture developing around the bikes, and it was wildly successful. The domestic market that was thought to have become saturated suddenly grew by 30 per cent, thanks to the new segment that had been discovered, and much of the growth was picked up by Yamaha. By the middle of 1981, Yamaha was within sniffing distance of overtaking Honda as leader in the Japanese market, just 2 per cent down on Honda's 39.3 per cent share.

This was like a red rag to a bull. Never before had Yamaha been so close to eclipsing their perennial competitors, and the company was directed to focus totally on achieving this milestone. New factories were built to meet the growth targets set within the company. In 1978 Yamaha had built 1.65 million motorcycles, and by 1981 this had grown to 2.66 million, with production and distribution facilities gearing up for even greater numbers in 1982.

There was, however, a massive flaw in the way the market share was reported by the Japan Automobile Manufacturers Association. The statistics were derived not from sold units, but from numbers leaving the production lines, and in the drive to take market leadership, Yamaha had lost sight of the demand in the marketplace and the result was enormous numbers of unsold motorcycles stacked in warehouses in both Japan and the USA. By the end of 1982 there were 500,000 unsold bikes in Japan, and another 390,000 in the USA. The total debt on this enormous inventory was estimated to be 250 billion yen.

As the consequences of the blinkered policy to overtake Honda became clear, drastic action was taken. President Hisao Koike, ironically the man who had saved Yamaha from bankruptcy twenty years before, stepped down, to be replaced in August 1983 by Hideto Eguchi, who came from the music division of the company. The financial results for 1982 had been even worse than anticipated, with a net loss of 23 billion yen, the first loss in the company's history. Drastic measures were taken to liquidate unsolved inventory, to lower production levels, reduce costs in the company and realize assets wherever possible. Perhaps most distasteful in the job-for-life culture of Japan was the need to lower staffing levels, and voluntary early retirement was offered, as well as an agreement with other Japanese companies for some managers to be temporarily transferred until the company could recover.

Developing the Virago Series

While all this played in the boardrooms of Japan, the fight for the export market continued. In the early 1980s, the yen was still relatively low in value with respect to the dollar, so prices were competitive and buyers could benefit from the company need to shift their unsold inventory. All the same, the bikes needed to be appealing, and of the V-twins, it was the Virago series that was most popular.

For 1982, the XV920 was brought into the Virago series, to create the XV920J, offering the extra punch brought by the larger displacement engine. The chassis was close to that of the 750, with the engine only slightly adjusted with respect to the sports tourer RJ that remained available. In line with the Virago 750, shaft drive was used for the final drive.

There were some attempts to improve the ergonomics of the series, with the 1982 Viragos having adjustable handlebars, but the riding position was still unsuitable for anything but short rides. Also the suspension was still difficult to set up to get both adequate ground clearance as well as a smooth ride. The engine was a peach, however, with a long wide powerband.

The XZ550, the Vision

Although little had changed on the 1982 XV920RJ, the sports tourer class had been joined by a smaller brother, the XZ550, known in the USA as the Vision. In fact the V-twin engine format was almost the only shared characteristic, as the 550 was a totally new design.

In order to avoid a long wheelbase, the V-angle had been pulled back to just 70 degrees, which made the use of a balance shaft essential in order to cancel the imbalance forces. It was an elegant design, situated just in front of the crankshaft, gear-driven directly, with the small balance weight rotating in the space between the flywheels. It resulted in an exceptionally smooth engine, further enhanced by the use of water-cooling, which damped down engine noise significantly.

Initially the V-twin was simply yet another streetbike; only later did the metamorphosis from TR1 to Virago occur.

The first of the Virago Specials was the 1981 XV750SP.

Even in the harsh lights of the studio, the Midnight Special version of the XV1000 looked very cool.

While described as one of the best V-twins available, the XZ550 was the victim of cost-cutting at Yamaha.

In contrast to the ball bearings of the Virago engine, the one-piece crankshaft ran on plain bearings with high pressure lubrication. The top of the engine was equipped with 4-valve heads, with the Yamaha-patented YICS system to introduce turbulence in the combustion chamber to improve ignition at all engine speeds. Rather complex downdraught carburettors supplied fuel to the engine, nestled in the V of the engine.

The frame was a bit of a hybrid, in the form of a double-loop perimeter design, with the engine acting as a stressed member. Monoshock rear suspension was becoming standard practice at the company, but cost saving prevented an adjustable shock being used, a foretaste of the forces that would result in the 550's premature disappearance from the line-up within a couple of years.

The general consensus was that the bike offered a tremendous engine in a flawed chassis. Performance was on a par with the 550 4-cylinder class leaders of the time, despite the use of just a five-speed transmission and shaft-drive final drive. Steering geometry was sharp and the bike was a little twitchy, and the lack of suspension adjustment really hurt the overall package. The expectation was that with a little work, the 550 could be turned into an outstanding mid-range

motorcycle and indeed the 1983 model was a lot better, with the mid-range carburetion flat-spot fixed and adjustable suspension.

But the model was axed at the end of the year, victim of the steps that had been imposed by Yamaha management to recover the financial health of the company. The XZ550 was an expensive model to produce, and the margin, with a weakening Yen and the depressed prices due to the attempts to liquidate unsold stock, was inadequate. In other times this engine could have formed the basis for a series of sports bikes that could have had Yamaha stealing Ducati's market, given the weakness of the Italian company in the 1980s. The world may never have experienced the aesthetic brilliance of the 916, ten years later. The XZ did survive for a few more years as the XZ400, in markets where it could command a decent price, but by 1987 it had disappeared completely.

Varying Fortunes in the USA

Meanwhile Yamaha's enormous US inventory of unsold bikes had caught the eye of the US government, who accused the Japanese industry of dumping machines in the US and selling under cost. In

Our fully-enclosed shaft drive system is virtually maintenance-free.

Offset cylinders help cooling air reach the rear cylinder. Which means no radiator, no hoses, no liquid-cooling equipment to spoil the Virago's clean, traditional lines.

Traditional instrumentation with white, easy-to-read faces housed in slim, chromed pods for a classic look.

Advanced monocoque frame is light yet strong providing low seat height, efficient engine cooling and nimble handling.

You can adjust the damping on the rear shocks for the most comfortable ride possible.

Our 1100cc V-twin engine features a 75°cylinder angle, leaving plenty of room for carburetion and cooling air.

Air-adjustable front forks are interconnected for easy setting.

Dual hydraulic front discs are slotted for plenty of stopping power

Smooth-shifting five-speed gearbox.

Over-and-under chromed pipes sound as good as they look.

Automatic cam chain tensioner reduces maintenance.

ABOVE: *The standard Virago look that was to last for many years.*   BELOW: *This is the 1987 line-up of the large-capacity Viragos.*

Virago 750/1100

The 535 became a very popular model with women, many appreciating the low seat height.

a fit of protectionist zeal and to preserve the iconic name of Harley Davidson, suffering badly under the Japanese invasion, extra tariffs were applied to all motorcycles imported from outside the US with a capacity exceeding 700cc. The tariffs could extend to 45 per cent for the largest bikes, and caught Yamaha especially heavily as they had no manufacturing facilities in the USA.

This resulted in a slew of 750s shrunk to just under the 700cc maximum, and one of these was the 1984 Virago. But it wasn't just a 1983 model with a smaller engine: a totally redesigned chassis returned to the traditional twin shock, with styling changes to bring the bike even closer to the appearance of the Harley. It was almost a knee-jerk reaction to the trade restrictions imposed by the US. Now Japan would target Harley and all its qualities directly, ultimately producing clones that were so close to the original it could almost be accused of copyright infringement.

The 700 was joined by a full-bore 1000cc model as well as the 500 that had first appeared in 1983. The smallest of the series used the standard Virago technology, but adopted the same 70-degree V-twin angle as had been fitted on the XZ550. These Viragos were all about styling, with everything else taking a back seat. Fat rear tyres, raked front end, stepped king and queen seats, flashy air-filter casing on the right-hand side of the bike, and chrome everywhere. These bikes were designed for urban cruising, nothing more or less, projecting a strong image of bad boy rebellion. Soggy rear suspension and back-breaking seating for the taller rider soon brought riders back to the core business of boulevard posing.

The Virago bloodline, which was to last for over twenty years, had been defined. Models came, models went. The 500 became a 535 in 1987, the 700 grew again to 750 a year later, once the dollar had become so strong and the yen so weak that Harley could stand on their own feet. In the meantime, the largest Virago had grown to 1100cc to ensure that power and power delivery would never be a reason to reject the Yamaha. Every year saw styling and cosmetic changes, but the world in general had moved on from the cruiser, and although the Virago held its position well compared to the opposition, the market had shrunk by the end of the 1980s.

All the same, Viragos continued to be part of the Yamaha line-up, with the XV250 appearing in 1988 and continuing to be available through

The first of the Star series to boost the custom image was the 1997 XVS Drag Star 650.

to 2008. There was even a 125 version built at the close of the 1990s. Over twenty-five years of Viragos is a great testimony to the success of the initial design.

A New Breed of V-Twin Cruisers: the XVS Series

By the mid-1990s, the Yamaha cruiser line, all Virago-based, was beginning to look dated. With style, over purpose or function, seeming to become a dominant factor in purchasing decisions, the excellent performance of the Virago engines was becoming less important, and the styling, felt by some to be rather ugly, more so. A new breed of V-twin cruisers was developed, sharing many of the main parameters of the Viragos, but few of the details. First a dry run was made in Japan, where the XVS400 was released in February 1995: it became an instant success, winning a Bike of the Year award.

Hitting Europe in 1997, the XVS 650 Drag Star was still a 70-degree air-cooled V-twin, with an engine that was a bored and stroked version of the 535 Virago. Not that anyone would really have cared, as the selling point was the cosmet-

ics dictated by the all-new chassis, featuring a double-loop cradle frame and concealed mono-shock rear suspension. The visual impact was impressive, the clean lines creating the impression of a hard-tail rear end with sweeping mud-guards front and rear. A year later the 1100 big brother also arrived, with all the right styling for the family photos.

The US had to wait a year for the bikes to arrive, when the 'Drag' part of the title was dropped and they were known simply as V-stars. Weight was up and performance down with respect to the Virago relatives, but these details were irrelevant; the new V-twin main-stream cruisers were a lot cooler, leading the series through annual styling adjustments right up to 2008.

The 1600cc Road Star

As the new millennium approached, acute rivalry broke out between the Japanese players for the high end cruiser market. In particular Yamaha and Kawasaki embarked on a battle to create the best large displacement mega-cruiser, with Suzuki and Honda contributing to the fun but with

Model	XV250	XV500	XV535
Year	1988	1983	1988
Capacity (cc)	249	493	535
Configuration	4-s V-2	4-s V-2	4-s V-2
Induction	4-valve sohc	4-valve sohc	4-valve sohc
Bore × stroke (mm × mm)	49 × 66	73 × 59	76 × 59
Gearbox	5-speed	5-speed	5-speed
Final drive	chain	shaft	shaft
Frame	spine	spine	spine
Wheelbase (mm, in)	1,490 (58.7)	1,410 (55.5)	1,520 (60)
Dry weight (kg, lb)	137 (302)	173 (381)	175 (386)
Power (bhp)	23 @ 8,000rpm	44 @ 8,000rpm	46 @ 7,500rpm
Torque (kgm)	2.2 @ 6,000rpm	4.2 @ 6,000rpm	4.3 @ 6,500rpm
Top speed (km/h, mph)	125 (78)	160 (99)	165 (103)

Model	XZ550	XVS650	XV700
Year	1982	1997	1984
Capacity (cc)	553	649	699
Configuration	4-s V-2	4-s V-2	4-s V-2
Induction	8-valve dohc	4-valve sohc	4-valve sohc
Bore × stroke (mm × mm)	80 × 55	81 × 63	80 × 69
Gearbox	5-speed	5-speed	5-speed
Final drive	shaft	shaft	shaft
Frame	double loop perimeter	duplex cradle	spine
Wheelbase (mm, in)	1,445 (56.9)	1,625 (63.9)	1,520 (59.8)
Dry weight (kg, lb)	189 (417)	214 (472)	225 (496)
Power (bhp)	62 @ 9,500rpm	40 @ 6,500rpm	56 @ 7,000rpm
Torque (kgm)	4.8 @ 8,500rpm	5.1 @ 3,000rpm	6 @ 6,000rpm
Top speed (km/h, mph)	170 (106)	145 (90)	170 (106)

Model	XV750	XV920	XV1100
Year	1981	1981	1987
Capacity (cc)	748	920	1063
Configuration	4-s V-2	4-s V-2	4-s V-2
Induction	4-valve sohc	4-valve sohc	4-valve sohc
Bore × stroke (mm × mm)	83 × 69	93 × 69	95 × 75
Gearbox	5-speed	5-speed	5-speed
Final drive	shaft	shaft	shaft
Frame	spine	spine	spine
Wheelbase (mm, in)	1,520 (59.8)	1,540 (60.6)	1,525 (60)
Dry weight (kg, lb)	213 (470)	220 (485)	221 (487)
Power (bhp)	60 @ 7,000rpm	65 @ 6,500rpm	62 @ 6,000rpm
Torque (kgm)	6.4 @ 6,000rpm	8.1 @ 5,500rpm	8.7 @ 3,000rpm
Top speed (km/h, mph)	175 (109)	175 (109)	175 (109)

(continued...)

Model	XVS1100	XVZ1200 Venture	V-Max
Year	1998	1983	1985
Capacity (cc)	649	1197	1198
Configuration	4-s V-2	4-s V-4	4-s V-4
Induction	4-valve sohc	16-valve dohc	16-valve dohc
Bore × stroke (mm × mm)	95 × 75	76 × 66	76 × 66
Gearbox	5-speed	5-speed	5-speed
Final drive	shaft	shaft	shaft
Frame	duplex cradle	duplex cradle	duplex cradle
Wheelbase (mm, in)	1,645 (64.8)	1,610 (63.4)	1,590 (62.6)
Dry weight (kg, lb)	261 (576)	321 (708)	262 (578)
Power (bhp)	62 @ 5,750rpm	90 @ 7,000rpm	145 @ 9,000rpm
Torque (kgm)	8.7 @ 2,500rpm	10.5 @ 5,000rpm	12.4 @ 7,500rpm
Top speed (km/h, mph)	170 (106)	190 (118)	180 (112)

Model	XVZ 1300 Royal Star	XV 1600 Road Star	XV1700 Warrior
Year	1996	1999	2002
Capacity (cc)	1294	1602	1670
Configuration	4-s V-4	4-s V-2	4-s V-2
Induction	16-valve dohc	8-valve ohv	8-valve ohv
Bore × stroke (mm × mm)	79 × 66	95 × 113	97 × 113
Gearbox	5-speed	5-speed	5-speed
Final drive	shaft	belt	belt
Frame	duplex cradle	duplex cradle	duplex cradle
Wheelbase (mm, in)	1,695 (66.7)	1,685 (66.3)	1,685 (66.3)
Dry weight (kg, lb)	305 (672)	306 (675)	273 (602)
Power (bhp)	74 @ 4,750rpm	64 @ 4,000rpm	85 @ 4,400rpm
Torque (kgm)	11.4 @ 3,500rpm	12.5 @ 2,250rpm	12.5 @ 3,750rpm
Top speed (km/h, mph)	170 (106)	160 (353)	180 (397)

Model	XV 1900 Roadliner	XV 1900 Raider
Year	2006	2008
Capacity (cc)	1854	1854
Configuration	4-s V-2	4-s V-2
Induction	8-valve ohv	8-valve ohv
Bore × stroke (mm × mm)	100 × 118	100 × 118
Gearbox	5-speed	5-speed
Final drive	belt	belt
Frame	duplex cradle	duplex cradle
Wheelbase (mm, in)	1,715 (67.5)	1,800 (397)
Dry weight (kg, lb)	320 (706)	314 (692)
Power (bhp)	90 @ 4,750rpm	90 @ 4,750rpm
Torque (kgm)	12.0 @ 2,500rpm	12.0 @ 2,500rpm
Top speed (km/h, mph)	170 (106)	170 (106)

ABOVE: Following in the Virago footsteps, 1999 saw this 1100cc version of the Drag Star hit the shops.

BELOW: Annual styling changes saw the 2005 1100 V-star appearing with a heavy retro look.

slightly less determination. The V-twin Vulcan had been the largest displacement cruiser on the market since the 1980s, but in 1999, Yamaha trumped Kawasaki with an all-new 48-degree V-twin, displacing just under 1600cc and named the Road Star.

This was Yamaha's first true challenge to the traditional 45-degree Harley, as previously the models had been built on Japanese common practice technology, then styled to produce the American cruiser image. This relationship was now reversed: the technology was dictated by the styling, resulting for instance in pushrod-activated overhead valves, with the distinctive chromed tunnel along the length of the cylinder, signature of the Harleys. Belt-driven final drive replaced the shaft drive that the Viragos and Drag Stars had been using. Of course the engine would need to be air-cooled, and where it didn't interfere with the styling, high technology could be used, resulting in ceramic-lined cylinders to help keep the engine well cooled.

Rather than attempt to suppress the vibrations from the unbalanced twin engine, it was accepted as being part of the package and no counterbalancers or rubber mountings were used. The worst of the vibrations were masked by the low engine speed, with a rev. limiter cutting in at 4,200rpm, before the buzz became unbearable. Engine performance was characterized by massive low-end torque, peaking already at 2,200rpm.

The long wheelbase and heavy weight had it tracking well in a straight line, but steering was adequately quick for corners, limited by the fold-up floorboards. Finish was excellent with thick gloss paint, lots of metal, and chrome, acres of chrome.

The XV1700 Warrior

The arrival of the Road Star prompted the others to introduce larger capacity bikes, resulting in Yamaha's 2002 response with the XV1700 Warrior model. Rather than exceed the displacement of the VTX1800 released by Honda the previous year, Yamaha chose to respond with a combination of lower weight and modestly increased engine size for their muscle cruiser. Aluminium was used to build the frame, and the complete front end and rear swingarm was lifted off the Yamaha R1 hyper-sports bike, complete with cast wheels.

The engine was fitted with fuel injection and far larger air filter volume, pushing power up to about 80bhp and bringing the quarter-mile times down under 13sec. But the price to pay for the increased performance was poorer ergonomics with an uncomfortable seat and riding position. By 2004, all the Road Star series had grown to 1700cc, with slightly different engine characteristics, better brakes and cast wheels.

The Roadliner Series

The battle wasn't over yet though, as rumours came of a 2000cc Kawasaki V-twin on the drawing board. Yamaha's designers got to work building a 2400cc prototype, but it was simply too much and felt really top-heavy and clumsy, so they limited the new engine to 1900cc, calling the model the Roadliner, with a tourer version, the Stratoliner. Following in the Warrior's footsteps, an aluminium frame lopped 12kg (26lb) off the weight of the chassis compared to the Road Star. With a dry weight of 320kg (706lb) this bike was still massive, although the first V-twin use of the EXUP valve to grace Yamaha's sports bikes for many years helped deliver good low- and mid-range performance.

A third version of the Roadliner series joined the pair in 2008, under the Raider epithet. This employed radical chopper styling with a raked-out front end and 21in front wheel, resulting in the longest wheelbase of any cruiser on the market. Suspension was well sorted though, and the handling in general was neutral and controlled. It was a good compromise between style and engineering, the large diameter exhaust mufflers snaking up and back to a 45-degree chop at the rear of the bike.

There were three versions of the Raider available with different styling, just as the whole Star series had become customizable. Yamaha had

Something a little special: the Silverado version of the 1999 Road Star.

started the Star company sub-brand back in 2005, to focus on the cruisers and their image, offering a multitude of special parts and apparel for those looking for something a little special. In the US, the cruiser market had become very important for the company, and they could claim the drive for individualism in this way, catching the owners before they drifted off to the aftermarket suppliers.

Full Dress Tourers: the Goldwing

The Virago, Drag Star and Road Star series were strong cards in Yamaha's efforts to displace Honda as the world's largest motorcycle manufacturer. Back at the start of the Virago series in the early 1980s, laying claim to be the 'greatest' motorcycle manufacturer in the world required not only higher production numbers but a complete line-up of models across the board that were qualitatively better than Honda's. Then in the mid-1970s Honda created one of the classics of the decade, which was to set the standard for its class for years to come: in 1975 the company released

the GL1000 flat-4, the Goldwing, classifying it as a tourer, but doing little to enhance its touring qualifications.

Honda seemed uncertain how to target the new model, sales were poor and its future uncertain at the end of the first year. It was turned into the benchmark tourer that it became, through the aftermarket accessory companies who developed the whole kit needed to turn the bike into a comfortable long-distance ride. By 1980, however, Honda understood that this was their opportunity to define the standards of the class, and the GL1100 rolled off the assembly lines as a full-dress tourer. Even smarter was the move of Goldwing production facilities to the USA in 1981, enabling them to avoid the currency fluctuation problems the other Japanese manufacturers experienced as the 1980s progressed.

Yamaha had nothing like the Goldwing in their line-up. There had been some attempts to produce full tourers with the Martini XS1100 in the 1970s, but these were simply opportunistic attempts to cover the touring segment with a kitted sports tourer. This would never appeal

ABOVE: Serious business as the Warrior XV1700 led Yamaha's challenge in the power-cruiser battle.

BELOW: 'Never enough' became the slogan for the hyper cruisers, and the XV1900 Midnight Star was Yamaha's response.

ABOVE: Full-dress 2006 Stratroliner, ready to rumble out of the darkness to the open road.

BELOW: The 2008 Raider was just a little more agile than the previous Roadliner series.

to the hardcore long-distance community that had developed around the Goldwing. Yamaha decided to create a purpose-built touring bike from scratch, to compete head-on with the Goldwing. It would launch in 1983 as the XVZ1200 Venture.

Yamaha's Reply: the XVZ1200 Venture

One of the most important aspects of such a flagship motorcycle would be the engine design and configuration. Honda had made no attempts to build a Goldwing class, rightly deciding that, while customizable, preferably with Honda-approved accessories, the power of the brand should not be diluted over different capacity classes.

Yamaha adopted the same philosophy, designing a new engine exclusively for the new tourer. While the flat-4 GL1000 had become an accidental tourer, Yamaha's design choice was more

calculated. The ideal balance between compact design, substantial power at all engine speeds and a comfortable ride could best be achieved from a water-cooled V4 engine. The twin-cylinder XVZ550 had appeared in 1982 and had been lauded by the press for its balance of elegance and innovation. The new tourer engine could follow many of the same design directions. A V4 endurance racer had been built at the end of the 1970s and this, together with the XVZ550, could form a baseline for the new engine.

Consequently, the V4 shared the same 70-degree separation of the pairs of cylinders, with balancer shaft at the front of the engine to cancel reciprocating mass imbalances. To cut any other distracting vibes that might get through to the rider, the engine mounting bolts passed through rubber sleeves at the frame attachment points. The large lazy engine could be spun to 7,000rpm thanks to the 4-valve head and double overhead cams, but power came in early and strong, with

Yamaha's XVZ1200 Venture super-tourer briefly outshone the Goldwing, but then lived on in its shadow.

Displacing 1300cc in its final guise, the Venture was fully equipped, but the flat-6 Honda GL1500 was a step too far.

just 3,300rpm showing on the tach at a comfortable 100km/h (62mph) cruising speed.

Handling was also a couple of notches above the Goldwing and Kawasaki Voyager competition of the time, thanks to good ground clearance and the full cradle frame. Air suspension front and rear was reasonably effective in giving the rider the adjustability to meet the road and load conditions.

A Short-lived Victory

The Venture was a slap in the face for Honda, displacing them from their position as 'tourer king' in one fell swoop. But it was to be short-lived. Despite some further enhancements in 1984, with cruise control and automatic levelling system, as well as other improvements for reliability, the introduction of the GL1200, with the Aspencade as flagship, brought Honda back into contention. There wasn't a clear winner between the two, although Honda were able to maintain a price advantage as the Japanese yen increased in value through these years.

In 1986 Yamaha responded with an engine that had grown to 1294cc to hit harder and it did offer better performance than the flat-4 Honda. There were improvements to the brakes, one of the Venture's weaker spots, and electric anti-dive front forks. Honda's answer came two years later with the 6-cylinder GL1500 – and at this stage Yamaha gave up the struggle, resigned to sell to those looking for a decent alternative to Honda, but not investing in major development. By 1992 the Venture was beginning to show its age as the competition moved on, and it was quietly dropped from the company line-up.

The thick creamy layers of paint and the attention to detail made the 1996 Royal Star the most expensive bike in the USA.

The Royal Star Series

Seven years later it was back, not as a Goldwing full dress tourer challenger, but as a tourer cruiser, decked out in the retro style of the mighty Harley Electra Glide, part of the Royal Star series that had been launched in 1996. The Royal Star was not a built-to-budget special, making the most of existing technology, cutting corners to make the grade and becoming a parody in the process: rather it was Yamaha's lunge to take the initiative in the evolution of the cruiser class, with styling that fitted the bill, inevitably leaning heavily on the American heritage of Indian and Harley Davidson icons. There would be no compromise in the design, and if it ended up being the most expensive bike available on the US market, so be it. And it did, despite being built around a version of the V4 engine that had powered the Venture tourer a few years before.

Long-distance tourers needed to be smooth, cruisers needed a raw edge to them, so the counter-balance shaft was junked. The engine was tweaked until the power had dropped to just 74bhp, but with the power coming in low down, thanks to tiny carbs and flatter cams and new transmission ratios. Red line was at 4,750rpm, but it was never intended to be run at that speed, with a flat power curve delivering strongly from 2,000rpm.

The large double downtube cradle frame held the massive engine, with an enclosed single shock lying along the longitudinal axis of the machine in front of the rear wheel. The build quality was exemplary, with thick, rich gloss paint over metal fenders and tanks and heavily chromed engine cases, exhausts and lights. All this was backed up with a five-year warranty and roadside assistance.

The Tour Classic version had a windshield, ox-hide saddlebags, even more chrome and a price tag of $15,399. It was the most expensive mass-production motorcycle available in the USA. It was this bike that was to morph into the 1999 Venture, with full front fairing and Electra Glide styling. The arrival and success of the 1999 V-twin Road Star eclipsed the Royal somewhat, and the high price and crowded cruiser line-up of the first years of the new millennium resulted in 2006 being its last year of sale.

The V-Max

Perhaps the original Venture Grand Tourer could have continued to challenge the Goldwing bloodline in the 1990s if development had continued or the company had marketed the bike more aggressively. Neither of these investments were needed for a bike that appeared shortly after the arrival of the Grand Tourer in 1983, related by the V4 engine that had been the Venture's greatest asset. There are a few models that have appeared in Yamaha's history that carved a niche in motorcycling history, for the qualities that gave them the charisma needed to be considered icons of the industry.

One of these is unquestionably the V-Max. Born in the USA, strongly influenced by the late-1970s renaissance of interest in hotrods and muscle cars, everything about the V-Max commanded instantaneous attention: its presence, its bulk, its intimidating styling and its total commitment to straight-line speed. It looked fast when stationary, and the rasp and growl of the exhaust told you it would not disappoint once it got under way. It was a monster, a beast, the first true muscle bike and a classic twentieth-century motorcycle, with design and technology forming the perfect complement to each other. This needed no marketing department to meet sales targets: it needed protection from impatient buyers.

It can come as no surprise to learn that the bike was developed under the guiding hand of Ed Burke, the Yamaha product-planning guru who

had been behind so many of Yamaha's US-born creations. But the design and engineering was executed by a small team of Japanese engineers, headed by Araki san and Ashihara san, seconded to California during 1983 and charged with producing a new bike. It needed to capture the spirit of the hotrod, the power of the dragstrip, yet be sufficiently practical for street use. The sketches that came out of the design phase look remarkably like the final product; because the bike was so original and totally aligned to the US market, perhaps no one in Japan felt able to offer constructive criticism.

Surprisingly, the toughest part of the development was the production of an engine with the right characteristics to match the spirit of the bike. The V4 Venture engine produced just under 100bhp, but had been designed for low- and mid-range power. This was fine for the initial launch of the V-Max, but the last thing the team wanted was a gutless wonder that fell on its face after a strong low-end punch. The ideal solution would have been a turbo, to kick in for the last 30 per cent of the engine speed, but it just wasn't practical to fit on the V4 configuration.

Instead Ashihara san, heading engine development, came up with the ingenious V-boost scheme, essentially emulating a turbo by feeding each cylinder from two carburettors from 6,000rpm, through the use of servo-controlled butterfly valves. The results were staggering, with the V-Max getting an enormous second wind as the valves cracked open and travelling faster, faster! It was the cherry on the cake, the adrenalin boost that all pseudo dragsters crave, that had them itching for the 6k kick at every stationary launch.

For a bike so focused on straight-line speed, it did a fair job in the curvery, although was no match for the sports bikes of the era. The double downtube cradle frame was similar to the Venture's, but conventional twin rear shocks were dictated by the styling. In anticipation of aggressive riding the rear shocks were quite hard, but the harsh ride was a small price to pay for the lack of squat under heavy acceleration. The rear tyre was massive on the small 15in rim, again a

Ten years after its first appearance, the 1996 V-Max was still one of a kind, and the iconic muscle bike.

combination of styling and pragmatism, in the need to get the claimed 145bhp to the road via the shaft drive transmission.

The only real criticism was that the bike was a true heavyweight, hitting the scales at over 260kg (578lb) dry weight. This, combined with the V-boost power drive, had the V-Max guzzling petrol at rates you'd normally associate with a large family saloon – but that was surely not on the potential owners' checklist as they stormed the US dealers.

It first appeared in metal at the 1984 US dealer convention in Las Vegas, where it was enthusiastically received, and it went on sale just in the US from the start of 1985. It was to be another year before it was homologated for Europe, emasculated by the lack of the socially unacceptable V-boost system.

Nevertheless it was still a tremendous success, and has become a cult bike with a dedicated, fanatical following. Given its slightly anti-social qualities, it was never really spotlighted by Yamaha, who adopted a slightly apologetic attitude to the V-Max – but that was just fine. It thrived, no

other manufacturer daring or able to produce a worthy competitor. Further noise, emission and federal and government social restriction hurt the power and torque numbers of the bike, but it lived on right through to 2007, with the expectation of a Next Gen V-Max on the horizon. Could it ever have the same impact as the original?

Glitz, Gloss and Bravura

From the early 1980s, Yamaha had embraced the cruiser custom market and developed a high profile among the Japanese manufacturers, using and re-using quite basic, unsophisticated V-engine technology. The company's success had come from their eye for the styling that would appeal to this market, building simple technology into a package full of glitz, gloss and bravura. As the pace of life continued to quicken over the years, the appeal of a laid-back, relaxed, short-haul ride became increasingly mainstream in the USA, and Yamaha served it well with generations of V-twins. That this could also lead to icons such as the V-Max was simply the icing on the cake.

9 One of the Crowd

With the dawn of the 1980s, Yamaha could look back on a difficult decade where the company had struggled to reinvent itself and its product line so it could exploit the marketplace, as this in turn was shaped by world politics. Most dramatic had been the tightening of emission controls in the USA, followed at a distance by Europe.

The decade had been Yamaha's period of transformation, marked by some engineering setbacks, as they built their four-stroke expertise to match their industry-leading two-stroke knowledge. There was also a commendable desire not to follow the pack, but to bring unorthodox and distinctive models to the marketplace, to test and tempt public opinion. This had resulted in a number of successes, most notably with the single-cylinder XT500 and its family, as well as the growing interest in the Special editions for the emerging mainstream cruiser market. However, Yamaha had chosen not to participate in the general drive towards 4-cylinder configurations for mainstream street bikes of 400cc capacity and above. In many ways synonymous with Honda, this design had been increasingly adopted by Suzuki and Kawasaki, but by 1980, the XS11 was the only Yamaha four.

The XJ Series

So the scene was set at the end of the 1970s for the 4-cylinder motorcycle to become the Jack-of-all-trades for the sports and tourer classes, and

The 1980 XJ650 was Yamaha's first move into mainstream mid-range 4-cylinder motorcycles.

While not a sportsbike, chassis and engine were good enough for hard, fast riding.

The 1981 XJ550 lost the shaft drive of the series and gained YICS to provide a cleaner engine.

Yamaha were enlightened enough to realize they needed to be in that market or face isolation into small niches in the face of the unstoppable march of the Universal Japanese Motorcycle. Once corporate pride had been swallowed, they settled down to building their own line of ubiquitous 4-cylinder engines, which would serve them well in the years to come.

It was decided that a single engine would be designed that could be used for both European and American markets, with chassis and cosmetics aligning the resulting motorcycles to the respective market requirements. In the US, the new models would build on the success of the Specials, with styling and ergonomics to match, whilst the European models would be more in the sports-tourer mould. This was the birth of the XJ series.

Although sharing the same basic design parameters, namely a double overhead camshaft 4-cylinder engine, with 2 valves per cylinder feeding a five-speed transmission and shaft drive final transmission, the first XJ displaced 650cc – but was not merely a shrunk XS11. It was designed so that the engine block was compact in both width and depth, resulting in a noticeably narrow engine. The alternator was removed from the right-hand end of the crankshaft where it was found on most of the 4-cylinder engines in the market, and instead was positioned above and behind the crankshaft, driven by a Hy-Vo chain, with the starter motor behind the alternator, driving it and the crankshaft. The transmission was also staggered, so that the extra shaft needed for the shaft drive did not overextend the length of

the engine. The result was an engine that would not compromise the chassis and frame design because of its bulk.

There was nothing innovative about the frame, featuring a double loop cradle frame with the usual headstock gusseting and reinforcement plates. With the price already pushing well past the competition, there was no money available for adjustable damping on the front and rear suspension, and the compromise chosen was on the soft side. Handling in general was good, but there was noticeable torque reaction on the rear wheel when feeding in the throttle, and that could upset the bike in corners.

Good as the ergonomics were for the European sports model, the Maxim, as the US model was christened, featured an awful riding position, caused by the curve of the handlebars and the slightly sloping, stepped seat. It was a good example of styling turning a good motorcycle into one that was uncomfortable for anything but the shortest of rides. This, together with the price premium Yamaha was expecting new owners to pay, depressed sales dramatically.

The XJ Secas

Fortunately there was a clear solution to the problem, and from 1981 there was a Seca version of the XJ available, close to the European models in appearance and functionality. 550, 650 and 750 versions were available, along with Maxim II versions of the 550 and 650. Acknowledging the ineffective design of the Maxim I bars and seat, these were updated for the new model, offering a slight improvement rather than a complete solution to the problem.

Other than the styling and riding position of the Maxim models, the steering was slower due to a longer wheelbase and greater rake and trail. The engine was also in a slightly different state of tune, thanks to a new cam profile flattening the power delivery a little. From a performance perspective the Secas were the better package, but if styling was the driver, this was irrelevant.

The 550 Seca

The 550 Seca was very much a clone of the 650 big brother, but did branch out on its own in a couple of areas. The shaft drive of the 650 and 750 Secas was replaced by a chain drive for the smaller model, offering a useful weight-saving in the process.

A new Yamaha feature was introduced on the 550, called 'YICS'. It consisted of a small extra sub-port just under the main inlet valve. In the head castings, a small passage was included that linked all the sub-ports and fed from the inlet tract between the carburettors and the cylinder head. As the inlet valve opened in the cylinder an extra small jet of fuel charge shot into the combustion chamber, causing increased turbulence and improving the combustion efficiency of the ignition stroke. The result was a cleaner engine and improved fuel consumption.

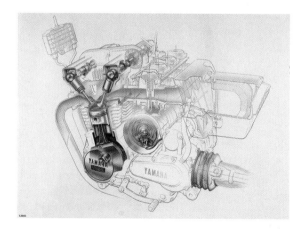

Some more Yamaha innovation was YICS, which raised combustion chamber turbulence, producing more efficient burn.

All told, the 550 was a great mid-range bike with good performance, handling and riding position. It still struggled to capture the public's imagination.

The 750 Seca

While there had been some cost-cutting on the 650 Seca model, this couldn't be said of the 750 introduced in 1981. Not only did it undergo a styling update that hinted at some of the cruiser credentials of the Maxim series, it was also given some seriously useful chassis improvements. Both front and rear suspension were adjustable, with four positions on the rear shocks and air caps on the front forks.

The biggest eye-catcher was the anti-dive front suspension add-on, linked into the brakes. As the front brake was applied, a small spring-loaded valve throttled the compression-damping circuit, increasing the resistance to compression. A check valve would crack open if a sharp bump was hit with the front brakes on, easing the compression damping restriction and thereby allowing the extra movement to be absorbed. It worked reasonably well, but whether it was worth the extra complexity and price is debatable. The 750 was also given the YICS treatment, but retained the shaft drive fitted to the 650.

Once again it was a good package, arguably the best of the contemporary 750s, but it was also 10 per cent more expensive, and this seemed to be enough to keep customers away in droves.

The Yamaha 650 Seca Turbo

As described elsewhere in this book, the early 1980s marked the height of the battle between Honda and Yamaha, not only in terms of volume of sales, but also in technological innovation. There was a very strong engineering curiosity present at Honda, which led to some strange decisions that didn't always make commercial sense. One was their attempt, around this time, to win the 500cc GP world championship with a four-stroke, severely hampered by the regulations on engine layout. Their ultimate contender was an inspired failure, a V4 with oval pistons and

ABOVE: Maybe the best 750 in 1982, but unfortunately the most expensive as well.

BELOW: Yamaha's contribution to the turbo world was the 1983 XJ650T.

XJ650T SPECIFICATIONS
ENGINE
Type .... 4-stroke, turbocharged,
DOHC, four
Displacement .... 653 cc
Bore and stroke .... 63.0 × 52.4 mm
Compression ratio.....................8.2 : 1
Max.power(DIN) ... 90.0 PS (66.2 kW)
@9,000 rpm
Max.torque(DIN)................8.33 kg-m
(81.7 Nm)
@7,000 ~ 7,500 rpm
Lubrication ....Wet sump
Carburetion..........................BS30 (4)
Ignition........... Transistor controlled
Starter system ....Electric
Fuel tank capacity ....19.0 l
Oil capacity............................3.5 l
Transmission.......................5-speed
Final transmission .... Shaft drive
CHASSIS
Overall length.....................2,200 mm
Overall width........................730 mm
Overall height..................1,355 mm
Seat height............................775 mm
Wheelbase ....1,440 mm
Ground clearance...............135 mm
Dry weight............................230 kg
Suspension
Front................... Telescopic forks
Rear .... Swing arm
Brakes
Front............Hydraulic double disc
Rear ....Drum
Tyres
Front 3.25 V-19
Rear 120/90V-18

*Technically complex,
awkwardly styled, expensive
and flawed, the Turbo was
only available for two years.*

Specifications and appearance of Yamaha motorcycles shown here may vary according to requirements and conditions and are subject to change without notice. For further details, please consult your Yamaha dealer. Always wear a helmet and eye protection.

YAMAHA

8 valves per cylinder that attempted to emulate a V8. It was brilliant engineering, but doomed from the start.

In general this was not Yamaha's way. For them, the most logical approach was the way to proceed, using ingenuity to refine, as a means to an end, rather than as a means unto itself.

Honda decided they would produce a turbocharged streetbike, mainly as a statement to their engineering skills, choosing to build this on the least likely of engine configurations, a V-twin. The CX500 was selected as the base engine, it being itself a rather quirky relic of the engineers' drive to be different with its water-cooled, narrow-angle transverse V layout.

In general, multi-cylinder engines are considered most suitable for turbo charging as the frequent regular exhaust pulses are most effective at driving the turbo. This is important to ensure the minimum of 'turbo lag', the bane of the turbocharger's effectiveness, manifesting itself as a delay between opening the throttle and the turbo speed picking up to deliver the dialled-up punch of a response. For Honda, this was an interesting technical challenge; a commercially successful motorcycle was of secondary importance.

Of course, if Honda were to launch a Turbo, Yamaha would do so too. They chose to take the XJ650 as a basis for their mid-range rocket ship, the 4-cylinder engine configuration minimizing, if not eliminating, the technical challenges.

The mission seemed to be to produce a distinctive-looking bike without broadcasting its use of a turbo to get the performance it offered. None of the turbo equipment was visible on the full wedge-shaped fairing fitted to the bike, with small badges on the sidepanels registering its forced respiration. The turbo itself was located just under the seat with a feed from the exhaust taken from the centre-section connector box. Rather than use fuel injection or place the turbo between the carburettor and the inlet port, it was placed so that it would blow air through the carburettors.

A complex two-section airbox fed the turbo, with reed and poppet valves to allow normal carburetion at low engine speeds and prevent overboost of the turbocharger. Special 30mm CV carburettors were used instead of the standard 32mm versions found on the standard engine. Anti-knock precautions were taken by having a system to retard the spark advance as boost increased, as well as a sensor to pick up the onset of detonation and also knock back the spark advance until the detonation passed.

With the increase in power, the bottom of the engine needed to be strengthened and steps taken to safeguard adequate lubrication and cooling. The oil pump was geared up to pump faster, and the oil-cooler, previously only found on European models, was standard on all Turbos. Bits and pieces from the 750's clutch were used to carry the extra power, but the transmission was unchanged.

So there was a lot of extra complexity, and all the turbo gear added 25kg (55lb) to the weight of the bike. Was it worth it? Not really. The bike was definitely more powerful, with the sort of peaky power delivery you could expect from a turbo-equipped engine. But it wasn't the tyre-shredding, black-line performance often associated with these types of bikes. It also suffered from the lag that Yamaha had attempted to avoid, so that jerking the throttle open at low- to mid-range engine speeds resulted in a noticeable delay before the engine responded. It was a characteristic that owners had to learn to accept, as there was no way to dial it out. Ironically, the best thing about the bike was the adjustable suspension that it now inherited from the 750, with air-assisted forks and four-way damping adjustments on the rear suspension.

Introduced in 1983, as the XJ series was eclipsed by the FJ series, the XJ900 was to last for many years to come.

The Last of the XJ Series

The Yamaha 650 Seca Turbo was available for just two years, and as Yamaha had to bite the bullet in their 1983 business and financial crisis, this was one of the first models to be axed. It had served a purpose, and demonstrated that whatever Honda could do, Yamaha could do too, perhaps even better. But it had nothing to do with mainstream motorcycling and keeping your shareholders happy. In essence by 1984, the XJ series was coming to an end as FJ models were announced and staked their claim as the mainstream 4-cylinder machines in the line-up. The 700 continued for a couple more years in Maxim form, being the 750 sleeved down to avoid protectionist tariffs applied to US imports.

An XJ900 was released in 1983, sharing the same engine design and many of the engine components as the XJ650/700/750, and carried in a twin-shocked cradle frame. Unfortunately

Once a bad wobble had been fixed in 1984, the XJ900 became a cheap, reliable, dependable, albeit unexciting motorcycle.

Model	XJR 400	XJ 550 Seca	FJ 600
Year	1993	1981	1984
Capacity (cc)	399	528	598
Configuration	4-s 4 cyl	4-s 4 cyl	4-s 4 cyl
Induction	16-valve dohc	16-valve dohc	8-valve dohc
Bore × stroke (mm × mm)	55 × 42	57 × 51.8	58.5 × 55.7
Gearbox	6-speed	6-speed	6-speed
Final drive	chain	chain	chain
Frame	duplex cradle	duplex cradle	duplex cradle
Wheelbase (mm, in)	1,435 (56.5)	1,425 (56)	1,430 (56.3)
Dry weight (kg, lb)	175 (386)	202 (445)	212 (467)
Power (bhp)	53 @ 11,000rpm	52 @ 9,000rpm	73 @ 10,000rpm
Torque (kgm)	3.5 @ 9,500rpm	5.5 @ 7,500rpm	6.8 @ 8,000rpm
Top speed (km/h, mph)	160 (99)	180 (112)	190 (118)

Model	YX600 Radian	XJ 600 Diversion/Seca 2	XJ 650
Year	1987	1991	1980
Capacity (cc)	598	598	653
Configuration	4-s 4 cyl	4-s 4 cyl	4-s 4 cyl
Induction	8-valve dohc	8-valve dohc	8-valve dohc
Bore × stroke (mm × mm)	58.5 × 55.7	58.5 × 55.7	63 × 52.4
Gearbox	6-speed	6-speed	5-speed
Final drive	chain	chain	shaft
Frame	duplex cradle	duplex cradle	duplex cradle
Wheelbase (mm, in)	1,385 (54.5)	1,445 (56.9)	1,435 (56.5)
Dry weight (kg, lb)	185 (408)	190 (419)	206 (454)
Power (bhp)	66 @ 9,500rpm	57 @ 8,000rpm	73 @ 7,500rpm
Torque (kgm)	5.3 @ 7,500rpm	5.3 @ 7,000rpm	6 @ 7,500rpm
Top speed (km/h, mph)	170 (106)	160 (99)	190 (118)

Model	XJ 650 Seca Turbo	XJ 750	XJ900
Year	1983	1981	1984
Capacity (cc)	653	748	853
Configuration	4-s 4 cyl	4-s 4 cyl	4-s 4 cyl
Induction	8-valve dohc turbo	8-valve dohc	8-valve dohc
Bore × stroke (mm × mm)	63 × 52.4	65 × 56.4	67 × 60.5
Gearbox	5-speed	5-speed	5-speed
Final drive	shaft	shaft	shaft
Frame	duplex cradle	duplex cradle	duplex cradle
Wheelbase (mm, in)	1,440 (56.7)	1,445 (56.9)	1,480 (58.2)
Dry weight (kg, lb)	230 (507)	215 (474)	218 (481)
Power (bhp)	90 @ 9,000rpm	81 @ 9,000rpm	97 @ 9,000rpm
Torque (kgm)	8.3 @ 7,500rpm	6.7 @ 7,500rpm	8.2 @ 7,500rpm
Top speed (km/h, mph)	200 (124)	200 (124)	210 (130)

(continued…)

Model	XJ 900 Diversion	FJ1100	XJR1200
Year	1995	1984	1994
Capacity (cc)	853	1097	1188
Configuration	4-s 4 cyl	4-s 4 cyl	4-s 4 cyl
Induction	8-valve dohc	16-valve dohc	16-valve dohc
Bore × stroke (mm × mm)	67 × 60.5	74 × 63.8	77 × 63.8
Gearbox	5-speed	5-speed	5-speed
Final drive	shaft	chain	chain
Frame	duplex cradle	duplex cradle	duplex cradle
Wheelbase (mm, in)	1,480 (58.2)	1,490 (58.9)	1,500 (59.1)
Dry weight (kg, lb)	239 (527)	227 (500)	232 (512)
Power (bhp)	89 @ 8,250rpm	125 @ 9,000rpm	98 @ 8,000rpm
Torque (kgm)	8.5 @ 7,000rpm	10.5 @ 8,000rpm	9.3 @ 6,000rpm
Top speed (km/h, mph)	210 (130)	225 (140)	210 (130)

Model	FJR 1300
Year	2001
Capacity (cc)	1188
Configuration	4-s 4 cyl
Induction	16-valve dohc
Bore × stroke (mm × mm)	79 × 63.8
Gearbox	5-speed
Frame	duplex cradle
Wheelbase (mm, in)	1,515 (59.6)
Dry weight (kg, lb)	237 (523)
Power (bhp)	145 @ 8,500rpm
Torque (kgm)	12.8 @ 6,000rpm
Top speed (km/h, mph)	260 (162)

The XJ600 Diversion was a competent, unintimidating ride for anyone looking for a taste of two-wheel transport.

The XJ600 engine was mildly tuned, with a linear power delivery that was especially well suited to novices.

the initial models were cursed with a very bad speed wobble at anything over 120km/h (75mph). It took a year to fix the problem with a modification to the half-fairing fitted to the bike, but by then the damage had been done and initially it struggled to sell. Yamaha persisted, and the bike built a reputation for a solid reliable ride. True to its character, it carved itself a small, inconspicuous corner of the catalogue, and year after year, as other models came and went, remained available for the no-nonsense conservative rider.

By 1983 it was clear that Yamaha were continuing to struggle to find a 4-cylinder sports package that would capture the public's imagination and sell in substantial numbers. The GPZ series from Kawasaki and the VF models from Honda had raised the stakes, and it was becoming critical for the company to build a model line that would enable them to challenge in this increasingly important class. Weakened after the 1982/83 crisis, a piecemeal approach was adopted for the introduction of two new sports models, the FJ600 and the FJ1100. The lack of any large capacity sportsbike was considered the most serious weakness, so a completely new design was funded for this model. A complimentary model in the 600 class was built from as much existing technology as possible, but with a strong marketing push, emphasizing the sports nature of the bike. Single-shock rear suspension was becoming ubiquitous on all sportsbikes, so for the 600, the chassis from the XJ400 that had appeared on the

Japanese market in 1983 was mated to a bored and stroked 550 Seca engine. The longer stroke helped get more mid-range torque from the 2-valve engine, while larger valves, with a longer duration coupled to larger diameter carburettors, increased the top end power as well.

The resulting engine, without the YICS fitted on older XJs and with a six-speed transmission, was the fastest of its class, close to many of the 750s on the market. There was a price to pay, though, in the form of a very buzzy engine, as the rubber mounting was ineffective, and from about 5,000rpm there was a very tingly vibe through the footrests and bars. There were also some carburetion glitches that had the bike struggling to get started and run smoothly.

Yamaha had in the past gambled that riders were prepared to pay a slight premium for the Seca that they considered to be a better bike, but the 10/15 per cent price difference with the competition was one of the reasons it was felt that the series had sold so poorly. For the FJ, they priced to match the competition exactly, but this meant, once again, the introduction of suspension with no damping adjustments. The compromise settings were a little too soft, but adequate.

The FJ600 bore all the hallmarks of a cobbled-together parts-bin special, designed to last a couple of years to plug a whole in the portfolio. This is how it was for the USA, where it was dropped after just two years as the FZ series took off. In Europe it continued to be available, marketed confusingly as the XJ600, until 1991.

The YX600 Radian

In the US, in the meantime, yet another parts-bin Special had arrived in the form of the YX600 Radian. Take a frame from the old-style twin-shock XJ550 Seca and add an FJ600 engine with a radical styling job including a 16in front wheel, and the result was the Radian. Some of the styling was a little reminiscent of the V-Max, so it had a muscle bike air about it, but it was intended as a budget Special and for that purpose it was perfectly suited. Vibration was much better that on the FJ, with very similar performance. The biggest handicap was a lack of ground clearance when pushed hard in corners, and this became worse when the alternator was moved back to the end of the crankshaft in 1989. But performance per dollar was high, and for five years it was snapped up by cost-conscious sports riders.

The Seca II/Diversion

From 1991, the FJ/XJ/YX 600 evolved into the XJ600 Diversion, known in the USA as the Seca II, a totally different motorcycle for a different market segment. It was built as a budget-priced, unintimidating yet competent motorcycle, for those looking for a solid, reliable, unobtrusive ride. And there were a lot of people looking for exactly that, as the 600 became a sales success, especially in Europe.

Engine technology was a basic 2-valve double overhead cam, as lifted off the first XJ models, with a mild state of tune, slotted into a cradle frame, with monoshock rear suspension and chain-driven rear wheel. Budget constraints prevented adjustable suspension, but Yamaha produced a good compromise for the sort of rider who would be interested in the bike, comfortable on the highway, and adequate for gentle rides through the countryside. A slightly more expensive model was fitted with a half fairing, especially useful for owners who used the bike for the daily commute.

In 1995, the two remaining XJ models were harmonized, with the 900 being slipped into a Monoshock chassis for another ten-plus years of service to the company. Coming with adjustable suspension and a shaft drive, it was a marked improvement over the previous F model, and despite its heavy weight, the 900 Diversion offered sufficient performance and comfort for both short trips as well as longer touring journeys, and built a reputation as a bullet-proof, reliable ride. Production was continued through to 2002.

The High Performance Superbike FJ1100

While the FJ600 had suffered a little at the hands of the corporate bean counters, no such fate awaited the FJ1100, as this needed to come off the assembly line as the best high performance superbike in the world for 1983. Arguably it did, although some gave the nod to the Honda's VF1000, known as the Interceptor in the USA.

With the 1983 FJ1100, Yamaha announced their intent to fight for the Supersports crown.

Engine design followed the XJ/FJ way, but with no YICS, a five-speed transmission and a chain-driven rear wheel. The 1100 also introduced 4-valve heads for the first time in the 4-cylinder series, an indication of increased interest in the design of the valve train for sports bikes. Slightly unorthodox cam profiles were used that would result in better top end power, but in fact the 1100 produced strong power at all engine speeds above 4,500rpm.

The engine was good, but it was the chassis that was the star of the show. A totally new frame

ABOVE: By 1986 it had become the FJ1200 and was moving inexorably towards the sports tourer class.

BELOW: The naked retro-styled powerbike class developed in Japan in the mid-1990s, Yamaha introducing the XJR400.

design was applied, with square-section steel tubes. Named a 'perimeter frame', the design had the engine lowered into a typical double cradle frame, with the top members of the frame splayed out around the top of the engine, with extra supporting tubes linking the top frame tubes with the front downtubes. The lack of central backbone enabled a low seat height to be adopted despite the tall engine, also giving full access to the top of the engine. The lower cradle members were bolted in place on both sides, their easy removal making engine access a lot simpler. A vertical rear suspension unit with linkages delivered the rising rate suspension with remote control of the damping and pre-load, allowing it to be built deep into the swingarm gusset at the rear engine mount.

This was the era of the 16in wheel, so steering geometry was chosen to balance the short wheelbase with the heavy weight of the full wet machine. The resulting motorcycle had a good balance between stability and steering sensitivity, and was lauded in the motorcycling press.

Two years after introduction the engine was bored out an extra 3mm, adding 100cc and 15bhp power, but it was no longer intended to be a supersports motorcycle. Instead it was moving inexorably into the area of the supersports tourer – that is, a comfortable high-performance mile-muncher, leaving the race-replica sports classes to the new FZ Yamaha series.

The 1986 model had a few extra detail changes to improve the fairing's performance and produce a slicker gear change, but was essentially unchanged. This left the model in an ambiguous position in the market, and 1987 sales were so poor in the USA that it was dropped from the line-up for a year to clear unsold stock.

For 1989 a few changes were made, the most visible being the move to a 17in front wheel, along with larger disc rotors and new front forks without the ineffective anti-dive system.

Two years later and some more changes were made to the chassis, to sharpen the steering and dampen vibration. Stiffness was increased through larger cross-section frame tubes, with slightly different positions of the cross-members.

With the FJ1200 engine and Ohlin tagged shocks, the 1994 XJR1200 had the pedigree for success.

The engine was now fully rubber-mounted, to reduce the vibration that the competition had managed to suppress more effectively. Some adjustments in the rear suspension dimensions were intended to improve the damping, and a new fairing design was applied. No attempt was made to improve the performance; comfort had become the main virtue of the FJ.

Final tweak was the arrival of ABS brakes along with a hefty price rise in 1992, but as with many of the automatic brake systems fitted to motorcycles, this was not popular, as it seemed to kick in far too early, well before the front wheel had locked. It seemed to be the last nail in the coffin for the FJ1200 and it was no longer available from 1994.

The XJR1200 Muscle Bike

'Dead but not gone' is perhaps the best description for the FJ1200, as it seeded its engine into the XJR1200 muscle bike that first appeared in Japan in 1994. Kawasaki had introduced a new segment variant with the Zephyr series, combining some mildly aggressive custom styling with a naked two-shock chassis, housing an engine tuned for mid-range grunt. They had the market to themselves for a couple of years, until 1992 when Honda introduced the CB400 to the Japanese market.

Within two years, all the factories had their own range of sports cruisers: Honda with the CB series, Kawasaki with the Zephyr/ZRX, Suzuki with the GSX and Yamaha with the XJR. Yamaha were quick off the mark, with the first bike available in 1993. With an engine measuring 55 × 42mm, the XJR400 had the same dimensions as Kawasaki and Honda, in what was otherwise a quite conventional design, housed in the ubiquitous steel double-cradle frame. Lots of chrome and black paint underlined the bad boy image of the bike.

A year later the XJR1200 arrived in Japan, with an FJ1200 engine tuned to give maximum torque at just 4,000rpm, at the expense of overall power at maximum engine speed. It was a good match of engine characteristics with bike image, allowing riders to launch themselves from stop lights with huge drive, the short gearing keeping them well ahead of all but the most powerful contemporary sports bikes. Smooth, straight roads were heaven on the XJR, until windblast became uncomfortable at close to legal speed limits. Sharp corners and bumpy surfaces were

The image was right, but the XJR was never quite as good as the competition.

something else, however, as the ground clearance was poor and suspension damping inadequate.

Despite the flaws, the bike sold well and established a fanatical following – and work on the suspension would transform the bike. From 1999, Yamaha took action themselves, with a larger 1300cc engine and what was described as a stronger chassis. Inexplicably, the only suspension change was the arrival of pre-load adjustment on the front forks, although front brakes from the R1 were adopted and steering geometry was tightened up to help the 230kg (507lb) bike to turn a little faster. An SP version of the XJR was offered, with adjustable Ohlins rear shocks and a special paint job, but the uprated suspension was only marginally better than stock and not worth the extra money.

Sales continued to remain steady, confirming that this had little to do with performance and far more to do with style. For 2004, the carburettors and exhaust needed to be changed to comply with emission regulations in Europe, and some token weight-saving was done with lighter wheels.

By 2007, it was really in need of a makeover, not least to ensure compliance to European emission laws. Carburettors were replaced by fuel injection, and the twin exhausts were replaced by a single can with EXUP as well as a catalytic converter. The suspension had always been a point of criticism and although still very soft, at least there was adjustability added for bump and rebound damping. Visually the styling of naked muscle bike was preserved and the wall of torque the

bike had been famous for was present and correct. For a design essentially twenty years old, it still offered a lot of fun per dollar.

The FJR1300

In 2001 it seemed that perhaps the FJ1200 had been resurrected to claim leadership again in the class it had once dominated, that of sports tourer. The FJR1300 was announced as a serious high-speed, long distance tourer, to challenge territory owned by BMW and the Honda ST100 Pan European. In fact, other than the model tag, there was nothing in common with the two models.

The FJR was built to be an excellent long distance tourer, with all the comfort that makes it possible to cover 500+ miles in a day, every day, for as long as the journey lasts. The performance of the bike was in support of this goal alone. To achieve this, the complete machine was built from scratch, sharing no significant components with other models, although some of the design principles applied to other bikes were adopted, when this made sense. The 4-cylinder 1298cc engine was fitted with traditional 4-valve cylinder heads, rather than the trademark 5 valves on the sportsbikes. Following the trend seen increasingly in large capacity motorcycle engines, fuel injection was fitted, with power to the five-speed gearbox through a hydraulic clutch. Catalytic converters were fitted to the exhaust system, which was not equipped with the EXUP valve of previous generations of engines.

In an attempt to eliminate any vibration from the engine, twin balancer shafts were positioned on either side of the crank. The engine was a fully stressed member of the frame, so the upper crankcase and cylinders were cast as a single unit. The frame was typical Deltabox, with a rather unorthodox rear swingarm, incorporating a tunnel on the left-hand side for the final shaft drive to pass through. Monoshock rear suspension was fully adjustable, as were the front forks. The bike was lavishly equipped with all the accoutrements required for hours in the saddle and with roomy panniers for the luggage.

Like a phoenix, born of the ashes of the FJ1200, the FJR1300 rose in 2001 to challenge for the sports tourer market.

By 2006, chassis and suspension changes seemed to have fixed any initial handling issues.

Engine characteristics were spot on, with very good low end torque minimizing the need for frequent gear changes; just a whiff of throttle was needed to pass slower traffic. Brakes were excellent, comfort and ergonomics very good, but handling left something to be desired, the rear shock being too soft for anything but the smoothest of surfaces, and the steering a little heavy. It was still a very capable tourer, and sold well in Europe where it was first introduced. For 2003 it arrived in the US and promptly took a 20 per cent share of the market segment, despite stocks quickly selling out.

In 2004 some of the weaknesses of the first model were fixed, with revised suspension as well as larger brakes with an ABS version available. A welcome change for taller riders was the increased height of the adjustable windscreen, allowing them to get their heads out of the wind blast. Two years later, a version of the FJR was available featuring clutchless gear changes, with a paddle operation on the handlebars or conventional foot shifting.

Other detail changes were made to the chassis, with a longer swingarm and repositioned footrests, as well as new bodywork and styling. The longer swingarm seemed to finally fix the marginal handling performance that had characterized the bike since its inception, setting it up to remain an important member of the line-up for years to come.

The XJ and FJ series that appeared in the 1980s were certainly not the most exciting of Yamaha's many motorcycle ranges. Nevertheless they were critical to the next steps that Yamaha were to take in the evolution of their four-stroke bikes, as it proved that they, like all their competitors had proved before them, could also build the Universal Japanese Motorcycle. Once the mundane had been mastered, the remarkable could be developed.

10 Some More Equal Than Others

For a decade, Yamaha had struggled to escape the shadow cast by their rival. Honda had the good fortune and foresight to have started the four-stroke streetbike revolution that had led to an almost universal adoption of the transverse 4-cylinder engine for all large capacity Sportsbikes. Yamaha had spent the 1970s fighting to find something different that could compete, but ultimately gave up and developed their own version of the Universal Japanese Motorcycle.

A New High-Power Engine

The XJ and FJ series were to prove the equal of all the other run-of-the-mill Japanese fours, and brought Yamaha the confidence and commercial foundation on which to forge their own distinctive line of four-stroke Sportsbikes. The FJ1100, the UJM that came closest to shaking off this demeaning moniker, had played an important role in rejuvenating Yamaha's tarnished image when it appeared in 1984. That single year, when it was arguably the best Sportsbike money could buy, was critical in giving the company enough time to complete the engine on which their future in this segment would depend.

Ironically, the stimulus to research and develop a new high-power engine had come from Honda. When they announced in December 1977 that they would compete again in the GP world championship with a 500cc four-stroke, many were sceptical that this could ever be successful. The scepticism deepened with the persistent delays in the arrival of the new GP contender, and seemed justified with its disastrous performance in the few 1979 GPs it participated in. At Yamaha, however, their respect for Honda was great enough for a crash programme to

be initiated to investigate how to create a four-stroke engine with comparable power to a two-stroke – exactly Honda's ambition. The programme ran from 1978 to 1980, essentially on stand-by to respond to any success achieved by their rivals.

Rather than the radical approach adopted by Honda for their NR500, involving oval pistons and 8 valves per cylinder, Yamaha experimented primarily with the shape of the combustion chamber in a four-stroke engine. The goal was to design a cylinder head that would allow very high compression ratios without stepping into the domain of detonation and engine failure. The design was also closely related to the valve and sparkplug layout, with single and twin plug options, as well as 4-, 5-, 6- and even 7-valve heads built and tested. Both 6- and 7-valve heads produced excellent power characteristics, but involved a very complex drivetrain and presented challenges in providing adequate cooling.

As the Honda threat waned, Yamaha's research in this field was shelved, but only after the conclusion had been drawn that a 5-valve cylinder head offered a good compromise between complexity and combustion efficiency, and hence power. A couple of years later it was this research that was used as the basis for the 5-valve Genesis engine.

Challenging for Superbike Glory: the FZ

By the start of the 1980s, the focus within racing had started to shift towards the four-stroke, especially in the USA. If racing success was considered to have an impact on streetbike sales, then that success needed to be in four-stroke racing. Yamaha had been able to persist for many years with their iconic TZ750, but its heritage was

Yamaha launched their 5-valve technology with the 1985 FZ750.

linked firmly with the 1970s. As interest in Formula 1 (open class) waned and Superbike focus grew, Yamaha found that they were not represented on the grids. Given their strong historical connection with motorcycle racing, this was unacceptable, and the new FZ would need to be capable of challenging for Superbike glory.

The Genesis Engine
The engine certainly didn't let them down. Producing a claimed 102bhp, it was the big, wide, consistent torque delivery that had pulses racing and tongues wagging. Once the bike was released, rear-wheel power levels were measured at 85bhp and climbing when the rev. limiter kicked in at 11,500rpm.

All this had been achieved through some sound, yet simple engineering principles. Continuing in the Yamaha tradition of a narrow, compact engine block, the generator was at the back of the engine as usual, but also the ignition pick-ups were mounted in the crankcase, with a trigger built into the outer webs of the crankshaft. The complete engine was tilted forwards at 45 degrees, primarily to enable near-vertical downdraught carburettors an uninhibited passage straight into the cylinder. Moving the centre of gravity forward would also add more weight to the front wheel to help keep the bike stable when under power over bumpy surfaces.

To accommodate the carburettors and their air supply, the fuel tank was built around the airbox, with a pump to deliver the fuel to the carburettors. Compression ratio was a high 11.2:1, significantly

higher than most streetbikes, but only reliable if the engine was adequately cooled, resulting in water-cooling for the cylinders, but not the heads.

Taking a leaf out of the FJ1100 book, the crankcase was designed to enable air under the descending piston to be pumped away, minimizing power loss due to compression of the air. It was claimed to be good for a couple of bhp at the crankshaft. A six-speed transmission was driven through a hydraulic clutch of the same design as the FJ1100. Demonstrating Yamaha's own hopes and expectations for the new engine configuration, it was dubbed Genesis.

The Frame
The frame was broadly also a replica of that fitted to the FJ1100, with box-section steel tubing painted black rather than silver. The shape of the wide, splayed upper members of the frame was necessary to provide the space needed for the carburettors and airbox. An aluminium rear swingarm was supported by a single Monoshock rear damper, with rebound damping adjustment. Air caps were fitted to the front forks. It was possible to dial in a good ride on the FZ, but it was very sensitive to correct damping front and rear as well as tire pressure and tire wear. It had all the trappings of a thoroughbred racer.

The Market
Yamaha chose to offer the bike in the USA as a full 750, rather than emasculate it to meet the 700cc upper limit to avoid extra import duties. Perhaps they should have offered both bikes to the US markets, as

the FZ was expensive compared to the VF700 from Honda, the king of the mid-range Sportsbikes in 1984. It was certainly faster and more comfortable than the VF in most situations, but the steering was less sharp and the bike laboured to match the Honda on tight roads. In addition there was a new contender to worry about, with Suzuki introducing their race replica GSXR750R, just as the first FZs appeared in the showroom. This bike clearly exposed the major weakness of the FZ: it was overweight, the extra kilos taking the edge off its performance. Suzuki had produced a 750 machine with very similar power numbers, but 32kg (70lb) lighter than the FZ and that is something any rider would notice. The GSXR was however a very focused bike and for those looking for a bike that was not just intended for blitzing bendy B-roads, the FZ was a better choice.

The FZ Family

The Genesis engine was intended to be the base for a new generation of bikes, and 700cc versions found their way into the 1985 FZX Fazer and the Maxim. The Fazer was a radically styled muscle bike, borrowing accents from the new V-Max, its lower weight making up for an engine less powerful than the FZ. It looked cool, but when pushed to deliver, was let down by the suspension and inadequate tyres. The Maxim continued in the line of the Special Editions with cruiser styling, with

the usual strengths and weaknesses. Both were built to a budget and offered good value for money, but were only to last for a couple of years.

In the domestic market, an FZ400 had already appeared in 1984, but using traditional 4-valve technology, and for 1985, it had been joined by a 250, running to 14,500rpm to produce the claimed 45bhp. There were some signs that the 750 had been rushed to market, as there wasn't even a version available for the Californian market for 1985. For 1986 this was corrected, along with a few small detailed, mainly cosmetic changes, including a double headlight to replace the previous rectangular unit.

The biggest news of the year was the appearance of the FZ600, styled to fit into the emerging FZ family, but in fact employing components lifted from other models. The engine was donated by the FJ600, no bad thing, as this had been one of the strongest aspects of the FJ. The 600 was transformed by being slipped into the chassis of the Japanese market FZ400R, featuring a small version of the FZ750 frame. The combination was devastatingly effective, as at last the powerful engine could benefit from the light chassis, and steering and handling came together perfectly. In the transplant, the engine lost a little top end, caused by the need to fit slightly smaller carburettors in the cramped space within the small frame. But if anything, this seemed to improve the appeal of the bike, as the lost power needed to be made up by radical steering, with a chassis that could not be got out of shape.

Frame-mounted cowling is very effective in protecting the rider from wind pressure.

Upswept handelbars, footrests and related components and a large-size single seat are designed to fit particular police bike uses. The freer riding position also helps in different riding situations.

Easy-to-operate hydraulic clutch.

21-liter large-capacity fuel tank (4-liter reserve). Increased fuel efficiency reduces the frequency of refilling.

Large-size single seat that keeps rider fatigue to a minimum even on prolonged patrol duties.

12 V 60 W/55 W square type halogen headlight incorporating a 12 V 3.4 W or 3 W twilight lamp.

Lockable saddle bags on both sides are standard equipment.

Ø 39 mm telescopic front fork with a preload adjustable spring.

70% aspect tubeless tire on a 17 in. front wheel for increased roadgrip.

Front dual disc brake that delivers strong, controllable stopping power in different riding situations. It's a Ø 298 mm floating disc type with opposed piston type 4-pot calipers.

The high power output liquid-cooled 4-stroke in-line four engine adopts a Yamaha original 5-valve DOHC system. The large dual-core capacity aluminum radiator and a 12 V 28 A large capacity AC generator give dependable performance even in prolonged idling or continuous low-speed cruising. A device to prevent sudden start-off or leaving the side stand down is also available as standard equipment.

Rising-rate rear Monocross suspension incorporates shock absorbers which can be adjusted for both spring preload and damping force.

18-in. rear wheel also carries a 70% aspect tubeless tire. Both wheels are a rigid aluminum alloy type with hollow spokes.

It takes a fast bike to catch a fast bike. Plod would have welcomed this over his BMW K75 'flying brick'.

At last Yamaha had a true scratcher's four-stroke dream bike, its pinpoint-accurate steering compensating for the hard seat and suspension. For a year at least it ruled the roost in the USA, arriving in Europe a year later. It was instantly recognized as the perfect bike for the mildly hooligan element of sports riders, and sold in huge numbers, especially in the UK.

Linking Track and Street

By the mid-1980s it seemed as if Yamaha's passion for sports motorcycles had been rejuvenated after a decade and a half focusing on building a mainstream set of four-strokes. Their commitment to GP racing was undiminished, with factory teams in the World Championship and an annual edition of the TZ250 production two-stroke twin racer. In the early days of the production racer there had been a tight bond between street- and racebike, but as the company moved towards four-strokes, this became increasingly tenuous. Although the RD two-strokes were marketed as siblings to the racebikes, they were more like cousins twice removed. Clearly the insights learnt in the development of racing two-stroke engines would have limited application to sports four-stroke engines, but increasing attention was being paid to the chassis design for racing machinery.

From 1983, Yamaha were focused on the use of the aluminium twin spar frame for their 500 factory racers, with others following suit during 1984. Just a year later, with the technology yet to become mainstream, Yamaha introduced their TZR250 street twin for Japan, fitted with what they called a Deltabox frame. A year later, their domestic four-stroke equivalent appeared with the same chassis, and the FZR400 kicked off Yamaha's standardization on this type of frame for their most serious sports models. Once again track and street were linked.

The new frame design had arisen from the intent to build a light yet strong frame, especially effective in resisting flex of the headstock under heavy braking and the twisting forces generated by heavy power application under acceleration. Traditional gusseting around the headstock and extra bracing tubes in a cradle frame design were the tools available to the chassis designer. Yamaha's approach was to eliminate the headstock/frame joint, a potential source of movement, and tie as directly as possible the steering head with the rear wheel mounts at the front of the swingarm. The massive spars of welded aluminium sheet would provide the torsional strength to resist the twisting forces at work.

The race track showed that the design worked, but five years earlier manufacturing technology would have been unable to mass produce such components. The company's heavy investment in automatic manufacturing processes, using, wherever possible, machine construction and assembly, now paid dividends, enabling precision aluminium frame welding to be integrated into the production lines.

The FZR1000

Finally in 1987, the world could enjoy the fusion of Yamaha's engine and chassis evolution with the 5-valve Genesis engine design mounted in the aluminium twin-beam Deltabox frame. It was fitting that a new model, the FZR1000, should showcase the pride of Yamaha engineering. It was the strongest, fastest motorcycle available with the most innovative chassis ever seen on a mass-production bike.

The same principles of engine design were used as on the 750, with canted cylinders and vertical downdraught carburettors feeding 5-valve heads. The power characteristics of the 990cc engine made it possible for the bike to deliver all the performance needed from just five gear ratios. The four-into-one exhaust pipe was felt by some to be the culprit for the mid-range dent in the torque curve, but it did contribute to the overall low weight of the machine. In fact it weighed in at exactly the same level as the 1985 FZ750, matching class lightweight, the GSXR1100 from Suzuki, and 20kg (44lb) less than contenders from Honda and Kawasaki.

Suspension was stiff, more to European taste than American, and lacking sufficient adjustments to please both. Likewise the ergonomics, which rightly concluded that the majority of owners would expect a racing crouch rather than a touring straight back. Reflecting a general trend in the business, the 16in front wheel found on the 750 made way for a 17in, offering a better compromise between sharp steering and stability.

There was no doubt that Yamaha were back in contention as supplier of the best sportsbikes money could buy. To underscore this, a limited edition FZR750R was also built, with the race-track, and specifically the upcoming World Super Bike Championship, in mind. The chassis was essentially identical to the 1000, with the same four-piston callipers providing huge braking performance on the front. There were a few refinements in the suspension, with a four-position rebound damping on the fork and ride-height adjustment on the rear shock.

Some of the engine components were strengthened, with extra clutch plates and stronger and longer conrods, and a larger oil cooler keeping temperatures down. A totally new set of ratios were found in the transmission, clearly geared for the race track. Much, much more would be needed to turn the bike into a true superbike racer, and Yamaha offered kits to liberate the serious power needed from the engine.

Yamaha's OW01.
World championship contenders and awesome on the road!

Yamaha's limited-production OW01 (FZR750R) superbike is no "replica racer".

It's the real thing. Pure racer!

A proven winner at World Championship level and coming ready-equipped with the right stuff.

Like flat-slide carburettors, titanium con-rods, dual-ring low-friction pistons, six close-ratio gearbox speeds and the EXUP exhaust pressure control which boosts and spreads the power.

Like the alloy-beam Deltabox chassis with genuine racing suspension and braking systems.

The kind of stuff that will make the OW01 a winner on the track as well as an exclusive and truly awesome road machine!

The bare essentials. Strip away the plastics and the OW01 was a pure racer.

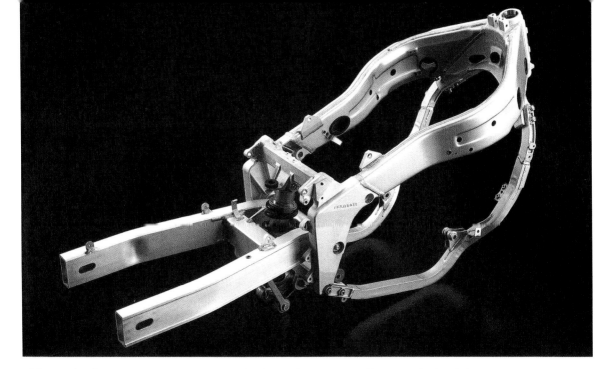

Yamaha's alloy "Deltabox" chassis: Handling to World Championship standards.

The most-advanced four-stroke engine on today's roads deserves a chassis to match and the Yamaha FZR1000 has just that! Wrapped around the power plant is an alloy "Deltabox" frame based directly on the design which won Yamaha both the 500cc and 250cc World Championships in 1986 road racing.

The "Deltabox" also proved capable of handling the bulk and power of our F1 and Endurance-racing "Genesis" four-strokes... on which the FZR1000 is so obviously based.

And this, of course, is why we are totally confident that the new FZR will be second-to-none when it comes to handling capabilities.

The "Deltabox" unit is constructed from high-grade aluminium sheet, fabricated into box-section beams that give it immense torsional rigidity.

Unquestionably, it is one of the strongest chassis on the road and, amazingly, it is one of the lightest! The main frame unit weighs only 12.2 kilogrammes.

Following Yamaha's "Genesis

concept", the FZR1000 chassis was developed in parallel with the motor, taking full advantage of the 45-degree forward inclination of the engine's cylinder block.

The upper chassis beams are splayed wide apart to accommodate the down-draft carburettors just behind the steering head.

These are covered by the dummy "front" of the fuel tank, which actually carries most of its load down behind the cylinders, where conventional carburettors would have been.

Weight distribution comes close to the perfect 50/50 front-to-rear balance, plus the centre of gravity is lower and the weight mass more-centralized.

Helping achieve this is the Monocross suspension layout, which controls movement of the box-section aluminium swinging arm by a De Carbon-type, gas/oil shock absorber. The main mass of the shock and its attendant rising-rate linkages are below swinging arm pivot height.

At the front end, the telescopic forks are made flex-free by the use of 41mm-diameter stanchions. These have a steep castor angle of 25.33-degrees (thanks to the high rigidity of the "Deltabox" frame) for quick but precise steering reaction.

The cast-alloy, hollow-spoke wheels are both extremely strong and light, with the consequent reduction in unsprung weight a definite aid to suspension performance. They carry wide-section, low-profile Pirelli MP7S radial tyres with ultra-high speed ratings and triple disc brakes. Dual 320mm units at the front and a single 267mm disc at the rear.

Chassis, suspension, wheels and brakes were all developed for the FZR1000 from Yamaha's World Championship-winning racers.

A superb pedigree. But then, of course, the Yamaha FZR1000 is a superb motorcycle!

So that's Deltabox. FZR1000 technology explained.

Yamaha FZR600:
bringing the "pure sports" approach
to the middleweight class.

Straight to the top of the middle weight ranking comes the Yamaha FZR600. A machine designed for those who specifically prefer the combination of light weight and the strong power delivery that the 'state of the art' 600cc engine provides.

A motorcycle where the emphasis is on all-round performance via a high power-to-weight ratio and razor-sharp handling. The kind of performance, in fact, that can get you over the twists and turns of the back roads quicker than anything else on wheels!

The FZR600 brings Yamaha's "Genesis concept" of totally-integrated engine and chassis design-thinking into the middleweight bracket for the first time. Designed from the ground up, the FZR is a lighter, more compact version of our highly successful FZR1000 and 750cc "racer replica style" supersports machines.

Just like those line-leaders, the FZR600 employs a four cylinder, liquid-cooled engine with forward inclined cylinder block and free-breathing downdraft carburettors. It's certainly not a scaled down 750, the double overhead cam powerplant is designed specifically for the middle-weight class, with the two most important design criteria in that category: power-to-weight and performance-to-price.

Just as with our bigger FZR models, the real core of the FZR600 is its "Genesis-type" four-cylinder engine with its inclined cylinder block that brings benefits in terms of both performance and handling.

The Genesis effect

Performance benefits because the forward slant of the upper engine allows the use of short, straight intake tracts and vertical downdraft carburettors. Its precise handling is enhanced because the "upper body weight" of the engine is moved further forward and lower down. Better overall weight distribution and a lower centre of gravity are the results.

It's a perfect example of the "Genesis effect". The design of one component used to positively influence the performance of another.

Four valves per cylinder

The FZR600 uses four valves per cylinder (dual inlet and exhaust) instead of the triple inlet, dual exhaust layout of the bigger versions. This is because our extensive flow bench testing showed that with the faster flowing, smaller volume ports, the four valve head, with the pent roof shape combustion chamber, performance was increased.

Deltabox frame

An engine that matches anything in its class needs running gear to suit. So we stayed true to the FZR specification and gave it a Deltabox frame based, like the rest of the range, on the chassis developed for Eddie Lawson's World Championship-winning Grand Prix machine.

The frame is constructed of high-tensile steel for added rigidity and durability, the impending weight penalty was minimised by a computer-assisted design that employs thinner gauge steel at the points of less stress. The results are a flex-free, precise handling sport bike!

Explaining why the FZR600 was such a good bike, albeit not quite CBR600-beating material.

Now we're talking. Deltabox frame plus 5-valve engine plus EXUP exhaust = FZR 1000.

Scratchers loved the FZR600, once the suspension had been sorted and new tyres were fitted.

Born of the domestic FZR400, the 1989 FZR600 had a powerful engine let down by poor suspension.

A fully kitted FZR750R Superbike, also known as the OW01.

How many 'R's can you get in a model identifier. The FZR400RR had a lot...

All the same, Yamaha could have done a better job in lowering the weight of the bike, as it was still much heavier than the Suzuki, although 20kg (44lb) under the original FZ750. When the World Super Bike Championship finally kicked off in 1988, the most successful Yamahas were Bimotas, running the 5-valve engines in their own lightweight chassis.

From 1989, the FZR750R became the OW01, with a new engine derived from the 1988 Suzuka 8 hour YZF750. Much was changed in the engine, now sloping at 40 degrees, with over-square 72mm × 46mm dimensions, reducing the stroke by 5.6mm. Full of racing components like the titanium conrods and aluminium fuel tank, the OW01 was never quite the success Yamaha had hoped it would be, despite the 2 TTF1 National Championship titles in the UK in 1990 and 1991 and the US Superbike title in 1991.

The FZR400

For 1988, the domestic market FZR400 managed to escape the country and was offered for sale in the USA and Europe. For California, once again Yamaha had to pull in the special services department to design some emission-reducing extras, and they came up with EXUP.

Given their two-stroke heritage, and especially the use of valves to modify the tuned characteristics of the exhaust pipe, Yamaha were able to kill two birds with one acronym. By placing a cutaway circular valve in the exhaust at the point where the header pipes converge, they were able to throttle the exhaust gases at a rate proportional to engine speed. At small throttle openings the pipe was almost blocked, preventing unburnt fuel leaving the exhaust. As the engine speed increased, the valve rotated and the restriction eased, the increased combustion efficiency producing cleaner gases. It worked well enough, but had the added benefit of increasing mid-range power delivery due to the back pressure caused by the obstruction in the pipe.

EXUP was reinvented as a power-enhancing standard feature on the FZR series. The 400 was, of course, what you would expect: a tiny, lightweight, agile race replica with a 14,000rpm redline and a significant power disadvantage to larger bikes, making it all the more rewarding when a focused rider used the sharp steering and his own skills to keep up.

The FZR600

While the 400 was for the truly hardcore racers, it was the FZR600 that appealed to many with

… but then it was indeed a race replica, a delightful little jewel of a machine.

the same ambitions, but less dedication. The two bikes were in fact closely related, as the 600 was developed from the 400 engine, so it had no 5-valve head, but followed the same design principles with a 45-degree cylinder block and full downdraught induction.

The extra engine capacity came primarily from an increased piston stroke, given the limitations imposed on wider bores by the original 400 block. There was danger in this approach as it resulted in a very high piston speed, and exposure to intense forces on direction reversal at TDC and BDC. This was mitigated with a quite conservative redline at 11,500rpm, a lighter piston and extra-long conrods to ease the forces on the cylinder wall. Valve diameter and attitude were modified, and the complete package worked wonderfully well, producing the most powerful 600cc engine in the world.

On the chassis side, however, all was not well. With the additional 'R', the 600 was, of course, brought into the Deltabox family, but the light aluminium version on the 400 was replaced by a steel version. Suspension was poor, a bad compromise between soft springs and over-damped compression valving. To make matters worse, skinny crossply tyres were fitted in the USA, with the steering sensitivity taking another hit in the process.

Nevertheless the potential for the FZR600 was clear, as better suspension and suitable tyres turned the bike into a racetrack winner, where it totally dominated the 600 class. For the 1990 model, some quick fixes were possible, with a wider rear wheel rim and radial tyres being enough to get the suspension to work far better. The cherry on the pie was the new four-piston calliper front brakes, straight out of the FZR1000 family of hyper-stoppers and welcomed by all riders for their power and sensitivity. The only thing to spoil the FZR's claim to being top 600 Sportsbike was the arrival of the Honda CBR600F2, which was close to the FZR in most things and a lot more comfortable to ride. CBR sales were to dominate the class for much of the 1990s.

Major Upgrade of the FZR1000

Despite just two years of production, in 1989 Yamaha invested in a major upgrade of the FZR1000 for the model year. Changes to both chassis and engine resulted in a more stable, sharper-handling bike with better low- and mid-range grunt, turning it into the class leader it had almost been from the start.

It was the combination of changes that was so important, as the engine needed to be more upright to enable the frame geometry to be

Model	FZ400R	FZR400	FZ600
Year	1984	1986	1986
Capacity (cc)	399	399	598
Configuration	4-s 4 cyl	4-s 4 cyl	4-s 4 cyl
Induction	16-valve dohc	16-valve dohc	16-valve dohc
Bore × stroke (mm × mm)	54 × 43.6	56 × 40.5	58.5 × 55.7
Gearbox	6-speed	6-speed	6-speed
Final drive	chain	chain	chain
Frame	duplex cradle	deltabox	duplex cradle
Wheelbase (mm, in)	1,385 (54.5)	1,400 (55.1)	1,385 (54.5)
Dry weight (kg, lb)	165 (364)	173 (381)	176 (388)
Power (bhp)	59 @ 12,000rpm	59 @ 12,000rpm	68 @ 9,500rpm
Torque (kgm)	3.7 @ 10,000rpm	3.9 @ 9,500rpm	5.2 @ 8,500rpm
Top speed (km/h, mph)	185 (115)	190 (118)	200 (124)

Model	FZR600	FZR600R	YZF600R Thundercat
Year	1989	1994	1996
Capacity (cc)	599	599	599
Configuration	4-s 4 cyl	4-s 4 cyl	4-s 4 cyl
Induction	16-valve dohc	4-valve dohc	16-valve dohc
Bore × stroke (mm × mm)	59 × 54.8	62 × 49.6	62 × 49.6
Gearbox	6-speed	6-speed	6-speed
Final drive	chain	chain	chain
Frame	deltabox	deltabox	deltabox
Wheelbase (mm, in)	1,425 (56.1)	1,415 (55.7)	1,415 (55.7)
Dry weight (kg, lb)	179 (395)	184 (406)	187 (412)
Power (bhp)	91 @ 10,500rpm	100 @ 11,500rpm	100 @ 11,500rpm
Torque (kgm)	6.7 @ 8,500rpm	6.7 @ 9,500rpm	6.7 @ 9,500rpm
Top speed (km/h, mph)	210 (130)	230 (143)	230 (143)

Model	FZS600 Fazer	FZ6	FZ750
Year	1998	2004	1984
Capacity (cc)	599	600	749
Configuration	4-s 4 cyl	4-s 4 cyl	4-s 4 cyl
Induction	16-valve dohc	16-valve dohc	20-valve dohc
Bore × stroke (mm × mm)	62 × 49.6	65.5 × 44.5	68 × 51.6
Gearbox	6-speed	6-speed	6-speed
Final drive	chain	chain	chain
Frame	duplex cradle	deltabox	duplex cradle
Wheelbase (mm, in)	1,415 (55.7)	1,440 (56.7)	1,485 (58.5)
Dry weight (kg, lb)	189 (417)	192 (423)	209 (460)
Power (bhp)	95 @ 11,500rpm	96 @ 12,000rpm	100 @ 10,500rpm
Torque (kgm)	6.2 @ 9,500rpm	6.4 @ 6,500rpm	8 @ 8,000rpm
Top speed (km/h, mph)	210 (130)	210 (130)	235 (146)

(continued...)

Model	FZR750R (OW01)	YZF750R	FZR1000
Year	1988	1993	1987
Capacity (cc)	749	749	989
Configuration	4-s 4 cyl	4-s 4 cyl	4-s 4 cyl
Induction	20-valve dohc	20-valve dohc	20-valve dohc
Bore × stroke (mm × mm)	72 × 46	72 × 46	75 × 56
Gearbox	6-speed	6-speed	6-speed
Final drive	chain	chain	chain
Frame	duplex cradle	deltabox	deltabox
Wheelbase (mm, in)	1,445 (56.9)	1,420 (55.9)	1,470 (57.9)
Dry weight (kg, lb)	187 (412)	195 (430)	209 (460)
Power (bhp)	121 @ 10,500rpm	125 @ 12,000rpm	130 @ 10,000rpm
Torque (kgm)	7.9 @ 9,250rpm	8.2 @ 9,500rpm	10.4 @ 8,500rpm
Top speed (km/h, mph)	235 (146)	240 (149)	230 (143)

Model	YZF1000R ThunderAce	FZS1000 Fazer	FZ1 Fazer
Year	1996	2001	2006
Capacity (cc)	1002	998	998
Configuration	4-s 4 cyl	4-s 4 cyl	4-s 4 cyl
Induction	20-valve dohc	20-valve dohc	20-valve dohc
Bore × stroke (mm × mm)	72 × 46	74 × 58	74 × 58
Gearbox	5-speed	6-speed	6-speed
Final drive	chain	chain	chain
Frame	deltabox	duplex cradle	duplex cradle
Wheelbase (mm, in)	1,435 (56.5)	1,450 (57.1)	1,460 (57.5)
Dry weight (kg, lb)	198 (437)	208 (459)	204 (450)
Power (bhp)	145 @ 10,000rpm	143 @ 10,000rpm	148 @ 11,000rpm
Torque (kgm)	11.2 @ 8,500rpm	10.8 @ 7,500rpm	10.8 @ 10,800rpm
Top speed (km/h, mph)	265 (165)	250 (155)	250 (155)

changed, with a shorter wheelbase and different weight distribution. Front-fork tube diameter grew to 43mm, and an entirely new rear suspension set-up was adopted, with new link rods that enabled greater damper movement, allowing softer springs and less aggressive damping.

The top of the engine was redesigned, resulting in a higher compression ratio and a claimed increase of 8bhp at maximum power. Bearings and conrods were strengthened to maintain the bullet-proof reputation it had developed. Although some attention was paid to the riding position, it was still considered very racetrack influenced, and even hardcore journalists for European magazines acknowledged that pleasure turned to pain after an hour in the saddle. The mirrors were still useless.

For three years the FZR was the king of the Sportsbikes, holding off the GSXR1100R Suzuki with some ease, despite its vices. Yet another update in 1991 brought upside-down forks, as was the fashion at the time, arguably stiffer with the thicker outer sliders clamped into the steering head. A year later, though, the king was deposed by the CBR900RR, the venerable Fireblade, setting new performance standards that left the FZR and all other competitors far, far behind.

Sportsbikes for the Domestic Market

Throughout the first half of the 1990s the FZR series remained the basis for Yamaha's four-stroke Sportsbikes. Various exotica appeared in Japan for the domestic market, such as the FZR250R EXUP and improbably named FZR400RR SP, offering riders a restricted engine in a racebike chassis.

For a couple of years unrestricted versions were available in Europe through parallel importers, and the lucky owners could experience the pleasures of 55bhp at the rear wheel with a close-ratio gearbox and fully adjustable suspension on a bike weighing just 175kg (386lb). After the 1991 upgrade to the FZR1000, nothing changed on the larger FZRs until 1994, when 'completely revamped' bikes were announced by Yamaha.

The most visible change was the styling exercise to follow the YZF750, which had appeared the previous year. Underneath the skin of the 600 there really was a new bike, but it was debatable if it was better. Frame design had changed a little, with the engine now a stressed member, and a claimed major increase in stiffness. It remained steel rather than aluminium. Larger diameter front forks paired off with rear suspension with rebound damping adjustment. All told, the bike felt roomier and less cramped.

In the engine a new manufacturing process did away with cast steel liners, the pistons running on the aluminium barrels with a composite-ceramic coating. Carburettor diameter grew to 34mm, and a less restrictive airbox was fitted. More seriously, engine dimensions had changed to give a wider bore and shorter stroke. The wider bore could have been used to increase valve area, but valves sizes were unchanged, although the stems were narrower and the included valve angle reduced. The whole valve train was lightened, and oval cross-sectioned wire used on the springs to allow more aggressive cam profiles to be used. The engine was now claimed to produce 100bhp, and to honour this achievement, the 600 gained another 'R', to be called the FZR600R.

Tough Market

It was an improvement unquestionably, but it was now Kawasaki's turn at the top with the ZZ-R600, with some claiming the CBR still to be undisputed champion. Few pitched for the FZR, which came up short in almost all areas. It took a year to reach the USA, where it was immediately rebranded to be the YZF600, although it was classified as an 'early release' model, so it could be found in showrooms mid-year 1994, priced well above the competition.

And the showroom was where most of the bikes stayed, the tales of poor suspension, high price and the far better Honda resulting in few buyers. By 1995 it was totally overshadowed, waiting for a new model to put it out of its misery. For the US market, a suspension upgrade was hurriedly applied, with a 41mm front cartridge fork and a new rear shock with remote reservoir. While they were at it, the front brake should have been improved, but it was left unchanged.

The 1996 US YZF600R was a lot better than the 1995 version, but was still down a notch on the Honda and Kawasaki competition. The FZR1000 had even fewer changes from 1994, although the six-piston callipers on the front made a good brake better, and the Ohlins fork looked sexy, but wasn't a lot better. In this guise it survived a couple more years as a good 1000cc Sportsbike, no longer cutting edge, but fully sorted and competent.

The YZF750R

The Yamaha model line was getting very scrappy and inconsistent during the 1990s, with Europe leading the marketing push for the top sportsbikes, and bikes taking a year longer to reach the USA. Yamaha USA often claimed problems getting the EPA certificates completed as reason for the delay, but in reality the European market was simply the battleground for sportsbikes.

Yet another line was created for the 1993 season in Europe, with a model code clearly trying to lever Yamaha's GP successes in the 500cc class. The YZF750R marked the company's re-entry into the 750 class for streetbikes, and was intended to form the basis for their continued participation in superbike racing as a replacement for the FZR750R, the OW01. Two versions of the bike were available in Europe, the YZF750R and the YZF750SP, with the intent that the SP formed the basis for racing. It wasn't exactly ready for the track, but the addition of a £5,500 race-kit would get you close.

Compared to the OW01, the YZF was intended to be compacter, with quicker, yet stable steering. The overall wheelbase was shortened by 25mm, and the steering head steepened a fraction. Unlike the budget-busting FZR600, the YZF was treated to a full aluminium frame, with steel castings to support the rear engine mounts and the swingarm pivot. Suspension was also of higher quality, with the R model at last getting rebound

A new generation 750 was introduced in 1993, the YZF750R.

damping adjustment on the rear shock, as well as upside-down front forks.

Most of the engine work was spent on the cylinder heads, with the same diameter valves plugging into narrower inlet tracts and entering the combustion chamber at a wider angle. 38mm downdraught carburettors fed the engine, with an EXUP-equipped exhaust helping the low- to mid-range power delivery. Reciprocating mass was lightened to help the engine spin up to the 12,000rpm redline, with a claimed 125bhp produced when it got there. Although the claim was a little high, measurements confirmed more than 100bhp available at the rear wheel.

The SP was 20 per cent more expensive, coming with fully adjustable suspension, 39mm flat-slide Keihin carburettors and close-ratio gearbox.

The YZF750R was a good bike, probably the best 750 available, although the Kawasaki ZXR750 was a strong competitor. However, the Fireblade was better than both of them and incredibly, the YZF was more expensive. This was a handicap from which the YZF never recovered, and stocks were only cleared after a couple of years with massive price reductions; the appearance of the Suzuki GSX750R SRAD was the final nail in its coffin.

The YZF600R: ThunderCat

The second generation 600cc sports bike that had been launched in 1994 as the FZR600R in Europe, and the YZF600 in the USA a year later, was not the success that had been hoped for. It briefly led the performance stakes, but the cost-cutting suspension components spoiled the overall package. At this time, Yamaha were having great difficulty matching the price of their bikes with that of the competition. In particular Honda were far better at building high-spec machines without missing the target price to market. If anything, the competition looked like intensifying, with rumours of a hard-core GSXR600 coming from Suzuki.

However, rather than go head-to-head with the hyper-sports rush that seemed to be developing, they chose to take a different approach. While continuing to develop the 600cc engine for more power and a flat and wide power delivery curve, they chose to target a sub-segment of the market with a more comfortable, less radically styled bike with plenty of mid-range power. They'd leave the market for a frenetic, rev-happy, twitchy-sharp race replica to Suzuki.

The result was the new YZF600R, known as the ThunderCat in Europe. It looked totally different from its predecessor, while in fact many components were unchanged. An extra 5bhp was squeezed out of the engine, with new cams and valve springs and lightened crankshaft and pistons.

This was a time of great experimentation in ram-air induction in both racing bikes and streetbikes. Large air ducts started appearing on many models, feeding fresh air into closed airboxes above the carburettors. On the ThunderCat, a central air scoop under the front headlamp split into two passages along the sides of the fairing into the central airbox. This ensured the carburettors a supply of cool air, unheated by the radiator at the front of the engine. The airbox was designed to increase torque through resonances caused by air flow into the box. Carburettors grew to 36mm in diameter, with a throttle position sensor plugged into the ignition to provide the right advance. All told, the new engine had a slightly better top end, and a noticeable mid-range punch.

Frame dimensions were unchanged, but at last, two years after the competition, fully adjustable suspension was present front and rear, and the

In 1996, the YZF600R ThunderCat arrived, with heavy restyling but only a few component changes.

brakes were as good, if not better than before. Aerodynamically the bike was well designed, thanks to many hours in the wind tunnel developing the fairing.

The seat was comfortable and the riding position relaxed. The whole bike was a balanced, well designed compromise, but not aesthetically attractive. In fact it was ugly, not bad enough to be interesting in itself, but just plain and uninspiring. The bike was the thinking man's 600cc Sportsbike, but this class is all about the heart, not the head, and no heart would beat faster on seeing the ThunderCat. It was to remain underrated for its eight-year existence in Europe. There were more thinkers in the USA, where it remained available up to 2007.

The YZF1000R; Thunderace

Appearing alongside the ThunderCat at the world launch in South Africa was big brother, the new YZF1000R. Like the 600, it looked totally different from previous models, but was in fact a mash-up between the YZF750R and the FZR1000, namely the chassis from the 750 and the engine from the 1000. It was a glorious fusion of the two, almost faultless in execution, giving the world an agile, sharp-steering, comfortable, hugely fast mile-muncher, as good as anything else on the market.

Not much had been changed in the engine, other than lightening of the crankshaft and pistons, which were now forged. Like the Thunder-Cat, the new 38mm CV carburettors were also fitted with a throttle position sensor for ignition adjustment.

At last Yamaha seemed to realize that they had been penalized so much in the past through inattention to weight, but now, with the YZF frame and with the use of new aluminium wheels, almost 15kg (33lb) was saved with respect to the FZR. It did hide this well, though, looking far bulkier than it felt when being ridden. Star of the show were the new front brakes, machined from a single casting, the four-piston callipers offering the best braking available on any bike in production.

No bike is 100 per cent perfect, and the YZF1000R clutch was still a little fragile, under hard use, like all the FZR and YZF clutches over the years. There was also a nasty band of vibrations through the footrest at around 5,000rpm, the legal cruising speed in top gear in Europe on the motorway.

There was also one other flaw, not with the execution of the design, but with the intent with the new bike. As on the Cat, it was intended to be the ultimate sportsbike for the mature rider, hence the subdued styling and sensible ergonomics. But the majority of riders wanted something

The Ace was still a little too heavy to race, but the huge torque from the engine made it a joy to ride on fast roads.

a little special, out of the ordinary, flashy, hinting of social irresponsibility. The ThunderAce was a superb machine, but it lacked that vital ingredient that made a bike successful, namely charisma.

Unlike the 600, the YZF1000R was never popular in the USA and was only available for a single year, 1997. In Europe it continued to be available through to 2003, not selling in large numbers, but proving to be as bullet-proof over time as its FZR predecessor.

The FZS600 Fazer

In an attempt to cover all the little sub-segments that existed in the most popular 600cc class, all the Japanese manufacturers had been busy for some years producing slightly different variants of the same package. It was a comparatively cheap way to bring a new model to market, with often mainly cosmetic changes or a few chassis or engine changes. Yamaha was as guilty as the others, with some of their efforts succeeding, and some not.

The Yamaha 600 Diversion, or Seca II, was a low-cost simple bike and had sold well for many years. In the USA, both the YZR600 and FZR600 were available for many years. In Europe it was felt that there was room for yet another 600cc model to fit between the plain Diversion and Sports YZR. It was a segment that Suzuki had been handily soaking up with their Bandit model, and Yamaha decided to give them a run for their money with the FZS600 Fazer.

Taking the Cat's engine, it was fitted with smaller carburettors and a new cylinder head, to knock off some of the top end but bolster mid-range torque. It worked well, with a strong engine at low engine speeds, but still managing a top speed of around 140mph (225km/h). A new chassis was built in the old style of tubular double-loop cradle holding the engine, rather than with the engine as a stressed member. There was no damping adjustment available on the forks or shocks, but both performed well, despite being a little soft. Brakes were excellent, coming straight off other bikes much faster and heavier than the

ABOVE: The 1998 FZS600 Fazer was the engine from the Cat slipped into a new chassis to produce a minor masterpiece.

BELOW: The Fazer was cheap, with a good chassis holding an engine with a fat mid-range. It sold in large numbers.

Fazer. A small half-fairing did a reasonable job of protecting the rider from wind blast, and the seat was well padded and comfortable.

The whole package worked very well, and sold at a budget price about 40 per cent cheaper than the Cat. Some testers were convinced it was better than its Sports brother, certainly when the massive price difference was taken into account. It was incredibly popular in Europe, soon displacing the Bandit as bestseller in its class, with Honda's effort, the Hornet, never really challenging its domination.

The FZS1000 Fazer

The success of the 600 led Yamaha to look a little more closely at their naked bike strategy. Although there was the retro-look XJR1300 muscle bike available, it was decided that there might also be a market for a sports naked bike. It might usefully be even more radically styled than the FZS600, given that this had also been intended for the practical rider looking for a competitively priced daily runaround with a bit of poke for the weekends.

By 2000, the rumours were flying around of a naked R1, and this is indeed what appeared in early 2001, the engine from the super-sports bike slotted into a low-tech steel tubular cradle frame. The FZS1000 Fazer was a worthy addition to the Fazer legacy. Not a lot had been changed on the engine, other than a heavier crankshaft to keep the front wheel down, and smaller carburettors to take the edge off the incredible power of the R1. Full adjustable suspension kept the bike well in control, and the slightly longer swingarm also helped to put more weight over the front wheel.

Almost everything about the bike was just right for its goal of stylish, naked sportsbike, with the small handlebar fairing doing a good job of protecting the rider and keeping rides quite comfortable over longish distances.

One thing they did get wrong, though, was the high price. A year later Honda had their Hornet 1000 ready, admittedly not as fast, but almost £2,000 cheaper! Furthermore Kawasaki had produced a ZRX1200S that was a lot heavier and much more old school, but also £1,500 lower in price.

The 2001 FZS1000 based on the R1 engine had excellent performance but was too expensive.

The FZ6

The FZS600 might have remained in the line-up for many years to come with occasional styling updates, as it was simply an excellent compromise. In fact it was killed off by stricter EU environment regulations that came into force in June 2003. Not only was the Fazer instantly illegal, but the same fate befell the V-Max, the Diversion, Ace and Cat. Fortunately there were enough pre-registered versions of the FZS around to fulfil demand until the completely new budget sport 600 became available late in the year.

The FZ6 followed in the footsteps of the 1000 by borrowing the R6 engine for the powerplant, with just a little detuning and adjustment of the fuel injection. Rather than the steel tubular frame of big brother, the FZ6 got its own aluminium spar frame, benefiting from the lower manufacturing costs of a new die-cast process Yamaha had just introduced. The rest of the chassis was quite conventional, but there was evidence of cost cutting in the lower spec brakes. Previously the R1-sourced callipers on the 600 had been one of the stars of the deal, but those on the R6 let the side down a little, lacking power and feel.

This was in fact a portent of worse things to come, as back-to-back tests between the old and the new Fazer demonstrated time and time again that the old bike was simply better at almost everything. The new R6-based engine lacked the healthy mid-range drive of the old Fazer, which in turn had made up for indifferent handling due to the under-damped and non-adjustable suspension. Suspension remained quite basic, although the settings were improved, but the peaky engine made the FZ6 a lot more effort to ride, needing to keep the R6 mill running above 10,000rpm to stay in the powerband. This was compounded by heavy throttle and clutch controls, making the bike just too much hard work to ride.

Disappointing Market Response

So the 2004 FZ6 was a disappointment, but at least the quality of the FZS1000 Fazer kept sales bouyant, despite the high price. This changed, however, with the 2006 launch of the FZ1 Fazer

Nothing was wrong with the 1000cc Fazer except the 20 per cent price premium.

replacement, also a totally new bike with a flawed engine. Once again the R1 was the donor for the powerplant, using the same formulae of heavier crankshaft and different cam profiles to take the edge off the top end and provide a fatter mid-range power delivery. But something went wrong in retuning the fuel injection, resulting in a snatchy throttle response in the engine mid-range.

Even though this was first commented on as early as the press launch, production models were just as bad and marred the overall impressive performance of the new flagship Fazer. The new frame was now a die-cast beam frame, with the engine clamped firmly between the beams as a stressed member. Front forks were upside-down with full adjustability, and the wheelbase and steering geometry tuned for a sportier performance. The contrast between old and new 1000 Fazer emphasized the different approaches adopted for the two bikes and the strong move to a sports rather than a touring ride. The styling was as strong as always, following the fashion for massive bulbous exhaust cans, but the problems with

ABOVE: The FZ6 replacement of the Fazer lost the character of the old bike through the use of the R6 powerplant.

BELOW: The naked FZ1 emphasized the radical styling, complementing the flawed engine.

The 2006 FZ1 complete with snatchy throttle response.

the engine meant it was a much less effective ride than its rivals. The 2007 version of the bike brought some relief, although it remained a weakness of the model. Both Fazers had stepped down from the top of their respective classes.

Sales of the 600 Fazer had plummeted from the new model, and for 2007 Yamaha attempted to improve the performance and image of the bike with the S2 version. A lighter throttle definitely improved the ease of use and there was in general a better throttle action, but the engine still needed high revs to perform, inevitable with the R6-based heritage perhaps. There was a new cockpit fairing and some mild styling changes, but the rest of the bike was left alone. ABS was now an option for both the faired and naked version of the bike. Priced at a level that was very competitive against the rest of the market, the FZ6 was in a strong position to snap up a decent share of the middleweight marketplace.

Over Twenty Years of FZs

There had been a remarkable polarization of the sportsbike segment in the twenty-plus years from the first FZ750 to the 2008 FZ models. Traditionally the top-of-the-range sports models had been the flagships for the company, showcasing their latest technology and innovations. Yamaha themselves had changed this, as they introduced the hyper-sportsbike R series in the 1990s, leading to a technology race to equip these radical sports-bikes with the most advanced features their engineering departments could produce. The mainstream sportsbikes slipped into the shadows, often inheriting technology a couple of years after the hyper-sports models. But that was all right, for what they missed in kudos as early adopter, they gained in the prestige of proven design and performance.

11 No Compromise

Yamaha celebrated its fortieth anniversary in 1995, and could look back with some satisfaction at four decades of motorcycle production, each of them marked with the design and development of a ground-breaking model that had changed the world of motorcycling. In 1964, the YDS3 had established the two-stroke as a dominant force in lightweight street sportsbikes, its position being consolidated by the 1973 RD350. For the

One of the most distinctive noses in the business first appeared in September 1997.

third decade the Virago had caught the imagination of, primarily, the American public and stimulated a surge of cruisers, which carved themselves a huge segment of the motorcycle sales market. The fourth decade should have been the one that Yamaha built the best sports superbike in the world; they came close, but ultimately it was the decade of the V-Max, the undisputed king of the muscle bikes. Surely it was time for Yamaha finally to create a superbike that was unquestionably the best in the world, which would stand as a beacon marking the moment when things would never be the same again. It was time to build a legend.

Changing the World

The story goes that this was exactly the line of the discussion that took place at the launch in South Africa in 1995 of the ThunderCat and ThunderAce series. Both bikes were essentially parts bin specials, excellent bikes as such, but not the sort of innovative, inventive, creative and fresh design that would change the world. So while the collective world press put the new sportsbikes through their paces in the warm February sun at the bumpy Killarney track, Japanese and European product planners sat down together to bat some ideas around.

The timing was fortuitous. A new president had been appointed in April 1994, the fourth in Yamaha's history. Takehiko Hasegawa had come through the ranks on the technical side of the motorcycle business, his first ten years with the company spent in the GP racing team. He had been involved in the development of the first 250cc GP racer, the RD48, and had experienced

Born for speed and styled to match.

the disappointment of the first trip to Europe in 1961, when it had been severely outclassed by the four-stroke opposition, notably the Hondas. Leading the team responsible for the engine development, he had transformed the engine during the winter of 1961/1962, while the financial storm had raged around the team as Yamaha tottered on the brink of bankruptcy.

Making its debut at the first race at Suzuka track in November 1962, the new 250, the RD56, was vastly improved, and ready for a serious challenge for GP glory. Hasegawa was standing at the pit wall when Fumio Ito powered out of La Source for the last time to take the chequered flag and win the Belgian GP in July 1963, with team-mate Yoshikazu Sunako coming home second. This was the first of many GP wins for Yamaha, and continued their history of close ties with racing. Hasegawa went on to run the GP team for the rest of the 1960s, with riders Read, Duff and Ivy. Technological and personal performance was in his DNA.

In 1990, Yamaha had announced a new corporate philosophy that they summarized as the desire to be perceived as a 'Kando-creating' company – not an easy word to translate, hence its inclusion in untranslated form in the mission statement. In essence it means a feeling of fulfilment and intense satisfaction at having met or exceeded your goal. Amongst the ways Yamaha intended to achieve this was through 'the creation of value that surpasses customer expectations'. When Hasegawa took office, one of the first projects that he authorized to be started was the creation of a new supersports machine, and Kunihiko Miwa was appointed to lead the project to realize this. He had travelled to South Africa for the launch of the new YZF machines, and sat down with Masahiro Inumaru, head of product planning for Europe. Inumaru had spent five years leading the US planning department at the time the XV1100 and V-Max appeared. On returning to Japan he had worked on the production of the FZR400R, which turned into a sensationally successful domestic model and formed the basis for many of the better FZR models that were produced. His philosophy was to focus on what was needed to address a particular segment, and to ignore all distractions that might prevent you achieving your goal.

In Inumaru, Kunihiko Miwa found a kindred spirit, with the drive and experience to push the project through to completion. His own ideas had led him to believe that the secret to the success of the project lay in a lightweight and compact design. Alignment with Inumaru was complete, as this was exactly the strength of the FZR400R of previous years. Together it was decided that the mantra for the development team would be 'No compromise'. And so they went to work.

Building the Legend: The YZFR1

The key to a compact motorcycle would be a compact engine block. This was not foreign territory to Yamaha, as they had taken design decisions at the start of the 4-cylinder Seca period to keep engine widths as narrow as possible. That was fine, but this engine needed to be narrow and short. This required some radical repositioning of the transmission shafts behind the crankshaft, with the mainshaft raised up above the axis of the crankshaft and the driveshaft tucked in partially underneath. The resulting engine was 8cm (3in) shorter than that of the YZF1000R. The short and narrow engine gave the designers a lot more flexibility with its positioning.

But they had some other requirements from the engine as well. With previous Deltabox designs, the engine had supported frame rigidity through engine mounting points on the spars. Now the frame was designed, with the assumption that major stress forces would be handled by the frame itself, enabling the spars themselves to be made slimmer and lighter. The engine construction therefore needed to be different to enable these forces to be absorbed without cracks developing at the mounting points. The solution was a single casting for the upper crankcase half, as well as the four vertical cylinders. The genius of the new design lay in this unique fusion of engine and chassis technology. This was innovation of the highest order.

Contemporary sportsbike perfection. The 1998 YZFR1.

Everything else was built around this integrated design. With cylinder dimensions of 74 × 54mm, the new engine had a smaller bore and longer stroke. The increased stroke helped preserve mid-range torque, while the smaller bore resulted in lighter pistons. Every component was inspected for potential weight reduction, delivering a 10kg (22lb) lighter engine. Cylinder head design was still based on the 5-valve principle, but with slightly smaller valves and new combustion chamber shape, good for a compression ratio of 11.8:1.

Transmission went up to six speeds, which meant extra weight, but was essential to get the most out of the 150bhp engine that was taking shape. The Mikuni carburettors grew to 40mm, retaining the throttle position sensor. Thinner-gauge steel was used for the exhaust to save a few grams, and the EXUP was slightly smaller but with its attitude now determined based on five parameters, namely engine speed, throttle position, gear, rate of throttle position change and road speed. The microprocessor had hit hard on roadbike design.

The wheelbase of the new bike was 35mm shorter than the YZF1000R, with the same rake and 5mm less trail. To keep the weight distribution even, not only was the engine canted forwards at 30 degrees, but it was positioned well to the front of the chassis, with an extra long swingarm to ensure adequate wheelbase for stability. Fully adjustable suspension was present front and rear, with lightened versions of the excellent Thunder-Ace brakes present. All told, the bike tipped the scales at 177kg (390lb) dry and 198kg (436lb) wet; for comparison, the acknowledged lightweight sportsbike, the Suzuki GSXR750 SRAD, weighed 179kg (395lb) dry and the Honda CBR900RR Fireblade 183kg (404lb).

On 15 September 1997, at a crowded press release in a large warehouse on an industrial site south of Milan, now owned by the Prada foundation, the YZF-R1 made its first public appearance with Yamaha superbike rider Scott Russell aboard. It had been a long and tiring journey for Miwa san and his team leaders Takanori Tsuchiya, head of engine design, and Wataru Tanizaki, responsible for the chassis. A team of up to fifty

Secret to the R1's success was the ultra-compact engine.

staff had worked long and hard to reach this moment. The response was positive, the striking white and red design of the new Yamaha clearly underlining their intent to make a statement with this new model. Later he was to pronounce himself satisfied with the results, claiming that the R1 was 'a bit like a woman. Beautiful to look at, but a real challenge to control'.

The rather jaded members of the world motorcycling press dutifully reported on the exciting launch of the new bike, and then sat back to see how far short of the hype the bike would really turn out to be. It seemed to have become standard practice to oversell new models, press releases running out of superlatives in praise of the new bikes. There was considerable scepticism as to whether Yamaha would this time be able to break the CBR900RR stranglehold on the class, or even match the crown prince, the GSXR750. However, it all became clear when they were invited to ride the bikes at the press launch at the Cartagena circuit in Alicante in Spain on 5 November 1997. This is a tight, twisty track that even a contemporary 600 would have trouble conquering – but the R1 took it completely in

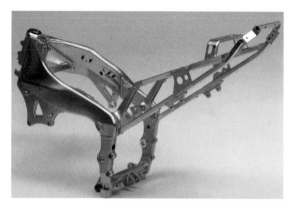

The beautiful minimalist frame of the R1 made possible by the compact engine.

Growing the family with the 1999 R6.

Although a streetbike, the R7 was really intended for this.

its stride. It was a perfect demonstration of the phenomenal capability of the new bike. Now it was the turn of the journalists to run out of superlatives: the R1 had made history. The legend had been born.

The R1 hadn't disappointed the press, and it surely didn't disappoint its new owners, many of whom had to wait months for their deliveries to happen. Even away from the track, in the real world of greasy surfaces and potholes, the R1 was magnificent. Tiny in size, yet with massive power and pin-point handling, it simply set new standards for sportsbike functionality. For some, including a few journalists, it was actually all too much and they insisted that the established order was correct, the Fireblade outselling the R1 in 1998, but this was reversed in 1999 and the R1 was sales king in Europe.

There had been a slight scare when a recall was issued to replace the clutch after some owners experienced lock-up when the thrust plate broke. There were also some problems with false neutrals in second and third gear, and at the next model upgrade in 2000, this was one area that received some attention. For the rest, it was an exercise in yet more weight reduction, losing another 3kg (7lb), and fine tuning of the chassis to make the bike more comfortable and to inspire more confidence on the road. It was enough: through 2000, the R1 still ruled the roost.

Sons of R1: the R6 and R7

It had soon become clear to Yamaha that the design philosophy used for the creation of the R1 had hit the mark, with R1 sales going through the roof and the bike referred to as the yardstick against which all others would be measured. It was time to do a repeat performance on the 600cc class, still the most popular for sportsbikes in both Europe and the USA. The same approach was taken towards achieving a compact, powerful engine by stacking the transmission shafts to save space. In contrast to the longer stroke engine that the R1 had used, power was sought on the new 600 by shortening the stroke and running the engine faster, extremely fast with a redline at 15,500rpm. Clearly it

Sjaak Lucassen loves his 2001 R1 so much he takes it with him everywhere. Mauritanian desert.

The Congolese jungle.

Trackday.

2003 marked the first major R6 upgrade, but the bike still came up short of the competition.

wasn't so easy for Yamaha to find the 120bhp they had targeted for the bike, and the higher engine speed was coupled to a ramair system of forced induction when at speed, as well as a compression ratio that crept up to 12.4:1. This defined the power characteristics of the peaky engine, with the most focused of riders needing to keep the tach above 10K to get the most out of the engine.

A similar design of Deltabox II frame was adopted, with engine mounting mounts on the sides of the upper cylinder/crankcase casting. Regular front forks with full adjustment complimented the rear shock, linked to a longer swingarm in true R1 fashion. Wheelbase was just 1,380mm, with slightly less trail than the R1 but the same rake at 24 degrees. Weighing in at 8kg (18lb) lighter than big brother, the R6 was as sharp a steerer as a 600 really could be without losing stability and getting twitchy. Like its big brother, the R6 unleashed a battle for the best minimalist 600cc sportsbike.

Although a good bike, the R6 was not as clearly dominant as the R1 had been. The peaky engine meant that the rider had to be totally committed so as to ride the R6 on the edge; a moment's lack of concentration and the bike would drop out of the powerband and the rider would have to knock it back a gear to recover. It was the four-stroke closest to a two-stroke that Yamaha had built to date. Hard-nosed riders loved it, but for many it was too extreme.

Even more extreme was the R7 that also appeared in 1999 in time for homologation for the World and National Superbike championships.

Cast in the R1 mould, this was a race bike with lights and mirrors, costing a fortune and needing as much spent on it again to run at the front in the championships. The biggest design difference between the R1 and R7 was the use of fuel injection to feed the engine, surely a foretaste of a future change on the R series. Although it had the potential for 160bhp with the full kit installed, the road bike was delivered with just 100bhp at the rear wheel to meet regulations in Germany and France. The Stage One Kit would push that up to 130bhp and cost a quite reasonable £750. You needed another £10,000 to turn the bike into a World Super Bike contender.

The new R7 should have been the WSB Championship winner in 2000 in the hands of Nori Haga, at last breaking the V-twin stranglehold, but Haga tested positive for high levels of ephedrine, was stripped of the race win and banned for the last race of the season. Instead of winning the championship, he finished runner-up. For Yamaha, the disappointment was huge, and their interest and investments turned towards the eagerly anticipated MotoGP class for 990cc prototype four-strokes. The R7 was discontinued.

Fighting for Top Dog

It was to be several years before the R6 underwent a serious upgrade, the original 1999 model having been enough to keep the Yamaha in contention despite the lack of development. For 2001 and 2002, new colours and decals were

Model	YZF–R6	YZF–R6	YZF–R6
Year	1999	2003	2006
Capacity (cc)	599	599	599
Configuration	4-s 4 cyl	4-s 4 cyl	4-s 4 cyl
Induction	16-valve dohc	16-valve dohc	16-valve dohc
Bore × stroke (mm × mm)	65.5 × 44.5	65.5 × 44.5	65.5 × 44.5
Gearbox	6-speed	6-speed	6-speed
Final drive	chain	chain	chain
Frame	deltabox	deltabox	deltabox
Wheelbase (mm, in)	1,380 (54.3)	1,380 (54.3)	1,380 (54.3)
Dry weight (kg, lb)	169 (373)	162 (357)	161 (355)
Power (bhp)	120 @ 13,000rpm	121 @ 13,000rpm	131 @ 14,500rpm
Torque (kgm)	6.9 @ 11,500rpm	7.0 @ 11,500rpm	6.9 @ 7,000rpm
Top speed (km/h, mph)	250 (155)	260 (162)	260 (162)

Model	YZF–R7 OW-02	YZF–R1	YZF–R1
Year	1999	1998	2000
Capacity (cc)	749	998	998
Configuration	4-s 4 cyl	4-s 4 cyl	4-s 4 cyl
Induction	20-valve dohc	20-valve dohc	20-valve dohc
Bore × stroke (mm × mm)	72 × 46	74 × 58	74 × 58
Gearbox	6-speed	6-speed	6-speed
Final drive	chain	chain	chain
Frame	deltabox	deltabox	deltabox
Wheelbase (mm, in)	1,390 (54.7)	1,395 (54.9)	1,395 (54.9)
Dry weight (kg, lb)	162 (357)	177 (390)	175 (386)
Power (bhp)	140 @ 10,000rpm	150 @ 10,000rpm	150 @ 10,000rpm
Torque (kgm)	7.2 @ 8,000rpm	11 @ 8,500rpm	11 @ 8,500rpm
Top speed (km/h, mph)	270 (168)	280 (174)	280 (174)

Model	YZF–R1	YZF–R1	YZF–R1
Year	2002	2004	2007
Capacity (cc)	998	998	998
Configuration	4-s 4 cyl	4-s 4 cyl	4-s 4 cyl
Induction	20-valve dohc	20-valve dohc	16-valve dohc
Bore × stroke (mm × mm)	74 × 58	77 × 53.6	74 × 58
Gearbox	6-speed	6-speed	6-speed
Final drive	chain	chain	chain
Frame	deltabox	deltabox	deltabox
Wheelbase (mm, in)	1,395 (54.9)	1,395 (54.9)	1,415 (55.7)
Dry weight (kg, lb)	174 (384)	172 (379)	177 (390)
Power (bhp)	152 @ 10,500rpm	180 @ 10,500rpm	180 @ 10,500rpm
Torque (kgm)	10.7 @ 8,500rpm	11.5 @ 10,500rpm	11.5 @ 10,500rpm
Top speed (km/h, mph)	285 (177)	295 (183)	295 (183)

about all the R6 could boast. The R1 was also left unchanged for 2001, but the year was important as the model found itself up against a new rival in the form of the GSXR1000 from Suzuki. The GSXR series had built their reputation on lightweight and powerful peaky engines, and the 1000 followed in this tradition, but with good traction from almost zero engine speed. At last, after three years at the top, the R1 came in second best.

Yamaha were now on a two-year development cycle, so all was put right with the 2002 model. Given how close to best-in-class the 2001 R1 had been, Yamaha might have been tempted merely to do some tweaking to regain the advantage. Instead the bike was almost entirely new. Fuel injection replaced the carburettors of old, with a design of integrated valves that responded to pressure changes in the inlet tracts. There were other small changes such as airbox design and anti-friction coatings on cylinder walls and piston rings. Reciprocating parts such as valves and conrods were made a fraction lighter.

On the chassis, the lessons learnt from the R7 were applied. An engine higher in the chassis would help the R1 to turn a little more quickly, so it was raised by 20mm (3/4in). The frame itself was now identified as Deltabox III, stronger and lighter, and with a detachable sub-frame. Great attention had been paid to the balance between machine and rider, resulting, amongst other things, in the exhaust pipe being pulled in closer to the bike. This in turn produced an asymmetrical rear swingarm so as not to foul the exhaust. Front fork diameter grew 2mm, and the stroke was reduced to minimize the change in chassis geometry as the rider braked and turned into a corner. To help get the power on hard and fast on acceleration out of the corner, the swingarm pivot point was raised 15mm (5/8in). Detail adjustments could be found everywhere.

The result was a faster, lighter bike, with improved steering and drivability, and which regained its position at the top of the heap.

For 2003 it was the turn of the R6. Essentially it was unchanged since its launch four years earlier, but now it benefited from technology proven on the R1. The same design of fuel injection was used, with 38mm throttle bodies rather than the 40mm equivalents on the R1, complimented with a larger airbox. The complete engine was reviewed to minimize power losses by improving crankcase ventilation, and attention given to increase low- and mid-range power delivery.

Reliability was considered, and it was decided to use forged pistons, with rings slightly further apart, to reduce piston rock, which would otherwise increase wear on the ceramic-coated cylinders. Deltabox III frame design was used, with the controlled filling die-cast manufacturing process reducing the number of welds to just two. The same process was used to create the new swingarm, slightly longer and with far fewer welds. The overall steering geometry was unchanged, the slightly shorter engine compensating for the longer swingarm. Lighter wheels, forks and exhaust all helped the bike to tip the scales at 162kg (357lb).

The 2003 model was a significant improvement, but the Honda CBR and Kawasaki ZX had improved as well and were arguably better than the R6. Many testers complained about the lack of radical styling, suggesting difficulty in finding something really worth criticizing. In fact all the Sports 600s had become so good that it really was a question of personal taste, with styling playing a major role in the final choice of the customer.

Redefining the R1 Series

One year on, and the R6 marked time while the R1 underwent a major upgrade, one that redefined the R1 series for the years to come. Cosmetically, ergonomically and technically, it was a massive change. Most striking was the cosmetic change, with the twin under-seat exhausts cleaning up the aesthetics of the bike to give it a superb, balanced look. In practice, the heat from the exhaust could, on a hot day in the middle of summer, raise the seat temperature to a level close to becoming uncomfortable. Nevertheless, the profile of the 2004 R1 was gorgeous.

The third-generation R1 was born in 2004, with a more powerful engine and stunning cosmetics.

Again there were many changes to the bike to counter the competition, with a strong new challenge being mounted by Kawasaki with the ZX10. The bore and stroke of the engine were changed to deliver a shorter stroke and higher compression ratio. Yamaha were looking for a top-end power boost and they got it, assisted by a pressurized air delivery system that would add another 6bhp to the power output at high speed, according to the factory. The engine was now redlined at 13,500rpm, an incredible number for a 1000cc 4-cylinder mill.

Continuing in the philosophy of integration between engine and chassis, the wider bores of the new block could be partially compensated for by the thinner crankcases that were used. This in turn was possible as the engine was no longer a stressed member, because by tilting it forwards to 40 degrees, the beams of the new Deltabox V frame could be built to run straighter between headstock and rear wheel pivot.

The frame was stronger, no longer needing the engine for added strength, but more GP technology found its way on to the bike with an 'upside down' swingarm, with the bridge gussets underneath the arm, and radially mounted front-brake callipers. Was the result the best supersports bike of 2004? It was debatable, owing to a very strong showing from Kawasaki and Honda, making a clear winner impossible to identify.

Yamaha celebrated Valentino Rossi's 2004 move to the race team with this rather plain R6 replica.

Radical Change for the 2006 R6

Things went a little quiet at Yamaha for 2005. The R6 did get a couple of changes, in the form of 40mm throttle bodies on the fuel injection, new upside-down front forks and the same front brake design as the R1. The fuel injection was not flawless; in particular sharp throttle changes seemed to drown the engine slightly, causing a stutter in delivery. For the first time the R6 was looking long in the tooth.

In hindsight, Yamaha can be excused for the half-hearted response to the cut-throat competition in the 600 class, given the drama of the upcoming 2006 R6 model. The same could almost be said for the R1, as the biggest change for the 2006 model year was the price drop to bring it in line with the class-dominating Suzuki. In fact, if you looked hard enough beyond the stunning graphics, you'd find a 20mm longer swingarm, resulting in more weight on the front wheel. Some tweaking to the valve guides added 3bhp, according to Yamaha, but the bike still felt a little flat in comparison to the Suzuki and Kawasaki competition. For those looking for the ultimate R1, a limited edition SP model was produced for just 500 lucky individuals. Exotica such as a slipper clutch, Ohlins suspension and Marchesini wheels were considered sufficient to justify the 50 per cent price premium.

The lack of development on the R1 was more than compensated for by the radical changes that were to be found on the 2006 R6. The combination of jagged colour slashes and swooping upper fairing lines, with the short stubby exhaust, resulted in an aggressive predatory look, reinforcing the hypersports image Yamaha were looking for. Underneath the plastics the bike was a total rework, marked by the use of new innovative technology in the form of the Yamaha Chip Controlled Throttle system. The YCC-T let the ECU system on the bikes control the throttle position on the fuel injection, based on the throttle position controlled by the rider; in short, fly-by-wire, poached from the Yamaha MotoGP M1 bike, in name at least. The fuel injection system had become very sophisticated, with a different throttle movement map for the top three gears as well as extra injectors for engine speeds over 6,000rpm. The engine was claimed to run to a redline of 17,500rpm, although in reality this was more of a marketing ploy, with the rev limiter kicking in at 16,500rpm. The engine characteristics were not so different from the 2005 version, except there was more torque and power throughout the curve.

The chassis was shortened and the steering quickened up, making this a very track-focused bike. Suspension adjustability went a step further, with both slow and fast compression and rebound damping, providing more choices than a typical road rider would want or need. Nice to know it's there, though, if the interest takes you.

As the ultimate 600cc hypersports model, the R6 was unbeatable in 2006, although for many riders it could be considered too focused for practical road use. Yamaha were aware of the possible aversion to such an extreme sportsbike and retained the 2005 model for sale in the USA, with a slightly lower spec suspension, but a significantly lower price tag as well.

Going into 2007, Honda's uprated CBR600RR somehow managed to combine extreme track performance with relative comfort and ease of use, the best of both worlds. In addition, Triumph had finally got their triple 675 right, challenging the 4-cylinder Japanese hard, with its sharp chassis and distinctive engine.

For 2008, Yamaha gave the R6 yet another performance update, with higher compression, variable inlet tract lengths on the fuel injection,

Radical as radical can be. A total focus on hardcore sports riding drove the 2006 R6 design.

Perfect for the track in 2006, but perhaps the R6 was too focused for the street.

and a new chassis. Yet more adjustability came in the form of ride-height at the rear, yet there was still no steering damper, a widely applied after-market accessory for 2006 and 2007 owners. If anything, the 2008 R6 was even more race-focused, and once again came up short in the real world of bumpy, traffic-congested roads.

Upgrades for the R1

2007 had been the R1's year for change, and again Yamaha brought in some new technology to differentiate through innovation. Complementing the YCC-T technology lifted from the R6 programme came YCC-I, the 'I' standing for 'intake'. The ECU was also in control of the intake trum-

Is this not an object of beauty? The 2006 R1 SP.

Capturing the lines for the 2007 R1.

LEFT:
Now the clay model for the 2007 R1.

BOTTOM:
The finished item in metal and plastic: the 2007 R1.

OPPOSITE:
The 2008 R1 was as uncompromising as its great grandfather of ten years before.

pets on the fuel injection, lifting them from their seat at high engine speeds. The result was long intake tracts for best power and torque at low- and mid-range engine speeds, and short tracts for top end. Fuel was now feeding a 4-valve cylinder head, the trademark 5-valve engine disappearing for good. The MotoGP programme had discarded the concept some years before, and it was felt that the narrower valve angle and more compact combustion chamber outweighed the lighter weight and better flow potential of 5-valves.

Yamaha also claimed to have redesigned the frame geometry, as well as the materials used for it, in order to tune the torsional rigidity of the chassis. It was debatable if this translated into a different feel for the bike on the road, though it might have been useful for the factory's increased interest in superbike racing.

The 2007 R1 package was unchanged for 2008, despite being considered overshadowed by the Honda and Suzuki litre hypersports bikes. In general it was felt that the engine was too peaky with inadequate mid-range torque to give the satisfying big push in real world riding. Ultimately it would often come down to brand allegiance and styling, and Yamaha had commendably ignored the move towards massive trumpet-like exhausts, retaining the under-seat tuckaway, keeping the lines tidy and sharp.

A Legendary Sportsbike

Yamaha had produced a new benchmark in sportsbike riding with the 1998 R1, and ten years later the bike was still a fine testament to the engineers and designers who had forced the rest of the world to play catch-up over all those years. For Yamaha, it unquestionably fulfilled the role of legendary sportsbike, joining the ranks represented by each of the Japanese manufacturers, with the Kawasaki Z1, the Suzuki GSXR 750 and the Honda Fireblade. Each of these bikes had pushed back the envelope, changing the standards by which sportsbikes were judged and establishing a new baseline for designers. They had simply changed the world of motorcycling for ever.

12 Dare To Be Different

'You've gotta be original, because if you're like someone else, what do they need you for?' This is a very astute quotation from Bernadette Peters, which captures the essence of the creative spirit that has shadowed the Japanese motorcycle manufacturers over the last four decades: the need to find the balance between inventing a better mousetrap and gambling on changing the world by launching an MP3 player with white earphones. For every iPod there are a dozen tales of Smith & Wesson mountain bikes and Sony Betamax video recorders.

There is risk in both situations, either of incurring the high costs of launching a model that flops, or of emulating another's success and being labelled a follower, not a leader. All the Japanese motorcycle manufacturers have experienced both faces of that coin, but they nevertheless had the courage to break out regularly from the status quo and cut a new path. The kudos garnered for the successes more than compensated for the scorn resulting from the failures.

The SR500

Many of the most successful leaps of faith that resulted in ground-breaking motorcycles such as the V-Max and YZF-R1 were attributable to the intuition and perception of veteran product planners such as Ed Burke and Masahiru Inumaru. Others have a less clear parentage, maybe just a casual remark, a couple of sketches, a low cost try-out, with the magic, almost intangible secret ingredient of correct timing, to bring it all to

The Big Single. Resurrected by Yamaha for the SR500.

Love it or hate it: the SR500 was a big seller in some markets and a dog in others.

fruition. Perhaps surprisingly, the bikes that did dare to be different were often built on components taken from other bikes. The components themselves were not important, it was their application within a new package that created the unique quality pertaining to the resulting bike. Benjamin Franklin's observation that 'Originality is the art of concealing your sources' seemed to be spot on.

The product itself need not be radical, although the thinking behind it often is. The SR500 came into existence through the unshakable conviction of one man, Shunji Tanaka. This simple, almost bland motorcycle came to be one of Yamaha's bestsellers in Germany and Japan, while receiving scant attention in the USA and most European countries. It touched a nerve, though, for the 38,336 Germans who bought one between its introduction in 1978 and the sale of the last, built up from spares, in 2005.

Tanaka's vision was to capture the spirit of the British single-cylinder thumper, which had all but disappeared from the street as the British motorcycle industry wilted and died. Following in the footsteps of the XS1, the clone of the dying breed of traditional British twins, the SR would be homage to the tradition of the large capacity single, simple, rugged and classic in look and feel.

Marketing guys told him he was crazy, the era of the big single was dead, not even dead long enough for some sales on the nostalgia ticket. They were certain it would bomb. Working with designer Atsushi Ishiyama, the pair started with the XT/TT 500 and began to adapt components to achieve the transformation to a Japanese-generation street single.

The engine basics were unchanged, with bore and stroke of 87 × 84mm. The crankshafts were not interchangeable, as the crank web diameter on the SR was increased. There were some detail changes to the piston, with a longer skirt to minimize rocking, and the inlet side of the cylinder head was fitted with a larger valve, fed by a 34mm Mikuni carburettor.

Conscious of the traditional difficulties of breathing life into British singles if the exact magic procedure were not followed, Yamaha thought to ease the problem by using CDI ignition along with 12-volt electrics instead of the 6-volt XT system. A number of other aids were fitted to help get the bike coughing and spluttering into life. A little lever was fitted to lift the exhaust valve so the engine could be turned over until a white mark on the camshaft was spotted in a small window on the cylinder head. Once the choke was activated and the throttle-set knob pushed up, a determined poke on the kick-start would usually have the bike lolloping away happily. Variations to the prescribed procedure were not advised, seldom resulting in the bike starting directly or until the flooded engine was clear.

The bike vibrated badly like all big singles, but this was not especially uncomfortable for the rider, despite, or perhaps even because of, the solid mounting of the engine in the frame. Rubber mounting for tank and footrests kept the rider isolated from the worst of the vibrations. The same frame, doubling as oil reservoir, was used as on the XT/TT series, with variations in tube diameter and gusseting. The steering was quickened with a sharper headstock angle, with conventional dual shock rear end and front forks.

The whole package was a competent rework of the classic single-cylinder design. The bike captured the fun of the lazy revving engine in a chassis that steered well, needing only light input from the bars. It was reliable, didn't leak oil or leave bits of itself behind on the trip, and cost just $1,489 when launched in the USA in 1978, or 4,380 Deutschmark in Germany. Twenty years later it was still for sale in Germany for 7,995 Deutschmark, virtually unchanged after all that time. There were regular colour changes and occasional larger facelifts as the SR was positioned as a 'classic', with a drum brake in the 18in front wheel that had replaced the original 19in item. There were some attempts by Honda to build a similar retro bike, but they never caught the imagination of the marketplace as the SR500 had managed to do, by daring to be different and succeeding.

The SRX600 and SRX400

Nostalgia is, however, a powerful emotion, and by the mid-1980s there was a strong interest in the bikes of the past, with many of the British and Italian bikes of the 1950s and 1960s that had been dismissed as obsolete, uncomfortable, unreliable and quirky, now lauded as classics worthy of collection and restoration. The big racing singles from AJS, Matchless and Norton were suddenly

The air of the British single café racer was well captured by the SRX600.

much sought-after collector's items with suitably heavy price tags.

Yamaha spotted an opportunity here, for a coordinated marketing action for the SR500, still going strong in Japan and Germany. The SR was given a more retro look with drum brakes and 'classic styling', and a new race-styled thumper appeared for the Japanese and European markets. The SRX600 arrived in April 1985, built around the 4-valve XT600 engine, with a modern twin-loop cradle frame built from square-section steel tubing. It was a curious mixture of prominently visible contemporary technology such as the frame, alloy wheels and disc brakes, coupled to the classic big engine, stubby exhaust and flat handlebars. It looked a little like a Special that had been built around a classic big bore engine.

It was quite unique. Performance was, as could be expected from a 40bhp single, nothing like that of contemporary 4-cylinder machines of a similar capacity. But it was quite adequate. In fact the appeal of the SRX lay exactly in its contrast to the UJM 4-cylinders that were dominating this class by now. It was minimalist rather than bulky, focused rather than universal, sharp not fluffy.

It came into its element on the twisty secondary roads of Europe, where its precise steering, firm suspension and good brakes gave the rider a buzz of confidence in stringing a line through a section of fast corners. The engine was a little disappointing as it was quite snatchy at lower engine speeds, resulting in a need to keep the revs up and change gear frequently; a few extra bhp and a fatter torque curve would have been welcome.

In Japan, the bike was a huge success; there was also a 400cc version to meet the Japanese licensing laws. An SRX250 had been on sale as well in Japan from 1983, with a modified XT250 engine in a double cradle frame and rather conventional styling. It found its way to the USA in 1987, with a pointy fairing and looking like an outcast from the FJ series.

In Europe the SRX6 was moderately successful, but inexplicably it flopped in the USA. Fortunately the initial production targets had been quite modest, with annual goals of 2,000 units of

It seems Yamaha thought the born-again biker was the target for the SRX, at least in Japan.

the SRX6 and 5,000 for the SRX4. Ultimately a total of 19,000 SRX6s had been sold by the time it was discontinued in 1991; in Japan there were 30,000 SRX4s sold over the same period. Over the years there were a few changes. In 1987, the front wheel dropped to 17in, with a single front disc and three-spoked wheels. The final version that appeared in 1990 used the XT engine with electric starter, in a Monoshock chassis. Although it was the best of the SRX singles from a performance perspective, the move to single shock chassis took the edge off the synergy with the bikes of yesteryear, and sales levels fell away sufficiently for Yamaha to call it a day and drop the series.

The SZR660 Super Single

But you can't keep a good idea down, and five years later yet another sports thumper was to appear, no longer styled in the past, but now making a fashion statement of its own. The SZR660 Super Single was a cross between the TZR125 chassis and the XTZ660 big trailie engine, and intended to be something different from the large capacity sports 4-cylinders that seemed to be the only choice for the sports riders. It was cobbled together by Belgarda, the Italian Yamaha importers, and marketed exclusively in Europe.

This was as attractive as it ever got, but strip the SZR660 of the plastics and there was a jewel-like race bike underneath.

The TZR chassis was very tasty, in the true Deltabox twin spar model, with rising rate, vertically mounted rear suspension, gull-wing swingarm to allow the exhaust to be tucked away, and upside-down front forks.

The XT660 engine was a slice of 5-valve Genesis technology, with water-cooling and 43bhp at the rear wheel. Look at the SZR660 stripped of its bodywork and it is a truly wonderful thing to behold, a compact street racer, with acres of aluminium and an engine topped with a larger airbox. With the bodywork in place the SZR660 is certainly striking in appearance, especially the blue model, with sky-blue fairing offset by the orange-red seat. Most reactions were that it was hideously ugly, although beauty is in the eye of the beholder. There was a full red version that was slightly easier on the eye, but it was a serious marketing mistake to create such an unconventional appearance.

Functionally it was similar in performance to the SRX, with a little more torque and power, but the same sharp steering and handling. On the down side it was less comfortable due to the even more compact and also static riding position dictated by the shape of the fuel tank. Also vibrations through the footrests were

bad, especially around cruising speed on the motorway; like the SRX, it came into its own on the country road and the twists and turns that characterize it in many countries. But not many people were able to see past the outrageous styling exercise and pay nearly £6,000 or 12,000 Deutschmarks for the excellent sports bike that lay underneath, and after just two years of sales in Europe, in 1997 it disappeared from the line-up.

The Super Ténéré XTZ750A

Yamaha's tradition of transplanting off-road engines into a series of road bikes was to be extended to the twins that had found their way into packages nominally labelled as dirtbikes. During the 1980s, the Ténéré variant of the XT series had proved very popular in some European countries, especially France. Although styled in the line of the off-road adventure bikes like those run in the African rallies, the bikes were not equipped in any way to be run off tarmac. They were statements of fantasy rather than intent.

Once this was understood, manufacturers could use their imagination to create a new model, unencumbered by the need to wrap the

The twin-cylinder engine was the star of the XTZ750 package, and went on to greater things.

styling around a core that could perform in the environment reflected by the image of the bike. The big twins that had been pressed into service in the African rallies had been stripped of excess weight and tuned for performance, but that treatment was never needed for street-based replicas. Yamaha exploited this new insight into consumer behaviour by building the Super Ténéré XTZ750A around a twin-cylinder engine with 5-valve technology.

The engine was a totally new design. It was as compact as possible, a virtue that Yamaha were frequently to apply in their engine designs over the years. Crank and transmission were staggered to reduce the length of the engine, and twin balancer shafts were fitted to reduce the vibration from the 360-degree crankshaft. The weights on the shafts, one ahead of the crank and the other behind, rotated in the space between the crankshaft webs, and were timed to pass through this space as it was freed up by the rotating big-end bearing. In true Genesis tradition, the 5-valve water-cooled cylinders were slanted at 45 degrees to enable vertical downdraught carburettors to be fitted, and also to benefit the weight distribution in the chassis.

The frame was quite conventional, with large-diameter backbone and square-section double cradle to hold the engine. Rising rate rear Monoshock suspension complimented the standard cartridge front forks, with two disc brakes on the front wheel and one at the back. Styling requirements dictated that the large aluminium bash plate was wrapped around the lower front frame tubes, under the engine.

The bike was tall and heavy, although steering was helped by the wide handlebars. The suspension was a little harsh for light riders, but satisfactory for most. The upright riding position was comfortable, and the fairing provided sufficient protection from windblast to make longer journeys a viable proposition. The star feature of the bike was the engine, which delivered a wide, fat band of torque and a decent maximum power output of a measured 60bhp at the rear wheel.

The Ténéré was to continue for six years from its introduction in 1989, and sold well in Europe, building a reputation as a good medium-distance tourer. Its engine was recognized as an ideal powerplant for a more street-oriented model, and two years after the XTZ, the TDM850 was announced.

Yamaha's greatest brochure image of all time? Introducing the Big Twin in the 1991 TDM850.

The family resemblance of the TDM 850 to the XTZ750 was still visible in 1991.

The TDM850

For this model the engine was lifted from the XTZ, the bore increased a fraction and a longer stroke crankshaft fitted. This was enough to add another 10bhp to the maximum power delivered, without destroying the strong torque delivery. The mill was slotted into a twin-spar steel Deltabox frame with 41mm front forks and suspension adjustable for pre-load and rebound damping. The high seat height and upright position were retained, the riding position felt to be one of the appeals of the XTZ. Striking styling with the double headlamps fronting the small cockpit fairing, coupled to dual short stubby exhausts, set the bike quite clearly apart from anything else on the road.

The design was right, but it was flawed in the implementation. There was too much play in the drive line, with a hesitation before the bike responded to an opened throttle. Gear changes were notchy and clunky, with a distinctive agricultural feel about them. The suspension was under-damped, the rubber mounts of the handlebar contributing to the vague steering. The fairing contributed a second blast of air to the rider's head, making high speeds uncomfortable because of buffeting by the windblast. Poor padding on the seat combined with the upright riding position meant that butt ache developed within the hour.

Upgrades for the TDM

The TDM had the potential to be a totally unique distinctive bike, if only it had either been good at everything or excelled in something. Instead it did neither and remained a bit of a sleeper, selling in reasonable numbers in some markets but flopping in others. It survived just two years in the USA, from 1992, because 'being different' was not enough to compensate for the rough edges and weaknesses. There were some updates to the gearbox in 1994, but generally little changed until a complete revamp in 1996.

Yamaha decided to add some more sparkle to the bike by giving it a revised and quite unconventional 270-degree crankshaft. This meant that the cylinders fired within 90 degrees of each other, resulting in a sound reminiscent of a V-twin. It was claimed that this improved the traction of the engine, just as the same modification had improved the traction on the 500cc 4-cylinder racing GP two-strokes, but this was more marketing imagination than reality.

Compression ratio was raised to add a few more bhp, and the gearbox was reworked to provide a slicker mechanism and to fix the slop in the drive train. Although the bike still had some difficulty running smoothly at low engine speed in high gears, in general the engine performed well, with clear improvements on the old model. The chassis was also a lot better, with the 43mm front fork, and better steering sensitivity now that the rubber bushes were gone. The biggest complaint was the rear shock, where although the damping was better, it was still inadequate.

In general, the new TDM was a great all-rounder, a lot closer to what it should have been from the start. To underline the new version it was also given a styling makeover, with swathes of vivid silver and yellow paintwork offset by the tinted screen and black headlight mounts.

It was with this model that the TDM really hit its stride in terms of sales, and it was immensely popular in France, Germany and Italy. By 2002, 75,000 units had been sold and it was time for yet another upgrade, in which engine capacity was taken up to 900cc. In fact there was a complete engine overhaul, following design principles being used by the R-series such as removal of steel liners to the cylinders, with the forged pistons running on ceramic composite plated cylinders. Fuel injection replaced the Mikuni carburettors, with an adjustable air intake system.

Although very similar in design, the frame was now aluminium, losing 11kg (24lb) in the process. This was useful, as the catalytic converters in the exhausts pulled back a few kilograms. The styling had quietened down a bit, but it was still clearly a TDM and still unique. It wasn't perfect, with uneven damping from the front forks, but it was good enough to satisfy a lot of owners throughout Europe.

The TRX850

For seven years during the TDM's lifetime it was accompanied by a sibling, with the same heart but a totally different skeleton and skin. Seeing the potential also to offer a lightweight large capacity sports bike featuring the unique parallel twin configuration, Yamaha designed a minimalist chassis to hold it. Although never acknowledged, the styling of the new bike was heavily influenced by the Ducati SS series of low-spec V-twins. Their most distinctive feature, other than the red colour scheme, was the heavily triangulated trellis perimeter frame. Back in 1992 Yamaha had equipped one of their domestic market 250 two-stroke twins

Re-styled and re-engineered, the 1996 TDM900.

The prettiest of the TRX models was never seen outside Japan. The 1995 TRX850 looking a little too much like a Ducati.

Although not seen before outside Japan, the TRX trellis frame had been used on a couple of domestic models before.

with a trellis frame; now it was scaled up to hold the new 850cc four-stroke mill from the TDM, featuring the 270-degree crankshaft, with the V-twin vibes, engine characteristics and sound.

The result was the TRX850, once again an unorthodox entry in the market. Generally the package worked well, with suspension that responded to fine tuning and an engine that shared the same positive qualities of the TDM. Sure, another 10bhp and a little more torque would have been nice, but it was fast enough as it was. Like the TDM, it suffered from drive-line snatch at low speeds in high gears, responding best to being ridden with the engine spinning above 5,000rpm. Its biggest problem was the competition in the form of Ducati themselves, as well as V-twin competition from Honda and Suzuki. In Japan, the TRX was an unqualified success; in Europe, however, it remained a marginalized bike, purchased by a small fanatical group of riders, but inadequate in number to enable it to survive the third generation upgrade of the TDM in 2002.

Creating the Distinctive Motorbike

Yamaha's approach to the creation of distinctive motorcycles had involved the use of existing technology, applied, with some adaptation when needed, to a new sub-class of machine. Rarely is it considered commercially viable to design and build a production motorcycle with totally new, unproven radical technology. This is the domain of the prototypes production behind closed doors, or non-functional concept bikes for high-profile trade shows, to project the image of innovation and creativity.

Sometimes the urge to experiment becomes too strong and the race track becomes the domain for experimentation and development, such as Honda had employed with their revolutionary and unsuccessful NR500 four-stroke racer. During the 1980s, in the post-NR era of GP racing, Honda had worked with French oil company Elf to test and evaluate the potential advantages to be gained with hub-centre steering as a replacement of the conventional telescopic front fork. Despite several evolutionary designs, extrapolating on the first designs by André de Cortanze, in practice the advantages brought by this design were not found to be significantly better than the best conventional telescopic forks.

The GTS1000 Sports Tourer

While the Elf programme was running at the World GP races during the second half of the 1980s, Yamaha licensed the RADD technology that James Parker had been developing in the USA. Perhaps Yamaha were hedging their bets should the Elf programme deliver some tangible results, but despite this not being the case, they

The ultimate compliment to the GTS was that it steered as well as a conventional motorcycle!

Model	**SR500**	**SRX6**	**SZR660**
Year	1978	1985	1997
Capacity (cc)	499	608	608
Configuration	4-s 1 cyl	4-s 1 cyl	4-s 1 cyl
Induction	2-valve sohc	4-valve sohc	5-valve sohc
Bore × stroke (mm × mm)	87 × 84	84 × 96	100 × 84
Gearbox	5-speed	5-speed	5-speed
Final drive	chain	chain	chain
Frame	spine simplex cradle	duplex cradle	deltabox
Wheelbase (mm, in)	1,400 (55.1)	1,385 (54.5)	1,435 (56.5)
Dry weight (kg, lb)	158 (348)	145 (320)	147 (324)
Power (bhp)	33 @ 6,500rpm	42 @ 6,500rpm	48 @ 6,500rpm
Torque (kgm)	3.9 @ 5,500rpm	5 @ 5,500rpm	5.5 @ 5,000rpm
Top speed (km/h, mph)	135 (84)	165 (102)	165 (102)

Model	**XTZ750**	**TDM 850**	**TDM850**
Year	1987	1991	1996
Capacity (cc)	649	849	849
Configuration	4-s 2 cyl	4-s 2 cyl	4-s 2 cyl
Induction	10-valve dohc	10-valve dohc	10-valve dohc
Bore × stroke (mm × mm)	87 × 63	89.5 × 67.5	89.5 × 67.5
Gearbox	5-speed	5-speed	5-speed
Final drive	chain	chain	chain
Frame	duplex cradle	deltabox	deltabox
Wheelbase (mm, in)	1,505 (59.2)	1,475 (58.1)	1,475 (58.1)
Dry weight (kg, lb)	195 (430)	199 (439)	198 (437)
Power (bhp)	69 @ 7,500rpm	72 @ 7,500rpm	80 @ 7,500rpm
Torque (kgm)	6.8 @ 6,750rpm	7.7 @ 6,000rpm	8.4 @ 6,000rpm
Top speed (km/h, mph)	180 (112)	205 (127)	205 (127)

Model	**TDM 900**	**TRX850**	**GTS1000**
Year	2002	1996	1993
Capacity (cc)	897	849	1003
Configuration	4-s 2 cyl	4-s 2 cyl	4-s 4 cyl
Induction	10-valve dohc	10-valve dohc	20-valve dohc
Bore × stroke (mm × mm)	92 × 67.5	89.5 × 67.5	75.5 × 56
Gearbox	6-speed	5-speed	5-speed
Final drive	chain	chain	shaft
Frame	deltabox	trellis perimeter	omega perimeter
Wheelbase (mm, in)	1,485 (58.5)	1,435 (56.5)	1,495 (58.9)
Dry weight (kg, lb)	190 (419)	190 (419)	246 (542)
Power (bhp)	86 @ 7,500rpm	80 @ 7,500rpm	100 @ 9,000rpm
Torque (kgm)	9.1 @ 6,000rpm	8.6 @ 6,000rpm	10.8 @ 6,500rpm
Top speed (km/h, mph)	210 (130)	215 (134)	225 (140)

Model	**BT1100**	**MT01**	**MT03**
Year	2002	2005	2006
Capacity (cc)	1063	1670	660
Configuration	4-s V-2	4-s V-2	4-s 1 cyl
Induction	4-valve sohc	8-valve sohc	4-valve sohc
Bore × stroke (mm × mm)	95 × 75	97 × 113	100 × 84
Gearbox	5-speed	5-speed	5-speed
Final drive	shaft	chain	chain
Frame	spine	deltabox spine	duplex cradle
Wheelbase (mm, in)	1,530 (60.2)	1,525 (60)	1,420 (55.9)
Dry weight (kg, lb)	230 (507)	240 (529)	175 (386)
Power (bhp)	65 @ 5,500rpm	90 @ 4,750rpm	45 @ 6,000rpm
Torque (kgm)	9 @ 4,500rpm	15.3 @ 3,750rpm	5.5 @ 5,750rpm
Top speed (km/h, mph)	175 (109)	185 (115)	165 (102)

Yamaha Omega Chassis : A Giant Step Forward.

Never before has a Sports Tourer been equipped with such an advanced frame and suspension system.

Designed to achieve previously unattainable levels of high speed stability, the GTS's new Omega chassis incorporates a technically advanced single-arm front suspension design and hub link steering with inherent anti-dive properties.

With a low centre of gravity and centralized mass, this sophisticated new system elevates the machine's handling performance way above the opposition.

And with ABS available on the GTS1000A, optimum rider control is assured.

Complex in design and expensive to build, the GTS only lasted two years.

decided to put their licence money to some use and developed the GTS1000 sports tourer for market launch. It was a revolutionary bike, with the front end comprising a single-sided swingarm pivoting on what Yamaha labelled the Omega frame, with a single suspension unit controlling its vertical motion. Steering was by means of a separate arm linked to the handlebars that contained at the other end the front wheel bearing, linked to the swingarm via a ball joint.

The problem that this was meant to solve was the perennial theoretical weakness of telescopic forks, namely their weight, stiction and chassis geometry change under braking. Potentially all these points could be addressed through hub-

centre steering, producing a better handling bike with more compliant suspension.

The GTS1000 was the first production motorcycle to put this design to the test. General reactions were that it was as good as a well set-up conventional telescopic fork, but no better. The steering felt heavy at low speeds, which was not surprising from a bike weighing 246kg (542lb) dry. It was using a detuned FZR1000 engine, with fuel injection and catalytic converters in the dual exhausts. Some felt that the presence of the catalytic converters compromised the whole bike, and also resulted in its poor fuel consumption. In order not to overload the catalytic converters, a sensor in the exhaust was used to adjust dynamically the mixture fed into the engine, requiring fuel injection to be fitted. Naturally no EXUP valve was present to help with the mid-range, so different cams were needed to boost mid-range at the expense of the top end. Compared to the FZR1000 EXUP engine, the GTS was down by 30bhp at the redline.

In many ways the GTS1000 was a true flagship, not only because of its radical chassis, but also because it used much of the most advanced technology of the day. But this all came at a heavy price, costing just under £10,000 in the UK and over $13,000 in the USA − and even then it was rumoured that Yamaha were losing money on every sale. It lasted just two years in the USA and only slightly longer in Europe, the last units being shipped in 1996.

The BT1100 Bulldog

For two decades Yamaha had been actively working to expand the traditional motorcycle market segments, perhaps more so than any of the other Japanese manufacturers. One other manufacturer had achieved enormous success in creating a totally new class of bike, the naked bike. Ducati had launched their Monster M900 in 1993, followed by 600cc and 750cc versions, and these had attracted a totally different group of riders, many new to motorcycling and certainly non-traditional Ducati owners. As always, the bikes themselves were not especially proficient, but Miguel

Launched in 2001,
the BT1100 Bulldog was
an imposing machine.

BELOW: The Bulldog at rest.

Galluzzi's styling exercise had captured the 'bad boy' spirit of motorcycles that played up to many non-bikers' preconception about biking culture. It was the ideal toy for the born-again biker, edging into mid-life crisis and anxious to experience more of the wild life before it was too late. By 2005, the Monster accounted for more than 50 per cent of Ducati's worldwide sales.

Japan was slow to pick up on this development in the market. For many years it was just Buell, with their Harley-engined street fighters that came close to the same segment, albeit with a far more focused and aggressive set of models. The whole Monster style seemed to be the domain of the Italians, with Cagiva bringing out Raptors and MV working on what was to become the Brutale. The Italian Yamaha distributor, Belgarda, was convinced that this was a missed opportunity and lobbied heavily for a Yamaha response. As a strong influence within the Yamaha European organization, they managed to obtain the go-ahead to develop a new model that would be Yamaha's statement in this segment.

The result was the BT1100 Bulldog that was launched in Milan in June 2001. Designed, developed and built in Italy, it made use of the venerable 1100cc V-twin engine that had been the heart of the successful Drag Star line, complete with shaft drive. After the extreme style statement of the SZR660 just five years before, Belgarda applied a little more self-restraint and designed a simple chassis with the engine integrated as a stressed member. The tall engine meant that the fuel tank was placed high, with the rider wedged against it by the sloping seat, but the riding position was not uncomfortable. Only pre-load adjustment was present on the suspension, probably dictated by cost as well as the assumption that the new owners were unlikely to be interested in fine tuning it anyway.

The engine was quite docile, with a little more torque produced by the redesigned airbox, but otherwise close to identical to the 65bhp Drag Star mill. With a weight of 230kg (507lb), this was never going to be a high-performance motorcycle and that was definitely not its intended domain. When pushed in the corners, the peg

extensions would soon grind, and once gone, the exhaust from the front cylinder would touch down, with the potential to lift the front wheel and crash. Thanks to the decent torque produced, straight-line take-up was good, and the brakes effective enough to knock off speed for the more delicate corners. But this was irrelevant, because the BT1100 was all about image, not performance, and in that department it was a winner.

The MT-01

Three years on, and it was time for Yamaha's next new project. Sadly the V-Max had fallen foul of EU environment regulations and had disappeared from showrooms in 2003. The loss was keenly felt at Yamaha, and a design team set about building a concept bike that had first appeared at the 1999 Tokyo motorcycle show. The MT-01 was the result, arriving in early 2005 to a shocked and wondrous motorcycle press. Yamaha must have known they had got it right when the first question asked was almost always 'What is it?'.

It was a 1600cc air-cooled pushrod engine, borrowed from the Road Star Warrior cruiser, slipped into a minimalist die-cast aluminium spar frame, with R1 sportsbike heritage. The fuel tank was placed high above the tall engine, sweeping down to a reasonably low seat height, with the rider seated comfortably in the angle as the exhausts arrowed back alongside the bottom of the seat to the back of the bike. It had a massive presence about it – everything seemed huge and intimidating, in a way captured so effectively in the V-Max thirty years before.

The engine had been reworked to produce torque at the cost of maximum power. The results were spectacular, with measured torque values off the scale when compared to other bikes. From 2,000rpm to 4,500rpm, the engine would produce three times the torque of an R1, still 50 per cent more than the sportsbike's maximum output. By 5,000rpm it was all over, but keep the bike in the torque band and it would fly.

Given the 240kg (529lb) weight and tall engine, it was not surprising that it was a heavy steerer, but the first class fully adjustable suspension provided a

Take a massive V-twin engine and add the minimum to turn it into a motorcycle. Result: the 2005 MT01.

Brutal torque levels for the MT01 were produced by the retuned 1600cc Warrior engine.

Despite its bulk, the MT01's steering was stable, if a little heavy.

Lacking some of the impact of the 01, the MT03 still scored high in the styling department.

very stable ride. It was what it was, nothing more or less: a naked muscle bike, with a totally different look and feel, and a huge fun factor thrown in with it. The biggest problem was the price, up at the level of the top-of-the-range Japanese sportsbikes. It took a lot of confidence for an owner to fork out that sort of money for a totally different type of bike, but those that did were rewarded with as much satisfaction as they could expect from any bike. Over 5,000 were sold in Europe in its first year.

The MT-03

A year later, building on the MT-01 styling, came a little brother, the MT-03. There was a nod to the MT-01 in the form of the dual round exhausts at the back of the bike and the high,

swoopy tank, but the heart of the bike was the 660cc single from the XT Adventure sports model line. Distinctive styling was once again a key driver for the design, and for the MT-03, this took the form of the exposed rear suspension unit mounted horizontally alongside the right-hand side of the engine. The original concept bike at the 1999 Tokyo show had featured this unusual design, but the production MT-01 had settled for a central rear shock underneath and in the length of the engine.

Some careful frame design on the MT-03 ensured that the asymmetrical rear suspension forces didn't upset the handling, which was pinpoint sharp and inspired full confidence in the rider. In contrast to the MT-01, the MT-03 was built to a budget, intended to be competitively

*Yamaha's own homage to the designs from the early days with the
1992 YD retro series sold in Japan.*

priced for the middleweight market for riders looking for a competent general all-round bike, with some design flair.

As always Yamaha had chosen a different approach, building on the single-cylinder power-plant in contrast to the twins and 4-cylinder bikes from Japan. Only BMW and Aprilia had passed this way before, but Yamaha's bold and distinctive styling had once again under-lined the originality and flair with which the company had for many years approached the aesthetics of motorcycle design.

From 2002, Yamaha had instigated a design philosophy that they tried to capture in the epithet 'Humachine Technology'. It was their attempt at capturing the balance needed between engineering expertise reflected in the technology, and design expertise reflected in the charisma or appeal of a motorcycle. Although only formally recog-

nized as a best design practice in the new millennium, in practice it had been applied from the very first days of the design work for the *Akatombo*.

With the YA1's colour choice entrusted to the small team of GK students, and their subsequent freedom to influence the YD1 and YA2, technology and design disciplines grew as equals in the company. While technical innovation was often hidden in the depths of the engine, design innovation resulted in a strong visual statement, appealing to the emotions of the observer.

Innovation is a risky business, but without it the world would be a blander place. Yamaha's contribution to the excitement of motorcycling had come from their willingness to innovate, often successfully, sometimes not. But their willingness to be different had enriched the world of motorcycles for everyone.

Coda

The high watermark for Yamaha Motor Co. business performance can be identified as 5 February 2008. Announcing the best financial results ever for the company, with motorcycle sales exceeding 1 trillion yen, the company felt quite justified in predicting the start of yet another record-breaking year for the business: the fiscal year 2008 would be the tenth consecutive year of sales growth.

Within a few weeks it must have started to become clear that there was trouble brewing, as orders dropped significantly. Slowing economies, high energy prices, instability in the currency markets: all were coming together to squeeze Yamaha and all the Japanese motorcycle manufacturers. By the time the Q1 2008 financials needed to be reported in April, there was a mild edge of panic creeping into the company, as all the important numbers started to tumble. By

July it was clear that Yamaha wouldn't even match the 2007 numbers, so the ten-year growth streak was broken.

Then things really went bad, as banks folded, the credit crunch hit, and major recessions developed around the world. What had been predicted to be a year of 4 per cent growth turned into a year of 8 per cent decline. Worse was to come, in that predictions for 2009 were for another 22 per cent drop in revenue, and major losses for the company. Factories were shut down for ten days in February and March 2009. This was drama on the scale of 1961 and 1983. With companies such as Chrysler and General Motors teetering on or over the edge of bankruptcy, would Yamaha be able to survive?

Yamaha were no longer masters of their own destiny. They had a good range of motorcycles,

Injecting some fresh blood into the sub-1000 cruiser market, the 2009 XVS950 Midnight Star.

ABOVE: Streetfighter styling for the new XJ6 led Yamaha's 2009 attack on the mainstream 600cc segment.

BELOW: Some very clever engineering had the 2009 R1 back on the top of the hyper-sports heap.

The pinnacle of Yamaha's sports engineering expertise was well represented by the R1.

The 2009 V-Max was Yamaha's statement of hope for the next fifty years of motorcycling individualism.

well represented in every segment of the market. Fresh blood was injected in the form of the new XJ6 mid-range, a streetfighter naked version, and the Diversion fitted with a half fairing and expected to live up to the enormous success of its namesake from the 1980s and 1990s. The engine was taken from the FZ6 Fazer and retuned for better mid-range and less top-end power, to make the bike easier to ride for the comparative novices who were expected to be the new own-ers. In some ways this reflected the failings of the FZ6 with respect to the FZS600 Fazer it had replaced in 2004: it was exactly these qualities that had made the first generation 600cc Fazer such an excellent middleweight in the first place.

For the YZF-R1, it was time for its bi-annu-al upgrade, and in the true tradition of the company, Yamaha took a slice out of their four-stroke race programme by emulating the firing order of the engine of their M1 MotoGP bike.

Model	XJ6	YZF-R1	VMAX
Year	2009	2009	2009
Capacity (cc)	600	998	1679
Configuration	4-s 4 cyl	4-s 4 cyl	4-s V-4
Induction	20-valve dohc	20-valve dohc	20-valve dohc
Bore × stroke (mm × mm)	65.5 × 44.5	78 × 52.2	90 × 66
Gearbox	6-speed	6-speed	5-speed
Final drive	chain	chain	shaft
Frame	diamond	deltabox	diamond
Wheelbase (mm, in)	1,440 (56.7)	1,415 (55.7)	1,700 (66.9)
Dry weight (kg, lb)	190 (419)	189 (417)	295 (650)
Power (bhp)	78 @ 10,000rpm	182 @ 12,500rpm	200 @ 9,000rpm
Torque (kgm)	6.1 @ 8,500rpm	11.8 @ 10,000rpm	17 @ 6,500rpm
Top speed (km/h, mph)	220 (137)	280 (175)	220 (137)

The so-called 'cross-plane' crankshaft resulted in a firing interval of 270°–180°–90°–180°, giving the engine a droning exhaust note reminiscent of a V-twin. Plenty of other changes were made to the engine, such as the introduction of a slipper clutch and secondary fuel injectors for high engine speeds, while the chassis was also adjusted for the balance between rigidity and flexibility. The styling was as striking as ever, especially the red anodized Deltabox frame on the white model.

But perhaps the most symbolically important announcement for the year was the new V-Max, press releases hitting the street as the financial crisis started to bite hard in June 2008. It was a tremendously encouraging statement for all those with a passion for motorcycling. In this world of increasing government legislation and restriction, environmental peer pressure and social responsibility, thrill suppression and mollycoddling, Yamaha was able to produce a 200bhp motorcycle with such a huge torque output that it was easily the fastest bike in the world, on a roll-on from 50km/h (31mph). There was nothing sensible about the V-Max at all: it was built solely for blistering, eye-popping, adrenalin-charged acceleration. It took the focused muscle-bike charisma of its legendary predecessor and cranked it up by 50 per cent. It was a testament to the free spirit of motorcycling: free to be different, free to be selfish, free to have fun.

But will we look back in ten years time at the V-Max in sorrow and regret, at an icon that represented the pinnacle of the Yamaha Motor Company? If the credit crisis doesn't kill the company, the pace of legislation and transportation reform may have killed the credo. Without the faithful, there can be no prophets. For over fifty years, Yamaha, along with their fellow Japanese manufacturers, have shaped the direction taken by the world of motorcycling. Given the depth of choice, the sophistication of the machines and the popularity of the sport, it can only be said that they have done a good job.

Yamaha's contribution has been significant. Moving from the champions of the two-stroke to the innovators of the four-stroke was a long and rocky path, with their share of bikes that came up short when measured by the harsh assessment of public appeal. However, it will not be these bikes that the world remembers, but the YDS1 and YZF-R1 and others of their ilk, the harbingers of change, the face of things to come, the future. Yamaha's future should be safe in the hands of its past.

Index